PEN___ BOOKS

A ___USAND___ ES FR___ ___OWHERE

Graham Coster was born in 1960 in _____ read English at
Cambridge, where he then worked until 19__ _____ t editor of *Granta*.
The author of one novel, *Train, Train*, he now writes regularly for *GQ*, the
Independent on Sunday and the *Daily Telegraph*. His other main interest is play-
ing the blues harmonica in Damn Right I Got the Blues, the band he
formed with his literary agent and the writer Ken Follett.

GRAHAM COSTER

A Thousand Miles from Nowhere

Trucking Two Continents

PENGUIN BOOKS

PENGUIN BOOKS

Published by the Penguin Group
Penguin Books Ltd, 27 Wrights Lane, London W8 5TZ, England
Penguin Books USA Inc., 375 Hudson Street, New York, New York 10014, USA
Penguin Books Australia Ltd, Ringwood, Victoria, Australia
Penguin Books Canada Ltd, 10 Alcorn Avenue, Toronto, Ontario, Canada M4V 3B2
Penguin Books (NZ) Ltd, 182–190 Wairau Road, Auckland 10, New Zealand

Penguin Books Ltd, Registered Offices: Harmondsworth, Middlesex, England

First published by Viking 1995
Published in Penguin Books 1996
1 3 5 7 9 10 8 6 4 2

Printed in England by Clays Ltd, St Ives plc

'I would not truck this brilliant day . . .'

– John Keats, *King Stephen*

Contents

Acknowledgements

Not a few people helped to make my travels and writing possible. To all of the following, thanks:

Andrew Southall, Henk Buzink and Tony Meddings at Fransen Transport;
Nick Smith, Trevor Jones and Charlie Maidment at Roadtrain;
Dick Schlichting at Kenworth in Seattle;
Mike O'Neill of Al Paul Lefton Company, Philadelphia;
Allen Koenig, Keith Derscheid, Bill Means, Earl Henry and the staff of Midwest Specialized Transportation, Rochester, Minnesota;
George and Peter Coumounduras and Tim Brown of Cargo Transportation, North Billerica, Massachusetts;
Angus MacKinnon, who first let me write about trucks for *GQ* magazine, where parts of this book appeared in earlier form;
and Sarah Sexton, for a quiet Dorset haven in which to write.

The publishers wish to express their thanks for permission to quote from the following songs:

'A Thousand Miles from Nowhere' by Dwight Yoakam,

'Down the Road' by Steve Earle, Tony Brown and Jimbeau Hinson, 'Guitar Town' by Steve Earle, 'Hold That Train' by Michael Robert King, 'Tell Me about It' by Bill LaBounty and Pat McLoughlin (copyright shared with MCA Music Ltd), 'The Wanderer' by Ernest Maresca, and 'Someday' by Steve Earle, all © Warner Chappell Music Ltd, London WIY 3FA. Reproduced by permission of International Music Publications Ltd

'I'm Moving On' by Joe Sample and Will Jennings, permission granted by Rondor Music (London) Ltd and MCA Music Ltd

'Stranger in My Own Home Town' by Percy Mayfield © Tangerine Music Corp, permission granted by Rondor Music (London) Ltd

'Please Come to Boston' by Dave Loggins, permission granted by MCA Music Ltd

'Prop Me Up beside the Jukebox (If I Die)' by Kerry Kurt Phillips, Howard Perdew and Rick Blaylock © Texas Wedge Music (ASCAP) and Songwriters Ink (BMI), permission granted by Affiliated Publishers, Inc.

'I've Got Dreams to Remember' by Otis Redding, Zelma Redding and Joe Rock © 1968 Irving Music Inc. (IBM) All Rights Reserved International, permission granted by Carlin Music Corporation, UK administrator and Rondor Music International, Inc.

'I'd Like to See Jesus on the Midnight Special' by Robert Seay and Dorvil Smith, permission granted by BMG Music Publishing

'Long Time Gone' by Tom McGuinness and Benny Gallagher © 1991 BMG Music Publishing Limited for the World. Used by Permission, All Rights Reserved

Part One

EAST

Chapter One

orry is the weak-chinned word we use in Britain: looks like 'worry', sounds like 'sorry'. Size does not mitigate – on the contrary, the bigger the worse: 'heavy lorry', we sniff, as in 'heavy cold'. The proper word, of course, is an emphatic riposte, a defiant clenching of teeth, sounds like something else altogether. So let's get it said straight away, in all its Anglo-Saxon uncouthness. *TRUCK!*

In Britain we like trains. We invented them. Therefore we don't like trucks. Trains keep to their own neat ribbons of rail and stop at stations a mile out of town; trucks barge through half timbered high streets and vibrate our Victorian sewage systems to pieces. A railway track says, 'within limits'; the tidal wave of spray that smacks you sideways on a rainswept M4 says 'free-for-all'. Trains run endlessly, mythically, through our literature and films, sweeping their charges towards dreams, freedom, romance. *Brief Encounter* was not sealed over a roadside cuppa in an A1 transport caff. Think of the famous TV serials constructed around other modes of transport – the juvenile idyll of *The Railway Children*; the stentorian rhetoric of *The Onedin Line*. Trucks got the careworn, lined shabbiness of *The Brothers*.

Now if we could only put more freight back on the railways, we lament, wistful for the sylvan branch line and the sprightly guard hopping out at the drowsy halt to pick up the milk churn and the crate of racing pigeons . . . But trucks, these days, carry 95 per cent of Britain's freight traffic. If you doubled rail freight overnight it would still take only 3 per cent of goods haulage off our roads. Even 85 per cent of European air freight actually goes by road, because it works out quicker, without all the handling involved in loading on and off planes and into and out of warehouses, than flying it there. Heavy trucks will, and do, deliver enormous quantities of things anywhere, even in the middle of the night, and right to your door, which is why everyone uses them, and hates them.

I, on the other hand, even like motorway service stations. I like the neatness of these staging posts, these twentieth-century coaching inns, to navigate yourself by as you motor the length of England. I like their middle-of-nowhereness. Rothersthorpe; Charnock Richard; Rownhams. Where on earth is Clackett Lane? I shall have to drive round the M25 one day to find out. To drive hundreds of miles and pull in, amongst so much hubbub, near to nothing! And I like the tranquil, plastic, piped-music goldfish-bowl ambience of motorway services: their Country Kitchens and their Granary Restaurants – anywhere but the countryside: somewhere utterly synthetic, telling you to move on, that here is nowhere, *that you're travelling*.

So it was not difficult to get interested in trucks. Through the picture-windows of the Country Kitchen the only view is the truck park. One swings in as another rumbles off, packing the parking area, all on the way from somewhere to somewhere. Here are working weeks, whole lives, even, measured out in Roadchef coffee spoons. I began to notice the same names on the sides of trucks – whether I was at Corley on the M6 or Thurrock by the Dartford Tunnel or Southwaite up near Carlisle. So who was Norbert Dentressangle, I came to wonder – and how did so many of his bright red tankers and trailers come to be scattered across the country? Why did all milk tankers and dairy produce seem to be pulled by trucks from Wincanton in Somerset? Who was Christian Salvesen – and what route had brought this Scandinavian to apparent hegemony in all Sainsbury's and Marks and Spencer's refrigerated haulage? But then amongst the recurring fleet names and liveries the one-offs started to stand out – the one-man bands, the guy driving obviously the guy who owned it. Name scrolled on the cab door, side window chequered with stickers and pennants to mark past journeys, the address Peterhead, Scotland, when we were sitting at Gordano outside Bristol, and the container on the back read MILANO ...

Once upon a time even our goods and wares travelled romantically. Bales of tea, rolls of silk, jars of spices, were dispersed across the oceans in East India Company schooners and clippers. Between the wars, mail would be carried from Southampton down through Africa to the Cape by Imperial Airways 'Empire' flying boats: Marseilles, Athens, Alexandria, Juba, Kampala, Nairobi, Mozambique ... These days we're trucked. Travel writers may still essay transnavigation of the globe by antique steam engine or renovated sail-boat, but trade doesn't. Almost everything that we need, everything we use, goes for some part of its journey by road, on a large truck. London Underground is currently scrapping its oldest underground trains and refitting some others: you can see the carriages travelling up the M1 to be broken up or tarted up – on the back of a lowloader. Steam locomotives are now also a common sight on our roads: as with the tube trains, it's cheaper to hoist them on to the back of a truck for a trip the length of the country than to shunt them there on rails. What safer, less unpredictable means of transferring valuable products across the world than to give them to a single guy, at the wheel of his own truck, and pay him to be the modern Paul Revere with the massive message? The Iraqi supergun made it as far as Greece by truck.

So who were these people in the cabs with curtains to pull round for the night? Were they the last nomads of the industrialized world? How far could you go in a truck – or rather, how far were you travelled by the goods in the trailer behind you? Films like *Thelma and Louise* stereotyped the trucker as the ultimate boorish sexist pariah – anything other than torching his wagon in a fireball of political correctness was too good for him – but how many people had met the guys who actually drove these things? Writers traversed the Andes on mountain bikes, or Cameroon with a donkey called Egbert, or the entire globe in two days fewer than Phileas Fogg: so many factitious justifications for long journeys that would only ever be made by travel writers in order to write a book about them. They never travelled by truck. And yet here were truck parks in service stations across Britain – call them *caravanserai*, if you like, if that gives a kinship with the great literary explorers of the East – that were everyday hosts to guys who'd just got back from who knew where. 'Mr Lewis', wrote Cyril Connolly once in incredulous admiration of Norman Lewis's travel book on Burma, 'can make even a lorry interesting.' It didn't seem that unlikely. Indeed, it was a reassurance. Travellers these days travelled over-loaded on all axles with literary freight, conscientiously equipped with and toiling through a whole trunkload of literary forebears for ironic counter-witness to their chosen territory. You couldn't even sail the Atlantic with Jonathan Raban without being required to read what Hilaire Belloc had written before him about the voyage to America. When I voyage to America I think about Elvis Presley and Howlin' Wolf. I've never read the modern American poets, but I do like singing in the car. Trucking wasn't travelling in anyone's footsteps, was travelling light. Mark Twain, Robert Louis Stevenson, Marco Polo, Mary Kingsley, Hector St John de Crèvecoeur – none of them ever wrote a word about trucks.

At a freight-forwarding warehouse at the end of the Central Line, on London's eastern outskirts, I met a man who drove to Russia for a living. FAST HAULING – NO STAULING! it said in huge letters stencilled along the side curtains of his artic's Tautliner trailer. Framed head-on against the drear grey sheds of the Hainault industrial estate, the green Scania – even dusted with road dirt, and still punched in above the left headlight from an argument with a Russian trucker – was the smartest, most *significant* thing in the road.

Pete, by contrast, was worn-looking, a lank of hair sagging down over glasses he often had to nudge up his nose. His black nylon-quilted parka gaped open behind him; he wore an air of shambling, dogged warmth. 'Pick a number,' the secretary of Owner–Operators, an association of independent lorry drivers, had suggested, scrolling at random through the membership list on his computer screen. Most of the forty thousand names were domestic hauliers – self-employed, one truck, up to the eyeballs on HP to pay for the thing; 80 per cent of truck drivers in Britain were owner–drivers. 'It's hand-to-mouth stuff,' he said, 'a very precarious existence. A quarter of them go bust within three years of setting up – and when I say bust, I mean bust. House and everything. Ah yes – now this guy does a lot of Continental work. Goes into Eastern Europe a lot. Runs it with his wife.' Pete, clopping back to his cab in his clogs, a sheaf of documentation in hand, twenty tons of china clay on board for the Turkish electronics industry, was heading off for the first time for Istanbul. 'One of the first requisites for being a Continental truck driver,' he'd advised me when I'd first reached him on his mobile phone, 'is to have half a brain. You wouldn't do it otherwise.'

We pulled out of Hainault at ten-thirty: twenty-something stops on the tube out into the thirties suburbs of Essex had seemed like a hike; Pete had been up since 4.00 a.m. and had already driven 250 miles to get here from his home base in Yeovil. As we made our way along the A13 bound for West Thurrock, where he was going to fill up with cheap diesel, he told me about Continental haulage. The distances: cross the Russian border at Brest and you *still* had another thousand kilometres to drive to Moscow. The cold: last time he'd been in Bulgaria the weather had just warmed up – it was only 25 below freezing. Pete's Cossack hat was still stuffed down the front of his dashboard. With the wind-chill factor when you're moving it might be minus 60 Fahrenheit, and then the diesel fuel turns to a waxy goo at the bottom of your tank, and you have to mix it with 20 per cent petrol to keep going. One night the cold had driven all of them in the truck park – even with their space blankets supplied by Owner–Operators – out of their cabs and into a hotel . . . except one. 'Bill Bailey – he'd never spend a penny of his running money on himself. He wasn't going in any hotel. The next morning when the others went to look for him they had to

break the duvet off him to get him out of his bunk . . .' The
risks: Pete had been held up and robbed in Moldavia –
'The oldest trick in the book – they let down one of my
back tyres. I lost my rag and got out to them . . .' Romania
– Pete didn't much like Romania: such poverty, such
thieving. Gangs of people wandering around in the middle
of the road pretending to be drunk: slow down and they
smash your windscreen. In Russia there'd been people
who'd never seen a banana – who'd pulled an empty corn
beef tin out of his lunch bag just to sniff its aroma . . .

We pulled up near the Lakeside Shopping Centre for the
cheap fuel. Here you could get 'red' diesel: untaxed fuel,
coloured with a red dye, intended for agricultural machin-
ery, which you were only allowed to use in a truck outside
the EC – so you filled up the belly tank on your trailer
with it and had it sealed by customs until you got out of
Germany. At only 22p a litre, instead of 40p for the 'white'
diesel you bought at normal filling stations, an owner–
driver like Pete, who had £1,000 in a roll of notes as his
running money to last him to Turkey and back, and whose
last Russian haulage agent had just gone bust owing him
£7,500, could save a lot of money.

'The ducking and diving,' said Pete, climbing back into
the cab. 'There's a lot of that. It's the free spirit – that's
what I like.' As we came out of the south side of the
Dartford Tunnel he got on the mobile phone to his haulage
agent to find out where was the best place to get a Turkish
visa. 'Go round the top of Greece, Pete,' boomed the
voice, 'and call in at Combatini. Darren got his there last
week. You put your passport in at nine and it's ready by
one.'

The characters – the kind of guys who did this sort of
thing for a living. There was Charlie: the customs men at

an Italian border post had refused to let him through until he came up with some new form he'd never heard of, so he'd chained himself to the customs compound for three days until they'd seen sense. There was Phil the Professor, a tatterdemalion university graduate who answered questions about his inconsequential vocation with a vaguely baffled, 'I got fed up . . .' There was Posh Pete, and there was the late, great Andrew Wilson-Young, a Middle East vet who waved himself through all tiresome border queues with a dismissive 'I'm British', and once circumvented a Kuwaiti law that all Western truckers must check into hotels overnight by pitching his tent on the lawn of the British Embassy, on the grounds that it was 'British soil'. I glanced at Pete's cassette collection, wondering how an international trucker sustained himself through the lonely small hours of a Bulgarian winter. Dorothy Squires; Bobby Darin: there was a lot of Bobby Darin. 'We don't all wear headbands and have hairy arses,' said Pete.

We pulled off the A2 into a new truckers' café Pete had heard was worth a look. On the cratered moonscape of mud the 38-ton Scania canted over like a splay-legged ox. By the time we had jumped out and discovered that the café was a battered caravan serving burgers and plastic cups of coffee through a hatch – you stood amongst the puddles to eat and drink – we could hear a splattering trickle beneath the truck. The red diesel was pouring out of the belly tank. We'd better get moving, said Pete – we'd be all right once we were on the level.

And trucks themselves. What Pete had really wanted was a Kenworth, a classic American truck, rugged as anything, Caterpillar engine that'd run for ever, cab the size of a small flat. We passed a French artic almost going backwards as we ground past it up the hill just outside

Faversham. 'He's overloaded,' pointed Pete as a police car with flashing lights pulled it over. 'That hill finds them out.' Since Kenworths up to 1973 vintage only had so far received UK type-approval, the finance company had preferred to lend him the money for a new truck, so he'd ended up with a sensible Swedish Scania.

And the sights. 'I've been to Moscow twice a month for six months,' Pete said, 'and I've never seen Red Square.' He'd been going to Athens for nine months before he got around to taking a look at the Parthenon: a dock strike had dragged on for so long that eventually there was nothing for it. He thought this Christmas he'd take his wife out with him on a run to Istanbul and they'd stay to see the Moorish palaces. 'I'm on my third marriage, Graham,' he said. When he did get a few days at home after several times to Russia and back and they went out to the pub in the evening, he said, and all his mates wanted to hear about his travels, he just sat there, couldn't speak – no words came forward. You had to remember how to use them again.

At the Gate services on the M2 we sat in the Yorkie truckers' diner – no plates for your sandwich, no serviette for your fingers. Pete cradled his arms around his mug of tea and confided to me – but I hadn't asked him – his ambitions. He wanted to take a load all the way to Pakistan: that was a three-month round trip. He'd met some Belgian guys in Brussels who were going all the way through Russia to the Chinese border – that sounded like a good one. And he wanted to do the frozen lakes in Alaska – 'a 40-ton truck travelling across a 300-foot-deep frozen lake!' When we got back to the Scania the red diesel was still splattering out on to the ground. We coasted down the hill towards Dover, Pete, now breathless with anxiety, shouting down the mobile phone to his wife that one of the tank seals must have gone: he'd have to stop the other side of the Channel and lose some time to get it fixed — couldn't lose £400-worth of fuel before he'd even got out of the EC. This was Thursday morning: the agent wanted him in Istanbul next Tuesday.

Pete dropped me at the gate to the ferry terminal. 'If you want to come out to Russia with me one time,' he called through the door, 'let me know.' Russia sounded the one. He hadn't told me much about the place — it was all inclement symptoms, and simply a long way: less a destination than a way of travelling, a kind of arduous climate. 'It's a very unforgiving country,' Pete had said. 'If you play the goat there you'll come unstuck. It gives you a keener sense of survival — that's why I like it. You find out who's quickest, in the Biblical sense of the word.'

But by the time I came to take him up on his offer, Pete was in trouble. He was slogging away on the Istanbul run — hadn't been given any more trips to Russia. The civil war in Yugoslavia had re-routed all Middle East-bound trucks up around Hungary, Romania and Bulgaria; with some of the border queues building up through there, and the breakdowns caused by all the extra wear and tear, a round trip to Turkey — normally a run you could do three times in 2 months — was taking 5 or 6 weeks, for no extra money. The last time I spoke to Pete he'd just got back: his voice was distant and exhausted — he sounded as though he was speaking under water. Later I heard gossip about him sitting for weeks on the docks at Hook of Holland, to stay away from the finance company; in any case, he'd just done this trip to Turkey in a hired, second-hand Hino. Then that had proved too battle-weary to rely on for another attritional Istanbul run — and by now there were difficulties renting another unit, and one day his phone went ex-directory . . .

I still wanted a truck to Russia. There were two compan-ies now going there regularly. Kepstowe's in Wandsworth, south-west London, ran tilts – framed wagons covered with canvas – and specialized in dry freight: their transport manager suggested I put up an advert in the depot on their drivers' noticeboard. 'If you say you've got blonde hair and big tits,' he said, 'you'll probably find they're a lot keener to take you.' And Fransen Transport, based in Kidderminster in the West Midlands, had white-liveried artics going into Russia with refrigerated trailers two or three times a month. Their headquarters were down a side road in the shadow of the town's huge British Sugar works: a small one-storey office next to a yard with a single truck in it and hardly space for another. These days trucks were too expensive to keep locked up at the depot: they stayed out on the road every day, paying for them-selves. Inside the office, just half a dozen people at compu-ter terminals. All the greasy stuff like maintenance was contracted out: you wanted the load as lucrative as possible, and in everything else you travelled light.

When I was young – I was going to write 'only', but I suppose this isn't *only* thirty years ago – I remember trailing down to the Surrey Street market in Croydon on Friday mornings with my mother and grandmother, a horrid bellowing mêlée of people shouting *Tamarders free bob a pan'* and glaring at you for the huge favour you were doing them by buying their produce, and shreds of tissue paper that once wrapped oranges sticking to your ankles as you slunk away: this was where you bought your fresh fruit and veg for the weekend. And I remember the year being divided into distinct seasons, a few weeks at a time – it was rather like the pop charts. Spring greens were coming *in*; old potatoes were still around but on the way *out*, and everyone was looking forward to the *new*. Oranges I never favoured: a very badly designed fruit that required far too much peeling and ripping and left you with a mouthful of pips and hands sticky with juice – but satsumas, an admirably user-friendly alternative, like a Terry's Chocolate Orange without the chocolate, came and went with disappointing ephemerality. There was one fleeting cusp during the summer, around the time of Wimbledon, when peaches were in: you had to eat them then, lots of them, because that was your only chance. Strawberries were so evanescent that if you went on holiday at the wrong time, then that was it for another year.

Nowadays, it doesn't grieve me to say we don't buy our fruit and veg from the market stallholder, don't have five pounds of Edwards, dusty and gritty, shot from the silver bowl of the scales into our basket along with a heap of mud-streaked spinach wrapped in yesterday's newspaper. We get them at the supermarket, all year round, never mind the weather: you can have *whatever you want*. Spring greens in the autumn, strawberries for Christmas Day, peaches in February, prickly pears, guavas, miniature potatoes: someone, somewhere, will have been growing them whenever you want them, and there will have been a truck to take them to your local Tesco's. I am surprised the orange is not as extinct as the dodo.

Temperature control, then: it is the medium for a minute-saving, microwaving modern existence. Nothing need be subject now to the elemental laws of heat and cold imposed by climate, season and distance. Perishable goods have a life-support system. That Mars Bar you buy off the kiosk in Oxford Street in the August heatwave may have melted during the ten minutes it has been out on the counter; but, thanks to a temperature-controlled truck, an oil worker in Qatar can eat an unmelted Mars Bar from Slough, England. And the modern trailer can be calibrated for any level of controlled temperature. You can turn it into a deep freeze to transport all the frozen lasagnes and chicken tikka masalas we buy at Marks and Sparks for our TV dinners; you can raise the temperature to a chill for all the dairy produce like butter and cheese and yoghurt, not forgetting the fresh-cut BLTs and coronation chicken sandwiches we buy for lunch; or you can turn the fridge motor off altogether and take advantage of the trailer's insulation to protect bottles of wine from freezing and exploding and vegetables from frosting when delivering them to Arctic regions where the outside temperature is way below zero.

But the history of temperature-controlled haulage is a chronicle of how technological sophistication has brought new markets and new patterns of trade. Twenty years ago a country like Ireland still had very few large trucks of its own – so British haulage firms with refrigerated trailers did a lot of business taking its hanging meat into Europe. Irish meat might go as far as American NATO bases on the Rhine or at Incirlik in Turkey – for a while it was a lucrative enough trade for vehicles to run back empty all the way from France for the next load. Before the terminal contraction of the British merchant shipping industry, there was plenty of work to be had in ship chandlery: meeting a P & O luxury liner at some Mediterranean port, for example, with a truckload of foodstuffs to equip the next leg of its cruise. But as more and more hauliers realized the opportunities in temperature control and bought their own trailers, the price for hauling a load of oven chips across a continent fell unviably low for many: so trucking looked to freight of higher values than comestibles that might reach new markets with benefit of refrigeration. Things like solid emulsion paint, electronics components, the chemicals for circuit-board manufacture, started travelling hundreds of miles in the fridge on the back of a truck. The more sophisticated the temperature control – computers and microprocessor to guarantee the most exact parameters of a specified climate – the more of a niche market a trucker could carve out.

Fransen's had been doing runs to the British embassies in Bucharest and Budapest for a while – their grocery shopping, really: then they got a contract for the Moscow embassy too, as well as the work taking out frozen foods and stocks of beer and wine to some of the bigger hotels who catered for the burgeoning constituency of western business people. A ground-breaking Pink Floyd concert out there had needed truckloads of comestibles for its army-on-the-move tour operation. 'At first we used to send our Russia drivers out with fan belts and all sorts of spare parts;' Fransen's Andrew Southall told me, 'now we don't bat an eyelid. But it can still be a hard job. You only need one bad breakdown or a bad crash there.'

Now the whole of Russia was just starting to open up. The first British trucks were venturing into Siberia. Domestic air freight was still very cheap in Russia, and normally a British shipping agent would have expected to truck a load for Siberia only as far as Moscow and then transship it on to an internal flight, but now western drug companies were beginning to send samples of muscle relaxants, skin treatments and anaesthetics into what they hoped would eventually become a vast new market – and such high-value loads could justify the higher cost of a truck taking them the whole way. Even then, internal Russian trucks could have undercut a British quote by half, but customers wanting to ensure the safe arrival of a valuable shipment would far rather send it all the way with one guy who literally would never let it out of his sight. Fransen's had recently been asked to take a consignment of film to Gorky – movie reels that had to be maintained at exactly 77°F the whole way – at double the Russian rate, because on the previous delivery the Russians' inexact temperature-control procedures had caused the entire cargo to be written off.

These pioneering runs into the Siberian interior some-times had to have a Russian soldier in the passenger's seat as mandatory military escort; a 9,500-mile round trip to Novosibirsk ended up on dirt track for the final 500-mile stage from Omsk, and found a big welcoming committee waiting at journey's end. That kind of assignment needed double-manning: two experienced drivers – one on his own would not see another western driver out there if he got into difficulties. Down on the Caspian and Aral Seas in Kazakhstan, oil and gas companies like Chevron and British Gas were engaged in big exploration and construction projects – prospecting was going ahead as far east as Baku. They all needed their Mars Bars and Primula cheese and Nescafé. But before any British trucker took on jobs like these he had the difficult task of accumulating enough information about the Russian interior to judge whether there'd be fuel supplies in the right places to get your truck all the way there and back.

Fransen's managing director, Henk Buzink, was peering over a further horizon. As container ships had grown in size, so the formerly hectic truck route from Britain down to the Gulf to supply the oil communities had all but dried up. By the time you'd queued for days to get through what had been Czechoslovakia and the borders of Hungary, Romania, Turkey, Syria, Jordan and Saudi Arabia, paid the punitive insurance cover for east of Turkey, and paid to repair the truck after the fearful battering it had received on the Middle Eastern roads, it was much cheaper, though much slower, to put the load on a boat. But now Fransen's Russia drivers were seeing Iranian trucks in Moscow. They must have found a route up from the south-east. Henk traced a line on his wall map eastwards from Moscow, swung his finger down south through Baku, and trailed it on. 'You look at the map and you start to wonder if it might be a good way all the way down to the Middle East – with no borders . . . !' Now *there* was a distant dream – and in the meantime, on the next truck going out, I was riding to Russia.

Chapter Two

Before Russia, I wanted to have a go myself. I wanted to try my hand at driving one of these things. A Class C + D + E licence: the toughest test of all – with it you could drive the biggest truck on a British road, a 50-foot artic. I could have gone to Wembley, on the North Circular. I could have gone to Purley Way, on the light-industrial fringe of Croydon. I could even have gone to Biggin Hill and driven round the lanes of Kent. But to learn to be a truck driver I went to 'The Best Place in the Whole Truckin' World'.

Truckworld, in West Thurrock, Essex – just up the road from where Pete had filled up with the red diesel he had then spilled all the way to Dover – alongside the Dartford Tunnel: one of the newest and biggest and most brashly self-publicizing truckstops in Britain – as the slogan says. At night there is something apocalyptic about the scene. The ocean-liner bulk of West Thurrock Power Station bears down on the approach, pouring steam into the sky. The horizon is skeletal with pylons and braided by the lights of the M25. Marooned in a floodlit clearing amongst grey warehouses and sheds and an intermittent wasteland of scrub and demolition site, a hundred truckers, curtains drawn, are tucked up for the night. As the catering combines have gradually bought up the old truckers' pull-ins on Britain's A roads and turned them into dainty Happy Eaters and Little Chefs with no room for an HGV to park, let alone overnight, places like Truckworld have become increasingly important. The driver heading to catch the ferry at Dover, or down from Scotland or even the Midlands and running out of hours on his tachograph, knows there is a safe place to leave the truck overnight, a hot shower, and some sort of a meal. But you wouldn't want to get hysterical about Truckworld. In any case, the sign that greets your entry sees to that.

Roadtrain had a fleet of red Scanias. A base at Truckworld meant a 10-acre lorry park for practising your manoeuvres. On a chilly Monday morning six of us huddled there at the start of our week-long intensive course in how to drive an HGV. There was Norman from Dagenham, who had just taken voluntary redundancy after twenty-two years as a chargehand gardener with the local council; Les, with constant repartee and a wheezing, infectious laugh, who delivered carpets across half of England for a firm in Basildon; Ivan from Tilbury, like Les a lorry driver already, but only passed for rigids and now wanting his artics licence; Robert, who'd captained supertankers in the merchant navy and was now driving a minicab; Eileen, whose husband had a haulage company and who wanted to be able to take on some of the driving; and me. Behind us the rush-hour traffic was tailing back on the new Thames Bridge. Beside us, a battered Scania, called Wanda.

The first lesson was coupling and uncoupling. Dropping Wanda's trailer was an immediate lesson in the hard physical labour of driving an HGV. You might need to deliver your trailer to Dover dock for it to go on a boat, and hitch up to another one to bring back. In which case you had to wind the trailer legs down with a big iron handle, pull the

air-brake lines off – the emergency line gave a loud report
of compressed air – and knock the locking pin loose on the
unit's greasy fifth-wheel coupling. Disconnecting the air
lines required clambering over the back of the unit and
balancing astride the tangle of grimy pipes; to get at the
locking pin you ducked and craned under the trailer. You
had to use your whole body, had to squat and wrench and
tug: it was a good way to start, out in the open, hands in
oily gloves, learning with your ungainly limbs the inert,
deadweight bulk of an 11-ton artic. I'd enlisted for this
Roadtrain course at its other branch at South Mimms; the
ex-army instructor there had signed me up with the clipped
warning that 'you will be in charge of a very large killing
machine'. The glamorous frisson of those words had already faded. Charlie, our yard instructor, a stocky little
man in his fifties, watched me rotate the trailer legs winder
with careful regularity. I must have looked like Windy
Miller on *Camberwick Green*. 'He's going to be here all
year,' he announced to the others, took over at quadruple
speed, and I wished I hadn't worn my fancy black lace-up
boots.

In the afternoon we watched Roadtrain's proprietor,
Nick Smith, on an instruction video. Smith was another
ex-army man – had come out of the Royal Ordnance Corps
and gone on the Middle East. 'It's not what it was,' he
said. 'In the old days you'd get into Dover after three
months away and say, "Hi, I'm back." Now they want you
to ring in every day even if you're only going to Spain.'
But he'd still rather be out on the road, he said – hated
sitting in one place like this all the time – and once in a
while even now he'd up and leave for the Continent with a
load. His head was efficiently shaved, his speech precisely
pugnacious, and his video began with early-morning kit

inspection. 'First Parade': all the things to check on your truck before you drove it away – everything from clean lights and lenses and registration plate to tyres with no cuts/bulges/bald patches/nails/stones. When he moved on to explain 'some of the expressions you'll hear used in HGV driving' my journalistic ear pricked up. DEAD GROUND: the hidden dip in the road on the other side of a blind summit, possibly hiding an oncoming wide vehicle. THE MEETING-POINT: the illusion of perspective that caused the two sides of the road to appear to meet as the road disappeared around a bend. If the meeting-point didn't open up as you approached you knew it was going to be a sharp one. THE CLOSING GAP: the diminishing distance between a truck's offside wheels and the white line in the road which told you it was pulling out, even if it hadn't signalled. LEAVING YOUR BACK DOOR OPEN: leaving space alongside you on a roundabout for a clever dick in a car to overtake you on your blind spot and force your trailer on to the kerb as you catch sight of him and swerve away. THE BUBBLE SYNDROME: safe procedure at roundabouts by thinking of them as crossroads with a bubble in the middle. I wrote them all down – what resonant metaphors for something! Like *Edge of Darkness* and *The Big Heat* they were spectral intimations of danger. I made mental notes of short stories to be called 'Dead Ground' and 'The Closing Gap' – all I knew was the rich and mysterious title and the unknown but evidently symbolic landscape. They're still unwritten. Once you've been at the controls of an 11-ton artic approaching a blind bend, or seen the back wheels of your trailer scour the grass verge in your wing mirror, metaphor seems – well, you just forget metaphor. Certain expressions, you understand, are coined in order to be used literally.

Then it was behind the wheel for the first time: Reversing Procedure. To pass the British HGV Class E test, you
have to be able to reverse a 50-foot tractor-and-trailer out
of a bay only half as wide again as the vehicle, round the
wrong side of a cone, and back into another bay on the
other side of the cone. The clearances are tight anyway,
and you're doing it all back-to-front in your rear-view
mirrors, but trickiest of all is the relationship between your
unit and your trailer. Steer your unit one way, and the
trailer – pivoting on top of the back of your unit – goes
the other. Steer your unit round fast, and the trailer swings
into motion only slowly. Ease off on the steering, and the
trailer will swing on round regardless until you steer the
unit in the opposite direction to correct it. I came to think
of an artic as a huge, wheeled crocodile, the tip of the
mighty tail taking an age to swish into slow motion, but
then carrying all with it.

But if you waited too long before correcting the swing
of the trailer, or, conversely, if you brought the unit round
the other way too quickly, then you jackknifed the thing:
the unit's wheels were no longer under the trailer, but
rather at right angles to it, and now you had no control
over the movement of the truck. Add in that, for reversing
practice, you had Roadtrain's two most knackered Scanias,
on both of which the power assistance came and went on
the steering, the accelerator pedal wobbled from side to
side, and the whole cab shivered and heaved unless you
got the idling pressure just right. Charlie had been runner-
up a few years ago in the Lorry Driver of the Year
competition: his reversing technique was as good as anyone's. When he showed us, he manipulated the wheel with
one hand, a slight pressure this side, a slight pressure that,
engine just ticking over, all eleven tons barely creeping

across the truck park. I couldn't think whether left on the steering wheel was the same as left in the mirror, and whether that corresponded to left or right in the direction the trailer moved, and which way to pull the unit if that turned out to be the wrong way. Engine roaring, clutch grinding and shuddering as I rode it, I yanked and hauled and the unit kangarooed from side to side, and the trailer just kept slowly, inexorably sliding on into that cone.

'Go and get that guy over there,' said Charlie. 'The one scratchin' his cobblers.'

So I jumped down and waved to Les to climb in next to Charlie, then joined Norman and Robert basking in the afternoon sun. 'When he told me to use my left hand I was fucked,' said Norman Bullock. 'I was *literally* fucked.' He'd also just bumped into one of his old council mates, back from passing his HGV test that day. 'I was on the gardens,' he told us, 'and he was on wheelie bins.' He looked over at me. 'There's a job you should do, Gray: the dustmen. They don't half work hard. *Cyeughh*. I done it for three days when they were short. The *things* people put in their dustbins. They put 'em in upside down – bags of *human shit*. You think, don't they have toilets that work?'

That evening – it was a bank holiday, and Truckworld was half empty – I walked over to the vast new Lakeside Shopping Centre next to the M25. I wandered amongst cool, antiseptic white halls and atria; fountains trickled; stylized model doves flew from the ceiling. The Food Court. The crafts hall. Marble floors. All these things brought here under one roof for you to buy; this emporium striving to be limpid and dappled and sexy as a swimming pool. It was the only landmark for miles around.

Back at Truckworld I had an omelette and chips in the cafeteria – such a mountain of chips I had to smother them in sickly brown sauce to make any impression on them. Huge wrecked weary men sat around, slumped and sated with huge meals. Truckworld remains the only place in the world where I have seen men eating lasagne *with* rice *and* chips *and* potatoes, and finishing the meal off with a Himalayan bowl of fruit crumble and custard. Most nights I'd get up from the cafeteria table cemented up to my oesophagus with starch and feeling like I needed a tow from a Scammell wrecker to pull me out.

In the bar there was Sky Sports football on the television. Between halves the presenter introduced Bob 'The Cat' Bevin – apparently their cheeky-chappie answer to Jimmy Greaves, but I could only see the contrast. 'I hear Wimbledon might be sponsored by *Durex* next season,' he twinkled – he'd obviously worked this whole routine out. 'I was thinking, their chairman, Ramsamy – of course, he's *not of these shores*, though he speaks very good English – maybe he doesn't know what they advertise. He thinks he'll be getting a few Old English sheepdogs on the telly!' The presenter chortled. 'Maybe he'll go along with it until the *bubble bursts*! But will he tell them to keep playing the long ball?' The studio fell about. Bob 'The Cat' beamed.

'You know that sign out the front?' one trucker was saying, pint in hand, to another. 'They're going to take it down in a few months and put up another one that says HAPPY CHRISTMAS YOU TRUCKERS.'

'That is what you call balaclava braking,' said Charlie as, stopping the Scania at the front of the reversing bay, I nearly put him and Les through the windscreen.

'Why's it called "balaclava braking"?'

'It's when you brake so hard your foreskin ends up over your head.'

The second day, and I couldn't get those air brakes. 'Like treading on eggshells without breaking them,' Nick Smith had sternly advised. They gave an 11-ton truck a shorter stopping distance than a family car – when 20 m.p.h. gave an unladen artic the momentum of eighty tons you saw why – and they were amazingly sensitive. Apply infinitesimal pressure, and nothing happened. A minute increase, and if you'd done it coming up to traffic lights you'd have had a nice tailback up your rear end. I was starting to appreciate the subtle combination of brute force and extreme delicacy you needed to drive a truck. That great pole of a gear lever I could just about get my little hand round – you had to ease it in, revving the engine just right when you changed down – but because it was positioned almost behind your shoulder you also had to brace your whole arm to reach and move it at all. Pete from Yeovil had driven in thick clopping clogs; Charlie had a pair of solid boots: they had the feeling of the pedals so fine they could just use the gravitational weight of their shoe to depress the accelerator or brake the right amount. We sat and watched a walrus of a man shoehorn himself out of a rigid van across the truck park. 'See, it's only the last few years you've had really big blokes driving trucks. Look at all these big things coming in here,' said Charlie, 'and a little tiny chap gets out. Great big blokes, they have trouble. Can't steer. Useless at steering.'

'I've seen some pretty big blokes in the cafeteria.'

'Yeah, and if you was to see what truck they had' – Charlie's accusing finger pointed at the Ford rigid – 'it'd be some fuckin' little four-wheeler.'

You couldn't manhandle the controls of a truck as you could your tiny tooty car. If you crashed the controls about it wouldn't go at all. Even taking that old Scania round the truck park was a lesson in how you had to drive a truck through the soles of your feet. You had to become aware of all your muscles, in order to learn not to use them.

Les had a go: did the whole reversing procedure with perfect smoothness.

'You've done this before,' said Charlie. 'Ain'tcha? You said you en't done it.'

'There's lots of things I done,' said Les. 'But I keep quiet about 'em.'

Charlie fished in his inside pocket for a piece of paper to draw me a diagram of the manoeuvre, but his hand brought out a photo. 'My son.' He was standing by a Scammell tipper with a yellow cab. 'Bought it for two thousand pounds. Runs a demolition business in Dagenham.' Now he'd found the old envelope he was looking for, and hurriedly turned it over. But on the back I'd already seen the list of all our names, in shaky black ink, the first day's covert assessment, and at the top was GRAHAM????

It was time for me to go out on the road. Roadtrain's road trucks were newer and in better nick, but they soon made me wistful for the ponderous, slow-reacting heaps back in the yard. They responded about as quickly as I could: the brakes on the truck my road instructor Trevor was taking me out in were hair-trigger sharp. This truck also had a splitter device on the gearstick: two ratios for each of the main five gears – in effect giving you ten gears to drive with. Going up or down hills you might want only to knock off half a gear – or go up one and a half. Each time it was changing down, of course, you had to depress the clutch, put the lever into neutral, rev the engine, and only then engage the new gear – remembering, of course, to have controlled the speed of the vehicle with the brake before the gear change so that the new gear would go in at the right speed. All this needed a precision, a method, and a momentum unnecessary in car driving – but I was now doing it out on the busy roads of south Essex. Our Scania with a full-length trailer on the back was hurtling through Grays town centre; along the dual-carriageway A13 with all the London traffic; round the windy, leafy lanes of Ockenden; through the narrow, mazy roads of an industrial estate; negotiating the busy roundabout beside the Lakeside Shopping Centre; pulling up at traffic lights and zebra crossings and level crossings.

But the complexity of all these traffic conditions is not merely in their adding more things to your list of things to do. The driver of a 50-foot artic – weighing thirty-eight tons if fully laden – cannot afford just to react, to respond to the road on the spur of the moment, or to change his mind in a trice. A truck is too big for most roads, which were designed for stagecoaches, not artics. Think of all those dithery middle-aged women in their little Metros, waiting an age and then shooting out of a side-road only when it's finally too late – or the hair-gelled well-wicked cat in the body-styled BMW Series 3, overtaking on the inside and daring the bus to take them on. Most people drive their car as if they're in one of those motoring sequences in fifties films, where the couple sit in the stationary soft-top with the road spooling pleasantly by on a back projection. Car drivers can get away with driving the little square of daylight through their windscreen. When you have eleven tons stretching 50 feet behind you, you have to drive the whole road, all around you, every second of the way. You're an ocean-liner captain looking through your telescope for icebergs. If there is another wide vehicle coming towards you on a narrow road it is already a factor affecting the speed you need to be driving at when it is still a quarter of a mile away. Approaching any roundabout, a truck driver has not only to drive his own vehicle but, as it were, to drive – in the sense you do cattle – all the other motorists around him. It's not arrogance born of size, but the only guaranteed safety for everyone. He has to keep tight in to the left if he's turning right – to exclude any unthinking motorist from nipping up on his nearside and getting clouted by the crocodile's tail as it swings round. If he's going left he has to move out to the right early, to give himself enough room to get the trailer round, and then move in left as soon as he's off the roundabout – Close Your Back Door – to prevent inside-overtakers trying it on. The trucker has to be aware not only that his vehicle is a long-tailed dinosaur that responds and moves in slow motion, its brain a long way from the tip of its tail, but also that his fellow motorists all assume that because they can dodge and wriggle and flit round him like kingfishers, so can he.

On my first outing, I watched the trailer's rear wheels brush the safety fence round a pelican crossing as I turned left. On my second, concentrating on driving the unit and forgetting about all that truck behind me, I pulled up at traffic lights blocking the entrance to a police station – an endorsable offence on the *driving instructor*'s licence if we'd got caught. 'I don't want to be here,' moaned Trevor, on the edge of his seat for the lights to change. On my third, I cut a right-hand exit from a roundabout too fine and took out a whole line of cones around the inside. A judicious distance down the road I told Trevor, 'I've always wanted to do that.'

'Slower . . . slower . . . SLOWER!' shouted Trevor

every time we approached a roundabout as I caressed and fondled and stroked that fucking brake pedal for *just* the right pressure and the thing kept rolling on and gathering speed until you found a touch more and *jolted!* to a halt. 'Slower ... brake well ahead ... smoothly and in good time ... Make me walk ... Make me walk ...' *Jolt.* 'Slower ... slower ... SLOWER!' – but we were coasting downhill, and I was trying to change down for the round-about and couldn't use the brake until my foot was free from revving the accelerator to put the gear in; the round-about was fast approaching and, because I'd come upon it so quickly the traffic that should have cleared was still on it, I'd have to stop and – *jolt!*

When I think back to learning to drive a car I can remember virtually nothing of where I drove: I know which district it was, but I can't even visualize the general neighbourhood, and I'm sure I couldn't then. But my memory of a week on the roads of Thurrock at the wheel of a Scania is as graphically specific as an aura. I can still see every road, every lay-by we pulled up in; that tight tree-lined bend; that arrow-straight main road where the tipper came at us round the roadworks; that A13 slip-road just after the London distance sign. You do drive every leaf, every kerbstone, every red and white cone, every bumpy manhole. It is fear, when you first take control of a big truck, that makes you do so; it is confident attention that later ensures you still do. It reminded me of how friends of mine with children would instinctively 'baby-proof' a room in a glance as soon as they entered, and how they'd talk of their infant children as 'life-enhancing': all those new things they noticed for you, and you noticed on their behalf. Eleven tons was a big baby to navigate along roads built for horse-carts.

'This is the hardest test you can ever take, Graham,' said Trevor more than once. 'Believe me: getting my licence was the hardest thing I've ever done.'

At our end-of-the-day test on the Highway Code Charlie had asked us, *How should you pass horses or animals in the road?*

Norman had written down, 'Put hazard lights on.'

'"Put hazard lights on,"' Charlie repeated in resigned amazement for the benefit of us all.

'That's 'cos he was on the dustcarts,' said Les Parker.

The Sky Sports was showing rugby league that evening. I watched the Widnes scrum-half Bobby Goulding try to shoulder-charge a brick shithouse of a forward and bounce off, concussed and foetal. The snaggle-toothed Glaswegian trucker next to me dissolved in cackling laughter. ''E 'it 'is fochen 'ead.'

In my dreams that night I watched a momentous accident. It was a Sainsbury's lorry – the driver's overalls matched its familiar beige and cream livery – but it was a *double artic*: not a rigid-plus-box trailer 'roadtrain', like they have in the States, but a unit with full-length trailer – and then *another* 40 feet of trailer coupled on behind that. The whole thing must have been 100 feet long. Sainsbury's, of course, run no such thing: the Ministry of Transport, sensibly enough, permits nothing anywhere near as gargantuan. But I'd dreamt it, and now this poor bastard, his Brylcreemed hair already flopping forward over his brow, was having to drive it.

By the time I was on the scene, safely to the side of the road – which plunged downhill as steeply as a Switzerland mountain switchback – it had already got away from him. Braked too late, misjudged the length of the bend, and he now was scrabbling and tugging at the wheel, never mind the silky power-steering, oversteering like mad to try to get out of his previous oversteer. As one trailer yawed towards me the other slewed away; the unit was already at right angles. A double jackknife! The driver had his cab door open, he was out of his seat and halfway down the steps, craning out in helpless panic for a clue from the heavy slow rippling of the crocodile's tail of trailers behind him as to how on earth he should wrestle that wheel to straighten it all out. In my dream I knew he had no idea, and neither did I. By now he'd lost it, whatever he did. To spare myself the inevitable carnage at the bottom of the hill I woke up, but not before I'd had time, grim, smug and disembodied, to shake my head to myself. I'd never leant out of the cab like that. I'd never lost it like that – he shouldn't have leant out like that . . .

Three families were sitting at breakfast in the cafeteria when we turned up the next morning. At least a dozen kids munched through heaped plates of toast. Was there a caravan site nearby? Were these folks on the way to their holidays? Were they *on* holiday – at Truckworld? As Les and Charlie and I strolled out into the truck park for the morning's reversing practice three black artics from a Barrow-in-Furness firm pulled away in convoy. In each the cab windows were crowded with small faces pressed to the glass.

Les brought out his cigarettes to show me how to do the reversing manoeuvre. His packet of Benson's was the trailer, and his gold lighter was Wanda. When he made the lighter nudge the fag packet backwards and round on the engine cowling I could see how to do it. He rested the packet on the edge of the lighter: 'Remember, the unit is *under* the trailer, Gray.' He pivoted packet on lighter. Yes, I could drive a packet of Benson's. Even though Les had done the reversing right first time Charlie was making him persevere at it, and when he got it wrong Charlie'd amuse himself by giving him painful whiplash swipes in the ribs. 'I'm paying to get fuckin' hit!' Les protested. 'I could go down the pub and get hit for nuffink!' He pointed his lighter at me. 'If you do that to him he'll snap.'

As I pulled up back at Truckworld after Wednesday's road driving, Trevor asked me if I was a very rich man.

To cheer myself up I went into the Truckworld shop and bought myself a Road Monster. It was a red six-wheeler American rig: big coffin-bonnet, silver twin smoke-stacks and fuel tank, and two trailers for a proper road-train, each loaded with real wood logs secured by elastic bands. The model was on a 1/64 scale: it even came with three little road signs and a red-and-white-striped miniature cone. You could keep your clapped-out Wanda. I spent the evening reversing unit and one trailer across my desktop, out of one bay (formed by my Highway Code and my chequebook), round the cone, and into the far bay (copy of *The Truck Driver's Handbook* and driving licence). I tried to watch how fast the Road Monster turned its trailer; how the unit moved out from under, and then back under, the trailer as you steered hard left, and then corrected to straight again. I deliberately jackknifed the Road Monster and tried to diagnose how I'd done it. By the end of the evening I reckoned I'd cracked the physics and the geometry. That left me with the problem of the mirror-perspectives putting it all back-to-front once you got into the cab.

On Thursday the mood amongst the whole class was suddenly sober and grim. Les and Ivan had been entered for their tests on the following Monday; for the rest of us the week's course was already half over. I watched Norman in the truck park practising his reversing, solemn and oblivious, fag dangling from his mouth, to and fro, time after time. Charlie – I could see the exact moment when he realized that the whole joshing, proto-military bullying of the here's-how-you-do-it-and-a-clip-round-the-ear-if-you-balls-it-up approach was never going to work on me – gave me one of the yard trucks for the morning, suggested I drive round the park as many times as I liked, and then work on the reversing in my own time.

It was the best thing, and eventually I cracked it. You used your mirrors as an alternative windscreen: looked through them, and pretended you were going forward. Then it became a question of the unit *pushing* the trailer – you could give it a nudge this way and a nudge that way like a sheepdog nosing a flock of sheep through a gate. And at last the steering corresponded: if you wanted the back of your trailer to go left in your mirror, you steered the wheel to the left. It worked! I still hit the cone, I still drove over the sides of the bays, I still turned the wheel too fast or too slowly – but at least I was doing it wrong in the right way.

In the cafeteria at lunchtime Les asked us if we'd heard the one about the Irish gynaecologist: 'Tried to decorate his hallway through the letterbox.' Then I noticed he had two tea bags steeping oxtail-soup brown in his mug. When everyone laughed Les shrugged at our lack of initiative. Nothing was too small for a bit of ducking and diving. 'It's the only way I'm going to get a decent cup of tea. Tea bag in your pocket . . . and then you pay for your cuppa!' There was a transport café up Edgware way, he added, where they made Yorkshire puddings the size of *plates*. 'But when you go for roast beef, they always put the Yorkshire on first, so you hardly get anything else on the plate. So what I do – you get all the roast beef and everything, bring it back to your place. *And then I go up for my Yorkshire . . .*'

I stayed to watch the evening's entertainment at Truckworld. Most nights they had a comedian and a stripper. The comedy was a hyperactive grey-haired man, machine-gun delivery, who told one joke about darkies with a black guy sitting right in front of him. The comedy was either dumb knee-jerk my wife/Irishman/Paki/poofter fare to raise a wheezing guffaw, or it was ingeniously and protractedly scatalogical. Some routines had a Wilkie Collins intricacy, but all the protagonists were cunts and minges, and wanking, and skiddies, and makin a tent wiv der bedcloves, and shit and semen in industrial quantities. Who went to the trouble of thinking all this up? Was it other truckers – did these mini-series of filth come out of a lonely empty day flogging some fucked old Foden down the length of the A1? The room swirled with cigarette smoke. Tonight the bar was full. The slumped truckers didn't laugh much. They weren't doing *anything* very much.

'Boatload of Veetnamese boat people, captain tries to dock 'em at Liverpool. Shop steward at Liverpool says (parodic Scouse accent), "We ehen't fochen techen them. Goe ter Brisstol." Captain goes to Bristol. Fuckin' harbour master says (parodic West Country accent), "Oy'm nart lettn' you unload them 'ere. Troy Tilbury." Captain sails to Tilbury, says to good old fuckin' East End docker, "I got a load o' fuckin' Veetnamese boat people on board, you gonna take 'em?" East End docker goes, "They on pallets?"'

Once or twice a month, according to the Truckworld calendar of events, they had a quiz evening. I'd have loved to hear the questions.

Then the disco lights were looping and raking across the

bar, and the PA was thumping out a heavy loud beat *bomp-a-bomp-baba-bompbompbomp*, and it was time to admire Amber, big doe eyes and a busty figure poured into black leather. Now the place was galvanized: Amber undid the leather flaps covering her breasts to let her nipples poke through, bent double a lot with her back to the audience and fingered her groin, and off came the leather top, and a thrill went round the room, and off came the leather hot pants, and when she was down to G-string and high boots it was time for baby oil over buttocks and crotch. When the G-string came off everyone was transfixed with excitement – there were guys standing on the snooker tables craning for a look. But as soon as Amber had shed everything the disco beat ceased. The lights went out. Pints were already being pulled again at the bar. Amber, still gleaming with oil, was quietly collecting her scattered clothes like a runner looking for her tracksuit.

In the morning I climbed into Wanda and took her a few times round the truck park – by now I liked that loose-limbed rattle of the flatbed in tow, bumping and swaying over manholes. A car was so small that even when you drove one you still felt like a passenger: now, in my throne-like driving position high above the tarmac, the big flat wheel like a desk to sit at and command, that big metal tail swishing from side to side behind me, I was really driving! I pulled up into the first reversing bay. Reach that cudgel of a gear lever over into reverse, and get Wanda creeping backwards on idle. Hard left wheel as quickly as possible to get the trailer moving out round the far side of the cone, until you're on full lock. Watch your front wheels to check they're not going over the side of the bay. As soon as you can see the back of the trailer safely heading past the cone, right wheel to bring the unit back round and under the trailer. Head back diagonally across the truck park over towards the far bay, checking in your mirror that the side of the unit's going to miss the cone. As soon as you can see the back end of the trailer framed by the sides of the far bay, right wheel again to start curving the trailer in – gradually, because you don't want to jackknife the thing. Once you've got the trailer turning in, left wheel to straighten up the unit under the trailer again so you back in in a straight line. When you see the rear line of the bay level with the bulldog clip Charlie's fixed on the trailer's rear-wheel mudguard: *stop!*

I jumped down from the Scania, leapt in the air and clapped my hands above my head as I ran over to Charlie.

'You didn't think you'd ever do it, did you?' said Charlie as he pumped my hand.

'Now you can go and buy your first Yorkie bar,' said Norman.

The final sessions of road driving were still no good – I couldn't work those air brakes any better than at the start of the course – but by now I knew this was the hardest thing I'd ever tried to learn in my life, and I wasn't going to be a truck driver in a week. I could reverse a 50-foot Scania artic through the full Ministry of Transport Test manoeuvre, though. I could do that. In the meantime, my mother would just have to buy herself a truck – some old Ford Cargo would do, I wasn't fussy – so I could practise on that. It's how you learn to drive a car.

Truckworld on Friday night had quite the deadest, most enervated disco I've ever encountered: the bar half empty as truckers tried to get home for the weekend, and half a dozen nervous and bored local girls sidling in to sit together with chins on hands. Was there *nowhere* else round here for teenagers to go?

For our final morning we had another video to watch, and Charlie to tell us about tachographs. The video took you through the whole test procedure, the camera following a Roadtrain Scania around all the roads of Dagenham, Thurrock and Ockenden we'd been rumbling along all week. The truck passed a gang of guys cutting the grass on a roundabout. 'Look at those dickheads!' exclaimed Norman. 'I worked with those bastards!'

When the video showed a Roadtrain truck carrying out the reversing procedure Les said, 'They was going to put you in this video, Gray. But they only had a 4-hour slow-speed tape.'

Charlie showed us how to fill a tacho disc in, and took us through the regulations on drivers' hours. We noted down all the exceptions to the rule, all the heavy industrial vehicles not required to operate with a 'spy-in-the-cab': tractors, combine harvesters, JCBs, fire engines, ambulances . . .

'Bird's Eye peas lorry,' said Les.

We all looked at him.

'Well, you've seen that ad on the telly, Charlie. "Straight from the pod to the plate." The peas lorry can't pull into a lay-by and say, fuck it, I'm on my nine hours' break.'

Then Robert had to leave and pick up his minicab to collect someone from Heathrow; he and Norman would be returning on Monday for another week's teaching to try and get them through. Ivan and Les were both to fail their tests first time – it was roundabouts that did for them, as it was with most HGV test failures. Trevor stopped his Scania at the Truckworld gates as I was walking off for the bus to Grays station, and I told him I'd be back, sometime.

In London a few days later, I was on a bus stuck in traffic tailed back from Islington all the way down the

Essex Road. I jumped off and walked ahead to find the reason. At the junction with Upper Street, a little Ford Panda was wrapped around the wheels of an Iveco artic loaded with bricks. The car driver had been lucky: he was standing with hands on hips talking to the traffic cop. *Bloody great thing — look how he's hogging the whole road — all thunder along as if they own it — if I'm quick I can nip past him now*: I could imagine it all. I couldn't have driven that truck yet, but at least I knew now why you had to let a truck driver close his back door in your face.

Chapter Three

The hardest part of this job, said Tony Meddings, was getting out of your own country. Fransen's had come up with a load for Moscow, and I'd met Tony and his Seddon-Atkinson Strato at a bond warehouse in Dover high above the town. Tony was forty-five, but with his receded white hair he looked, like Pete from Yeovil, a lot older. It was quarter to seven in the evening already. Still becalmed at the docks with none of the TIR carnets ready yet or customs clearance given, we were looking at a midnight ferry. November: beneath the ivory-white cliffs a freezing mist tingled in the floodlights.

Tony had made five pick-ups in the last twenty-four hours to fill up the refrigerated trailer. He'd tipped his previous load the day before down in Bristol – 'I thought, I'll be home tonight. It's only forty-five miles away' – but then Fransen's had phoned to say he had to be in Reading first thing in the morning. 'You try to get home, but you don't always make it. The last time I was home was four or five weeks ago, and that was only one night.' Home was his daughter's house in Evesham – he was divorced from his wife. So he'd driven up the M4 and overnighted at Colnbrook, and then been at Novacold in Reading for 6.00 a.m. to load 31 cases of frozen lamb saddles and 25 cases of gammon steaks. Then on to another cold store at Wey-

bridge in Surrey for 105 cartons of ice-cream. Then 30
cartons of frozen Cornish pasties, 12 cases of Brussels
sprouts, 5 of baby carrots and 5 of sweetcorn, all from
Dunton Green. And on to Dover to the Hibberts bond
warehouse, where we'd taken aboard 275 kegs of beer, and
185 cases of wine.

We were going to the Red Lion pub, Moscow; the
Savoy Hotel, Moscow; and the Baskin Robbins ice-cream
parlour, Moscow. The frozen food was for the pub's bar
meals: I knew what cuisine I'd be having to sample when I
finally got to Russia. Baskin Robbins was getting the ice-
cream from Weybridge, and also two boxes of parts for its
freezers, a late arrival by express van from Maidstone, and
100 cases of 'plastic kitchenware' – little ice-cream spatulas
made in Croydon. The wines were for the Savoy – a
consignment put together by Grants of St James's, a subsidi-
ary of Allied Breweries, who were also the joint-venture
partners in the Red Lion. It was an impressively cosmopoli-
tan selection: Pouilly Fumé, Chablis, not to mention a bit
of Beaujolais; Villa Maria from New Zealand; Chianti and
Frascati; and Errazuriz Premier Chilean Wine. All this
alcohol had obviously done a good deal of trucking already.
The beer was more familiar: John Smith's bitter, Skol lager,
and plenty of Guinness – some for the hotel, and the rest
for the pub. The load was completed with a few boxes of
Luminarc 'Elegance Hi-Ball' tumblers for the Savoy, and a
box of standard Guinness drip-mats. At the Dover docks
weighbridge we were right on our 38-ton weight limit.

Our unit was, as Tony put it, 'a bit of a poser's truck': a
special customized version of the Strato of which only ten
had been made. Polished alloy wheels; a Globetrotter twin-
bunk high-ceiling cab, fared in and streamlined at the back,
which allowed you to stand up inside it even when you

were over six foot; leather seats; fuel-line heating to prevent the diesel waxing up in the pipes in extra-cold weather; and a weight-transfer option on the rear wheels that allowed Tony to shift sixteen tons of the payload on to the drive axle to give added traction on hills and in snow. Add a 400-horsepower Cummins engine, a silver paint-job all over – for an image of frosty hygiene Fransen's usually painted its trucks plain white – and, to confirm our elite status, 'Silver Knight' scrolled in red across the aerofoil on top of the cab. Not, I was congratulating myself, something you could ever mistake for a *lorry*. But Tony wasn't the kind of guy, it was already clear, to let this sort of thing go to his head: he, I soon found, was quite happy to talk about mere 'motors' and 'lorries'. The flash Harrys who worried about that sort of thing he called 'romancers'.

'You get a lot of them in this profession,' he'd been saying in his soft Worcestershire burr as we'd rumbled down from the bond warehouse into the town, darkness already fallen. 'Oh, they're the best drivers of the lot, they are. Some of them, they've only come to Dover to pick up a trailer from import and deliver it in England. They've never been abroad in their lives, but they'll have heard everyone else talking.

'But if you're going to be a romancer you've got to be good at it. You'll meet him in Watford, with a tilt from the dock' – it was the commonest trailer around – 'and he'll have a louder voice than anyone. He'll *just* have got back from Tehran, and already you'll hear, "Hark at him!" like – and soon he's got his audience. Well, you can't do Tehran these days . . .'

But Tony had been on the road long-distance for eighteen years, and it was he, and not the romancer, who had the Silver Knight.

'I've never been to Moscow, though. It's one place I haven't been. I took five guitars, a set of drums and a pool table to Kiev for that singer, Ian Gillan. Took that to Kiev – it was only a ton, couldn't believe that. But Moscow's a new challenge.'

It was nearly eleven before we were through customs – four and a half hours after we'd arrived on the dock. We went into the Sealink office to confirm our ferry, and there Tony bumped into a couple of home-town mates from Evesham he hadn't seen for months, and we adjourned to the bar. Lennie, a wiry Yorkshireman, ran an F-reg MAN with his wife Maggie as Mag-Len Haulage; but this time he was double-manning with a guy in a denim jacket called Don, who muttered something about being an off-duty policeman. It was unclear how permanently Don was off-duty: he rolled his eyes and craned his neck inside his jacket and sighed that it was 'a long story' and something to do with 'a domestic incident'. Edgar, a new boy to Continental trucking, who'd just been talking about the dynamite birds in Italy, had a small Volvo. Both trucks had car parts from Dagenham on board: Edgar was going to Hungary, Lennie to Istanbul.

Settled down with a Pils, Lennie leaned over to me when he heard about my assignment and gave me his opinion. 'I'm getting to *dislike* this work,' he exclaimed. 'All the "baksheesh", that's what gets to me. I pay £700 a month HP on my truck – it's not new, but it's all right, it's only three years old. I've never missed a payment and I've only got another fourteen months to go. And £800 a month insurance, and £3,400 a year road tax, when I'm abroad nine weeks in ten. There's only about three hundred of us in this country doing this work –'

'This country doesn't want a haulage industry,' said Don in amazement.

'– and then I get to a Hungarian border crossing and the policeman goes to drive off with my passport and it's seventy quid to get it back! The time before I had to give my pen to some other policeman – and the Hungarians, they're always arseholed. And the queues! We were *eighty-nine hours* at the Hungarian border last time. *Eighty-nine hours!* And there's *no* sanitation. It's not on.'

A rumpled, paunchy man with a shock of unbrushed hair and a filthy Bosch T-shirt was shambling over to join us. He peered at us in dazed scepticism through thick spectacles that had slipped to the end of his nose.

'It's Mr Mole,' said Lennie. Mr Mole slumped down next to Tony and puffed on a fag. Here was another Middle East stalwart: he and Tony had crossed paths on the road to Istanbul for the last fifteen years, and he was on his way there yet again.

'Look at him,' said Tony. 'Where've you been?'

'I just changed my clothes,' complained Mr Mole in a broad Huddersfield accent, brushing at his grease-smeared T-shirt. 'Clean on.' He smiled sagely through his cigarette smoke.

'Did you hear about his prang in the lay-by?' said Lennie. '*Priceless*. He parks up for the night in the same one every time out. Never looks where he's going. This time it's got three ton of gravel dumped in it.' He went *smack!* with his fist into his palm. 'Blind as a fookin' *bat*.'

Tony was getting up and fingering the leg of his smart sandy-coloured slacks. He looked at Mr Mole. The legs were already streaked with black grease. 'I'm getting back to my truck.'

Lennie, Don and Edgar followed us back to the truck

park. 'Let's have a look at this here camion,' said Edgar. They scuffed and picked around the Silver Knight, admiration ill-concealed behind worldly disapproval. A couple of German truckers walking across the park stopped before the Silver Knight and looked it up and down the way you undress a woman with your eyes. 'I don't like them there wheels,' said Edgar, toeing the polished silver-alloy hubs with his boot.

We drove round to the ferry loading-ramp. I browsed through Tony's copy of the *Sun* and read the story of 'randy trucker' Richard Burley, whose wife found out about his summer naughtiness abroad when his French lover put a picture of him and her together in the paper to try and find him.

'That's all it was,' complained Richard, 'a fucking fling ... How do you think I felt when she was handing pictures out all over the place? My wife has given me a hard time   I'm lucky to have any b***s left.'

At 11.30 p.m. we rumbled on to the *Pride of Bruges*, left the truck on the booming, roaring cargo deck just in front of Lennie's MAN and went up to the restaurant. This boat – 'an old banger,' said Tony; 'the worst of the lot' – had been converted into a cargo-only ferry: the Zeebrugge route no longer carried cars or foot passengers. If a truckers' restaurant called the Carvery, with linen tablecloths, thick carpets, blue-waistcoated waiters and freshly squeezed orange-juice in slender goblets, was not a legacy from First-Class passenger days, and not taking the piss, but offering only well-meaning hospitality, then it wasn't working. These drivers were weary and irascible – midnight already, and still no food – and after many hours hanging around on the quayside they were in no mood to wait even minutes for their meal. At every waving knife and 'Oi, *where*'s my food?' the waiters padded to and fro, smoothly, implacably, rigidly courteous. They obviously got this every night. On the next table Lennie was throwing a wobbly because he still hadn't got his mixed grill. Don had sent his gammon back a second time because the potatoes were hard. The place was done up like a leisurely luncheon salon in a time-expired department store, and here, in the middle of the night, it was making a hundred battered truckers behave like stroppy dowagers. Mr Mole pulled a chair up at our table and wagged a hand at the steward.

'Was that "*garçon*" or "arsehole"?' inquired the steward with unctuous aplomb.

Mr Mole wanted to know what was for starters.

'Melòn balls in port.' The steward smirked. Mr Mole went for the mixed grill, and after a few pulls on his cigarette started getting impatient.

I asked him if he was taking Ford parts as well.

'No. I'm a professional,' said Mr Mole. 'Them's for the rank and file. I'm taking cigarette filters, me.'

Lennie was at his elbow. What was this, he wanted to know, about Mr Mole losing eight hundred quid in Sofia?

It was a complicated tale about four transvestites knocking on your cab door when you pulled up for the night and offering you all kinds of favours until you shooed them away and thought you'd seen the back of them, and I only followed it in snatches. They couldn't have been the same as the Bulgarian prostitutes whose expert attentions Mr Mole was now extolling? 'The first one – finger straight up your arse', he mused in satisfaction. 'And while you're lyin' back going' – he mimed gaga prostration. How many of *them* were there in his cab? Or was this how Mr Mole had lost his money?

Lennie was moving eagerly in for the kill. 'And where was your wallet?'

'It were in me trousers on't seat.'

'And where were your glasses?'

'They were on't dashboard.'

'I've never known *anyone*,' exulted Lennie, 'get in *so* much *trouble*!'

Three and a half hours of sleep in a throbbing cabin later we were back down on the truck deck and engines were thrumming into life around us. But the Silver Knight's ignition switch clicked meekly, and Tony had to fix up a jump start from Lennie's MAN to get us off the boat. 'These smart new fancy trucks,' said Lennie. At 5.00 a.m. we rolled off the *Pride of Bruges* into a foggy glowing dark. The bars, caves of orange, were still open in the dock area. We all met up at a truckstop on the outskirts of Zeebrugge for a coffee, and Edgar bought himself a brown leather wallet with TRUCKERS embossed on it. Lennie and Don were going to have a couple of hours' kip and then go non-stop to get into the former Czechoslovakia before the end of Saturday. In Germany HGVs weren't allowed to drive on Sundays until ten at night. 'Just a piece of shit,' said Edgar when Lennie told him of our flat battery. 'Yer fookin' dipstick,' said Mr Mole through the window of his white Volvo. He poked the cigarette he was rolling at me. 'He'll be pushin' and shovin' yer all the way there.'

We were heading for a truckstop just outside Hanover, some six hundred kilometres away. By the end of today Tony would have used up his weekly hours' limit on the tachograph, so even without the Sunday HGV ban we'd have to lay up for a full twenty-four hours. By mid-morning we were calling in for diesel at Wenlo, a sylvan residential suburb on the Dutch border, at a gas station where Fransen's had credit. Fifteen hundred litres filled up the belly tank under the trailer as well as the main tank on the unit: by periodically pumping fuel across, Tony would have enough now to get us all the way to Moscow and perhaps back into Poland. Across the road there was a Saturday morning dog-obedience class. Ranged in neat formation across the dewy field like a passing-out parade, Afghans and spaniels and setters stood to attention beside their owners in the thin drizzle.

We crossed into Germany at half ten; it was six o'clock and dark before we got to the truckstop at Mellendorf, after a long crawl through the rain where the autobahn had been reduced to a single lane to allow tree-felling on a steep embankment. After the flat grey cruise past cities like Dortmund and Essen – all concrete cuttings and under-passes and flyovers – wooded foothills had swelled around us, magnificently shading from emerald to orange to copper to magenta. It was to be the brightest splash of colour around us the whole way.

Sleeping arrangements in a long-haul truck aren't bad. There are twin bunks behind the seats, rather like couch-ettes on European trains, and when, as in the Silver Knight, it is a 'Globetrotter' cab (the term was coined by Volvo, the first manufacturer to offer an extra-high cab roof specification), you can stand up in the morning to put your trousers on. Curtains – I don't know whether you could specify Liberty's fabrics, but these were a kind of grey weave, just the thing if you didn't want to think about curtains – could be unzipped from inside the hanging wardrobe where the driver's clean clothes could stay neatly pressed, and pulled around all the windows. In older trucks you had to keep the engine running all night if you wanted to keep the heater or the air-conditioning on, but newer models had a cab heater running off a separate small tank of diesel. A little tabletop pulled out over the transmission casing: that was the breakfast table for the morning cuppa. But imagine sleeping in the kitchen, or having your fridge in your bedroom – and that fridge the size of a house: the noise of the motor on a refrigerated trailer takes getting used to. When the thermostat-controlled motor – positioned literally just behind your head – switches on, it's not with the gentle New Age hum of the fridge you keep your milk and yoghurts in, but the loud bray of a lawnmower. It took me that first night to learn not to hear it.

A Liverpudlian guy was working in the Mellendorf gasstation shop. He'd come out nine years earlier with the army, married a German woman and now worked for IKEA, the furniture warehouse. When IKEA set up on the North Circular he had had the chance to transfer back to England, but though he was having to work weekend shifts here to make ends meet he said he still couldn't afford to go home. The truckstop had been quiet for three weeks, he said – nothing coming through. You went crazy trying to find things to do. Impassive and helpful, he passed on lurid tales of the road beyond his becalmed kiosk. 'We've had several western truckers shot at in Russia in the past few weeks. The guys in the smart trucks – the Mercs and things. If you don't stop and give them everything they shoot you – and the police, they just stand by and whistle!'

There were about twenty trucks laid up at the Autohof for the weekend: Danish, Hungarian, Norwegian – but there was space for a hundred. On the Sunday morning Tony did his housework – always did his housework on Sunday mornings. He had a Mr Sheen aerosol for the windows; he polished the wheels; swept the dust off the dashboard and gearbox console with a fine-bristle paint-brush; hung a conifer-shaped air freshener to dangle above the windscreen and exude the vanilla aroma of Johnson's Baby Lotion; and secreted little bags of pot pourri in the glove compartments in the doors.

Truck drivers, it seemed, fell into two kinds, the house-proud and the hovel-dweller. Tony's orderliness paled beside his tales of two colleagues. Barry, we'll call him, never moved out of his cab the whole time he was in a place like Moscow – spent ten quid on himself the entire round trip, begrudging even a beer or a cup of coffee out. He'd taken a truckload of frozen food all the way to Bucharest to supply the Michael Jackson tour, and passed up a free room in the five-star Intercontinental Hotel to spend twelve days sitting tight in his nest, cleaning and polishing. Company driver he may have been, but had nevertheless passed a law that no one else was allowed to drive his motor. 'You could eat your dinner off the inside of his fridge,' said Tony. 'When he put his truck in for service he told the mechanics he wanted his cab kept *spotless*. One of them said to him, "You're a fussy sod – you treat this thing like it's your fuckin' home." He said, "If you were living in here forty-seven weeks out of fifty-two it'd be *your* fuckin' home."'

George, meanwhile, had collected his truck from over-haul to find a mechanic had been smoking in the cab. The garage had had to pay for the interior to be valeted *twice* before he was satisfied that the last slight whiff of smoke had been expunged. Such men were the equivalent of the gypsies whose caravans have painted porcelain chimney-pots and lace curtains. Their home happened to be on wheels: no reason not to spring-clean it as spotless as a semi. Tidy, hygienic individuals like this got put on fridge work: the kind of well-scrubbed guy you'd want handling your frozen fish fingers; the ideal courier the drug company would want to see turning into their high-tech plant to pick up an expensive pharmaceutical consignment.

The hovel-dwellers, on the other hand, took the scout-camp approach to nomadic life. Never mind the dirty underpants and fag ash everywhere – that was easy. Such men kept sacks of coal on their bunk-beds to fuel summer barbecues beside the trailer, and impregnated curtains and seat covers with cloying greasy odours and fat splashes from huge breakfast fry-ups on a Camping Gaz inside the cab. Tony knew one driver whose dedication to squalor had managed to knock a good thousand off the resale price of his truck.

After the housework, Tony sat and sorted out his paper-work – bringing his log sheet up to date, totting up his running money expenditure, checking that all the CMRs, the insurance forms, tallied with the TIR customs forms and the suppliers' individual invoices. Border officials would seize on any discrepancies, and that would mean long delays. I went for a walk into Mellendorf village. It was a high, bright, blue day, a slumbrous Sunday morning; not even a breeze. From the truck park, zigzagged with big metal hunks of truck, the straight tree-lined road led between fields of pasture and sugar beet. Families wobbled past on cycles, out for a weekend ride. On the village outskirts a gaggle of kids was jostling at the gates of the ice rink, fluorescent skates in hand. A silent railway line crossed the road at an open level crossing, an empty platform. The village was so quiet it was like a film set. Only a single bus and a couple of BMWs broke the silence hovering over the flat landscape, and walking there and back took me a good hour and a half.

It was my first experience of the way trucking travel leaves you on the outskirts of things. The trains slide into a central station, and even late at night there is always bustle – electric carts clanking trolleys of mailbags behind them; and expectancy – restless passengers scuffing up and down the platform waiting for their connection. Here we were, however, off the autobahn, down the road from the village, twenty kilometres from the city, conveniently nowhere, hiding out for a day where we weren't really welcome and didn't fit, until we could rumble off again and leave the neat, manicured village to the slumber it hadn't realized we hadn't disturbed.

At quarter to ten that night engines roared into life in the truck park so drivers had time to build up the air in their brakes and transmission, and at ten precisely a convoy of artics and roadtrains pulled out under a gleaming ivory full moon. It was another sharp, clear night, and by two in the morning we were past Berlin and running through forests of spindly birches. The American Forces radio was giving helpful tips to new arrivals. 'Cultural shock can bring depression, irritability and dislocation,' quavered the announcer in clotted Cronkite tones. 'But a sense of humour can help accommodate you to your place away from home. And then begins the adventure of exploring this new country . . .'

A quick stop for a cup of tea at Straby petrol station fifty kilometres from the Polish border, next to a Lada crusted silver with the thick frost – its sleeping inhabitants were swaddled thick in blankets – a shivery piss among the infant pine trees, and then on to the border post at Frankfurt-am-Oder.

Border posts are like busy railway stations without the trains: all the commotion, the restless travellers, the echoey clamour underneath the platform-length strip-lit canopies, an arena of cold daylight in the night – but no theatrical cleansing arrivals and departures. Instead, edgy inching forward; pulling over to the side; parking up; or a limitless, apparently purposeless, wait. Charlie Watts was once asked to describe the experience of twenty-five years playing with the Rolling Stones. 'Five years playin',' came the sepulchral reply, 'and twenty years waitin' around.' For the European trucker it is all much the same: waiting to get going, and then the faster you go once you're moving the quicker you get to the next wait. Worse, the driving – the bustle, the expedition – is the solitary part. The attention and interaction of people once you finally reach the border is no reward, but rather a denial of welcome and the imposition of chaos. No one knew you were coming, no one asked you to come, and certainly no one seems to know what to do with you.

This time we were lucky. Twenty minutes trudging around from office to soldier's hut under the floodlights froze the feeling out of our hands but established that Poland no longer required or issued visas for entry – last time Tony had been through he'd needed £5 and a passport photo. A Chaplinesque customs woman with a heavy black moustache passed the TIR papers and, miraculously, at four-thirty in the morning, after just three-quarters of an hour, we were free to go. All the time we were there elderly orange and white Polish coaches, loaded low on their suspension, were lumbering in, windows streaming with condensation and weary passengers stretching and yawning and nuzzling their faces into their seats. They were all returning from day trips into Germany, and customs clearance for them looked as if it was going to take a long while.

It took twelve minutes, once out of the border gates, to drive past the queue of trucks, two and three wide, waiting to get into Germany: there must have been five miles of them. They were stopped from entering Germany until ten o'clock Sunday night and now, said Tony, they'd got to the border and were having to wait until the agents they needed to furnish their customs documentation started work again on Monday morning. 'We saved half a day there.' That queue could as easily have been on the other side of the border.

On, under a full moon haloed with orange-brown clouds. Airliners squeezed thick toothpasty contrails across the sky. Little kiosks, open by the roadside in the middle of nowhere in the middle of the night, had wicker baskets and clay pots hung up for sale on racks. At 6.00 a.m. we stopped in a bumpy lay-by in the forest for a few hours' sleep, woke up to a cloudless blue sky, and set off again in the middle of the morning, six hundred kilometres ahead of us to the Russian border at Terespol. With a lot of the highway across Poland neither dual carriageway nor bypassing the towns, it would be about a $10\frac{1}{2}$-hour drive.

We were virtually transnavigating Poland in a day, so Poland impinged only as an unravelling frieze through the truck window. On the approach to Poznan we passed through little sandy-coloured towns and villages; the other side of the city – a sprawl of factories and blocks of flats, scrubby belts of trees and allotments we wound among on broken, humpy roads – smooth new motorway stretched ahead across a vast plain of fields. A white horse pulled a plough; a farmer shovelled manure on to his small patch; an old woman in a headscarf bent astride the railway tracks oiling the points. Then we were among the evening rush of central Warsaw: the trams, the red and yellow McDonald's signs, the skyscrapers and slabby flats – for the first time today a landscape in which the 50-foot truck felt small instead of huge – and an hour and a half later pulling into the truck park at a motel at Siedlce.

Just as we'd been leaving the Carvery on the *Pride of Bruges* Edgar had taken me aside and nodded after Tony, solemn and pensive. 'He's one of the best you'll find,' he murmured. 'He was one of the pioneers of the Middle East.' So that evening in the motel restaurant I asked Tony how he'd first got into Continental trucking.

He'd been driving trucks ever since he was seventeen – limited at that age to 3-tonners. When he was twenty-four, by now driving artics for Spiers and Hartwell in Evesham, the boss had said he was thinking about going overseas, and Tony'd said, why not? 'So, on the 15th of November, 1974, I picked up a load of Old Spice aftershave in Swindon, to go to Jeddah. The boss said, "I've never been overseas myself, but in this briefcase here is everything I've been told you'll need" – and that was it. I went through France, Italy, Yugoslavia, Bulgaria, Turkey . . . and every time I didn't know where I was going I just asked somebody. Picked up with some Germans on part of the way – found my way there by word of mouth. It took me exactly one month: I got back the 15th of December. Then, on the 2nd of January, I went back out.

'From there he built his trade up, and in the end there were eight of us going out. But then another company came along and undercut us, and the boss said let 'em, I'm not going overseas any more. Of course, by then I'd been doing it eight or nine years, and it was in my blood. So I left him. It's like a disease – you can't get rid of it. It cost me my marriage – literally, she said, it's the job or me. I tried not doing it for a month ... But I'm only happy when I'm driving, like. I go back home for a couple of days to unwind, then I want to get back on the road. The longer the trip, the better it is.'

A bank-managerish man with slicked-down hair was playing tripping, shuffling songs at a Hammond organ, bleating out quavery vocals far too close to the microphone, a male Edith Piaf.

'And what was your longest run?'

'That would have been Karachi – back in '75. That was Old Spice aftershave again. This was in the days when you used to be able to transit Iran and Afghanistan. I got down to the Pakistan border, and I was there for twenty-two days, because the importer in Pakistan wouldn't pay the import tax. There were three of us went down there, and that trip took us thirteen weeks and two days. You've either got it in you or you haven't. You've got to have patience – if you haven't got that you might as well give up. Before the Gulf War there were queues from Turkey going into Iraq fifty-five K's long.' Another thought occurred to Tony. 'You've got to be a headbanger, really. A nutto. You've got to get it into your system. You see, now the winter's coming in the summer boys are all packing up. They'll just be doing Belgiums and internals all winter. A lot of drivers don't even know how to put snow-chains on.' Tony hadn't had time to get home before coming out, so he was heading for Moscow in November with thin cotton slacks, no gloves, and clogs on his feet. He'd bought a quilted tartan shirt at the truckstop in Germany but only ever wore it open and flapping about him. He said, 'I don't like to be all done up.'

The music jigged and nudged along like the signature tunes to bad regional TV quiz-shows, but the dining couples at the end of the hall — there was some kind of conference in — leapt up to dance, galumphed boisterously about, jitterbugged and whooped and clapped hands. When we went back to the truck, a roadtrain full of steaming, monotonously groaning lambs had pulled up in the freezing frost.

In the morning there were three Dutch trucks parked in front of us. 'Heijden Transport,' said Tony as we had our first — at 4.00 a.m. it was hardly morning — cuppa. 'That's the firm we used to load Mars Bars from in Holland. Can't touch 'em any more. The last job I had, we were delivering Mars Bars from Slough to Saudi, Qatar — Kuwait was the main one. They'd give you some samples when you loaded at the factory. Well, when I say samples I mean boxes. I did that job for eight, nine years. Snickers, M & M's . . . Bountys were the ones that made me sick. Now I just *cringe* when I see them.'

An hour and a half's drive between white frosty fields, a pink sky ahead of us and huddled figures stomping their feet at the roadside as they waited for the works bus, and we hit the border queue at Terespol. Six-thirty. Click off the ignition, and silence. Three hours later, and the light had come up on a pale sunny winter day. Crows and choughs wheeled over the fields. A woman cycled across the rutted, frozen earth towards the river. A gang of workmen pottered at the roadside hacking earth out of an embankment. There was time to watch, minute by minute, the thick white covering of frost on the fields thin and recede and disappear. There were still nine trucks, mostly Russian artics of the state-owned Sovtrans company, ahead of us before the barrier, and as many more had drawn up behind.

I stayed in the cab in the Polish border compound while Tony went to clear his customs forms. Soon a crowd of Russian truckers had built up around the Silver Knight. They paced around it, poked at the freezer motor controls, argued in front of the radiator. One man looked up through the windscreen and gave me a headshake and whistle of bewildered admiration. There was a knocking on my door. What kind of engine did this have? asked their spokesman in German. And what was the horsepower? And what kind of gear-box? And who made the cab? Eventually – I was stumped on the gear-box – one of them pointed to my notebook, drew a big *A* in it, and frowned in inquiry. The German-speaker explained that they drove DAFs – he pointed to their white cabs across the compound – and they couldn't understand why the Silver Knight looked just like a DAF but had an 'A' rather than 'DAF' on the radiator – especially since Fransen Transport in Cyrillic script above the windscreen suggested it was even more Russian than their trucks. I told him that this Strato was built with the same cab as the DAF – probably the same engine, too. And what country made Atkinsons? I seemed to remember that Seddon was American, but Atkinson was English – or even Scottish? – but wasn't the whole firm owned by the people who built combine harvesters? By now our pidgin German was defeating both of us. What of the roads ahead of us that they'd just driven to get here? I asked. As far as Minsk, he replied, they were fine – but beyond Byelorussia: he shook his head. '*Sie sind gefährlich.*' They'd had rain and snow in Moscow, then the sun had come out, and then the night-time chill was freezing the melting roads. There had been lots of accidents, he said: '*Viel Glatz. Sie müssen vorsichtig . . .*' You must be careful.

Tony got back in the cab and drove us across the bridge to the Russian side. 'There's an English guy ahead of us. Comes from Redditch, just down the road from me, and he used to work for the same guy as me in Folkestone. He got here at midnight, fell off his perch at half three. He was that Merc up at the barrier – he was only about nine trucks in front of us.'

'What do you mean, "fell off his perch"?'

'Nodded off. They don't wake you up. You're sat up, trying to keep moving forward – fall asleep and you don't know it. You think you've only been off for a minute, and then you see the truck that was in front of you's about ten ahead. Really gets your goat.

'Another tip, when you're in a queue like that. Never go right up to the back of the truck in front. Because if he can't start, you can't get out. I've learnt my lesson the hard way. Especially in the winter, when the brakes freeze, or the diesel waxes up. But don't leave enough space for another truck to get in.

'The other thing we say is, *throwing your teddy in the air*. I think I invented that,' Tony reflected. 'It means losing your rag, like. Throwing a wobbly – you know, at a border queue, or at customs.' The air in the *Pride of Bruges*'s dining-room, then, had been thick with teddies.

We pulled up over the inspection pit in the Russian compound for the soldier to shine a torch around and check for stowaways hanging underneath. A kid in an army uniform, gun slung over his shoulder, dragged a listless Alsatian amongst the trucks. The currency control officer climbed in the cab, dished out a couple of declaration forms, and helped himself to a Rennie from Tony's packet on the dashboard. He coughed and patted soothingly at his chest, and popped it in his mouth.

The English guy, who had a Rod Stewart cockerel-cut and a wife in Warsaw he saw on the way between Holland and Russia, showed Tony where to go in the soaring brutalist customs hall – he had a truckful of Mars Bars to get to Moscow *tonight*. I studied the mural by the entrance: tractors, space rockets, women with circular melon-breasts. Factories pulsed cotton-puffs of smoke; shining angular youths scythed corn straight and solid as fence palings; iron arms lifted dumb bells, hurled javelins. Beneath it a residually militaristic reception from spotty youths in greatcoats was speeding through twenty tons of chocolate bars.

Chapter Four

For some reason in-car cassette-handling is not part of the driving test. The correct control of air brakes may be a matter of 'treading on eggshells without breaking them' – but is there anything more delicate than the one-handed extraction of *The Very Best of Little Feat* from its case without the sleeve insert falling out, twirling it over with drum majorette's fingers to position it for Side Two, 'Texas Twister', and ejection of Joe Ely's *Lord of the Highway* to allow its insertion? It is driving's equivalent of boogie-woogie piano: a left hand like God, and the absorbed disengagement of your subconscious for this intricate task, so that your whole conscious mind can remain clamped to the road, your right hand to the wheel, and a basilisk stare missing not a single cat's eye. Finesse is invisible: the art is in your car, even yourself, resting unaware that any transaction has even taken place until (volume, bass and balance already subtly adjusted) those rear speakers suddenly inflate with the guitar on superfast idle, straining for the brake to be released, and then the rhythm section bangs in to sweep us away!

Driving, like music, is a sensual art: for years I never dared to learn to play a musical instrument, dismissing myself as not-a-physical-kind-of-person, more a brainwork specialist – until one day I thought, but you drive a car . . .

There is a smooth safe grace in good driving. It is not about pumping adrenalin, not a crude heavy power-flexing, which is why all those guys in the Golf GTi Cabriolets with the bass-drenched funk turned up loud enough to drown a Jumbo jet are missing the point (as well as intimidating the rest of us). It was when I blew my speakers one day on the M11 near Bishop's Stortford that I realized: Little Richard's 'Good Golly Miss Molly' is great rock and roll, but bad driving. I slowed down after that. Music, like driving, is controlled motion: the tick-over of an engine hits a beat as regular as a drum machine; the white line down the middle of the road marks out the bars; the landscape rises and falls, looms close and fades away, like a chorus. 'That band are *motoring*,' we nod to each other down at the pub. The motor mechanic deals in components like the *rocker* arm on the piston. There's nothing better, in my opinion, than a good blues *chug*.

But our cars, our cabs, are also listening booths. Driving, for most of us, is the only time when we *really* listen to music. At all other times, music plays as backdrop – to the hoovering, the cooking, the washing-up, the dinner-party conversations; all this inharmonious, dissonant activity. The car and the cab are the soundproofed, secluded study: a guitarist in a band I once played with used to say it was only listening to a tape in the car on the way to the rehearsal that he finally got the hang of the new songs he'd been trying to learn all week.

You need to be on your own, of course. Driving is definitively solitary. At such times, the driving music you play can then – must – be matched with exquisite, incredible precision to the atmosphere of the moment. From the first bars of a new tape you know – even if a few seconds ago during all that nimble manipulation routine it had seemed a good idea – whether it is *quite* right enough for your mood. Just as Rebecca West said that sitting down to write was important because it forced her to discover what she thought, so music when you're driving alone makes you find out what you feel. Driving towards something: the prospect of setting out, the anticipation of encounter – it all becomes clear in the spangled, stinging guitar lines of Tom Verlaine; the slow trundle back across London after a night out – that weary sanguine retreat is the voice of Jimmy Witherspoon. Generalized regressive 'no i'm not going to': George Thorogood's *Maverick* is being nudged up to top volume. In those peaceful hours of solitary confinement in motion – when you could drive the length of England without a thought of loneliness or isolation – you can be, entire and uncompromised, you.

It can't be more specific and less moody than that – not in Britain, at least. Unlike the United States, we don't sing our surroundings. Billy Bragg once composed a song about the A13 from London to Southend as a tongue-in-cheek way of proving that it was not Route 66. We hate our roads: the M25, the M1, the M6, the M4, the North Circular, the Blackwall Tunnel – they are all symbols of our incompetence and confusion, and we wish they didn't belong to us. 'I'm goin' out west out to the coast . . .'; in America that means California; over here it would have to be Llandudno. So Americans mythicize their country into being by singing its Highway 49 and its Highway 61 and taking pride in being 'On the Road Again'. Stuck among the contraflows and tailbacks that we resent as our roads, we retreat into singing ourselves, switching on the car stereo to remind ourselves not where, but who, we are.

I had a whole bagful of tapes with me for the trip to Russia. For an entire life on the road, Tony Meddings had:

four. All his others, he said, had been nicked, but he was vague as to the specific losses. His collection comprised:

1 Tammy Wynette's *Greatest Hits* (Vol. One)
2 Tammy Wynette's *Greatest Hits* (Vol. Two)
3 *Truckin' USA* (country music compilation)
4 *Heavy Haulers* (country music compilation)

These first miles of Russia were nothing to look at – we were slowly floating across a wider, emptier version of East Anglia, the flat, pale fields a vaster Cambridgeshire, the birch forests lining the road a huge Thetford Chase. Snow in the lay-bys, where men stood next to their Ladas offering black-market diesel out of a jerrycan, showed the bad weather the Russian truckers had hit on their way to Brest. Now a cold sun was out.

'Shall I put a tape on?'

Tony shrugged. He was happy, I could see, just driving. Music would be something to keep awake to.

What was the right music for this slow accumulation of mileage – transferring distance in front of you to distance behind you? If Tony had only four tapes to last us another three thousand miles we'd better save them for later. I rummaged around in my bag.

Brass blared, a harmonica wailed, the rhythm section stomped in *bompa-bomp-baba-bompbompbomp*, and Elvis Presley growled about being 'a ssstranger in mah own home tairn'. *The Memphis Record* was my favourite Elvis album, the only and the last time since the Sun Sessions when he'd truly sung his socks off – but it wasn't right now. This was too loud and insistent for the present bleached, empty moment. Right now, the two of us in this cab here, music was like having a third person in the cab. I switched it off

and we ground on in silence. Sometimes you just don't
have a thought in your head, or anything to feel.

By late afternoon when we stopped for a break a bright
clean moon was up ahead as the sun was still setting
behind us. Puddles were frozen over; the fields and verges
were white with light snow. A beaten-up Rover 3500
pulled up with its occupants rotating their hands to suggest
we change some money. Two kids materialized from nowhere – there wasn't a house visible as far as the horizon –
to wave packets of Marlboro. A Polish trucker borrowed
our wheelbrace to wrestle unsuccessfully with his leaking
back tyre: the nuts were on too tight to budge. Tony said,
'If he just kept going instead of messing about with that
he'd get there.'

It was half past seven – fourteen hours since we'd got
up and set off – before we found the motel outside Minsk.
Between the border and the capital, both Minsk and Smolensk, where the motels had yards guarded and locked
during the night, were the only safe places to stop over –
park up anywhere by the roadside and you risked the load
disappearing by morning. It wasn't brigand country, just
poor. We parked nose-to-tail in the muddy truck compound
– artics were jammed in with barely room to manoeuvre –
and went in search of some beer. On the steps of the motel
we bought some furry Cossack hats from two guys with a
Lada and a Great Dane. Tony tried on one in brindled
grey rabbit fur; I should have settled for the same, but for
some reason bought myself a chocolate-brown sheepskin
effort that would have looked more at home on the head
of Raisa Gorbachev. The Russians struck their arms out
like circus tumblers in campy ironic salutes of 'Ah!' and
'Oh!' and 'Ay!', secreted away our Deutschmarks and had
to restrain the gangling dog – it was as high as a small

horse – from snapping the hats straight back. The Lada dematerialized in seconds.

In the torpid bar a television was showing a dubbed Australian soap opera with the sound turned down. The picture of moroseness, the barman thrust down cans of cheap American Schaefer beer in front of us. Peter Gabriel's plaintive voice floated out of a radio tuned to an American station. Two prostitutes in black with incandescent red lipstick – just pretty young girls – swanned over and moued and smirked at us: we hadn't even any cigarettes on us they could bum. The TV screen had switched to footage of Boris Yeltsin striding into a dour stone doorway.

I said to Tony, 'The weather in Moscow looks all right.'

But then Yeltsin was talking to the Queen, and Prince Philip was standing by in his ceremonial military regalia. This was Buckingham Palace: in Minsk we were watching pictures of the Russian president who was over in England. Yeltsin in London to build diplomatic bridges and trade links with the UK; our Silver Knight heading for Moscow with Cornish pasties, ice-cream spoons and Guinness. Then the leader of the Labour Party, John Smith, came on, talking in his adenoidal tones about recovery – and it turned out that the monolithic stonework framing *him* was Moscow, where he was attending some international social-ist congress. All these goldfish-tank windows on elsewhere, one image inside another, like the set of Mischa dolls Tony had just bought out in the foyer for his daughter. Back at the truck he pitched his rabbit-fur hat on to his bunk and said, 'I'm going to have all them dogs after me when I get home.' I was beginning to recognize the characteristic contradictory voice – a saturnine Jeremiah who was thoroughly equable – of the English trucker.

It must have rubbed off. In the middle of the night – it was far enough below freezing for thermals, socks and a woolly hat in bed – I jumped out of the cab for a piss and landed in a puddle of diesel. I chucked the diesel-slick socks out of the window, and my sleeping-bag reeked for days afterwards. I drifted back to sleep, and into a dream in which a television interviewer was thrusting a micro-phone under my nose and asking me about Prince Philip. Diesel fumes needling my nostrils, I scoffed, 'Well he doesn't do any bloody work for a *start* . . .'

When I felt my way through the darkened foyer at six in the morning to clean my teeth in the Gents someone was playing Space Invaders in the pitch dark. All you could see were the flashing lights, all you could hear were the thumbs and fists hitting the console, the dogged *thump-thump*.

Since pulling out of the Zeebrugge truckers' café on Satur-day morning and leaving the Istanbul crew to their pre-dawn naps we hadn't spoken to anyone properly – just odd exchanges of information with other drivers – and we wouldn't until Moscow, and even then it would be hardly a Babel of voices. Had I not been along for the ride Tony would have been alone: he had a big heap of paperbacks in the locker above his seat – the other long-distance guys called him the Library – and he'd have sat and read in the evenings. In the summer months he stowed his garden chair in his trailer box and sat out in that beside his truck. But, so much of the time, no one to talk to. He'd been to the doctor a couple of times, he told me, because sometimes he found himself slurring his words. 'I read books all the time,' he said, 'but I couldn't read a passage *out* to you.' He couldn't pronounce the names of the places we went through at all – he said, 'Teespol' and 'Slerdeechee', 'Minx' and 'Soblenks-I-can't-say-it'. He called a Renault truck a 'Ranulph'. The doctor had told him he could find nothing wrong: it was probably to do with him being on his own so much of the time.

But there was also, I was finding, a peaceful safety in non-communication. Most of the enforced interaction a truck driver had was hostile, attritional: the customs official, the border guard. Safe inside your cab, safe tucked away in the corner of a bar, you weren't challenged. It was a broad, profound solitude. All the time you were away no one accosted you, quizzed you, called your way of life into question, no one set you a different example. Back in Evesham, Tony told me, he paid the bank ten pounds a month to look after all his finances: pay the mortgage, deal with all the bills. He didn't even have a cheque-book – just lived off the running money Fransen's gave him for each trip and had a hole-in-the-wall card to get cash in Dover whenever he needed to stock up his trailer box at Tesco's. Imagine paying for everything in your life with pocket money, at forty-five! Then you drove away from all those problems, and you kept driving. Who, I thought, wouldn't yearn to travel this light? When you could watch the world through the TV set of your windscreen, when you'd closed the door of your little spotless house-on-wheels, you'd made yourself a serene home.

The water had been frozen in the kettle when we tried to make a cup of tea before setting off. The fuel-line heater was on when Tony turned the ignition: the light stayed on half the morning – without it we'd most likely have been caught out by the cold and unable to start. There were seven hundred and twenty kilometres to go to Moscow, an endless straight road through birch forests, snow-lined

from last night's powdery fall, and the dreamy thoughtful-
ness of driving to deliver – someone else had done all the
thinking about why.

I dipped into breakfast: the bag of fun-sized Snickers
bars I'd brought with me from England and was fast
getting through. A couple of fun-sizes and a can of Coke
was a good enough sugar hit to last you a few hours. I'm
allergic to cow's milk, so too much milk chocolate is not a
good idea, which ruled out the trucker's stereotypical
snack, the Yorkie bar. (Actually, apart from Trevor, my
instructor at Roadtrain – and he insisted someone had
bought him his as a present – I never saw a single trucker
eating a Yorkie bar. It's kind of man-sized, and you're
supposed to grasp it like a wheel-wrench, but no one at the
advertising agency that came up with the marketing cam-
paign can ever have eaten a Truckworld blowout. Most
truckers – sedentary all day every day, no exercise and then
an unavoidable mountain of starch in the evening –
watched their weight and tried to avoid munching calorific
snacks, but many still ended up with bellies that pushed
their jeans down on to their hips.) Mars Bars: a little sickly
to scoff at seven o'clock in the morning, and rather obviously just sugar, toffee, sugar, caramel and sugar. But
Snickers are different. They have peanuts in them. Nuts are
protein, protein is good for you, and so you can have
Snickers for breakfast – indeed, any meal of the day – in
the knowledge that they are as nutritious and healthy as a
plate of egg and bacon. There are other classic foods that
will do the trick: indeed, the top three could in truth be
permed endlessly to satisfy all one's daily dietary needs for
ever, but since Crunchy Nut Cornflakes, Burger King
cherry pie and bacon sandwiches made with sliced white
bread were unavailable on the road to Russia, and unsuitable

in any case, for consumption in a moving truck on poor roads, it was fortunate that long-distance trucking has made the multinational Snickers bar ubiquitous.

The sun rose and glowed through the tops of the silver birches. We passed villages of tiny weatherboarded dachas. Kids skated in the middle of a frozen lake. The dual carriageway we'd followed since Brest petered out with more than six hundred kilometres to go. There were huge earthworks in progress as Russia built the next section of the motorway back towards Moscow – topographical confirmation of the traffic of vehicles like ours it wanted to see heading across its border towards the capital. All the new concrete bridges were far too high for the road either side: we hit each one with a crash, and Tony sighed to himself, thinking about the stoppers in the beer kegs and the glass bottles of wine. We passed two of the Dutch trucks parked alongside us at Siedlce pulling off the road into a lay-by in the forest – almost certainly to buy some black-market diesel. Tony wound down his window a crack, poked a Hob-nobs wrapper out, and said, 'Get it in the bin every time.'

When we stopped for a tea-break Tony filled in his diary. Besides the running-sheet he kept for the company – meal expenses, fuel, winter clothing – he had his own battered five-year desk diary, and every day he filled in where he'd stayed the night, where he was heading, how many kilometres he'd done, what he was carrying, where he loaded, and where he tipped. He was one of a select few British drivers in possession of an EC 'Green Card' – which meant that he could load and unload all over Europe, wasn't restricted to loads originating in or destined for the UK – bringing him more places to go, but also keeping him away from home for weeks at a time. His

life was structured forwards for him, and in his diary it was
mapped backwards, day by day. Tony riffled through the
pages for me, and stopped at random somewhere in 1992.
'Here we are. This is back in April . . . Oh, I was going to
Yugoslavia. So I loaded in Widnes – firm called Shearings,
one of the top-of-the-range chemical companies. Straight
to Dover – that was the 31st of March. I caught the ferry –
you have to catch the one from Western Dock, the special
chemicals ferry. There we are: "03.00 Sealink to Dun-
querque." France, Belgium, Germany – that was the 1st of
April. Then I've got: "Germany-Czech 8½ hours." That was
a border queue at Schoening. Then Friday 3rd: "Big queue
at Ryka. Try to jump queue but turned round. Many
trucks." I was there for 8 hours 40 minutes – that's the
border out of Czechoslovakia into Hungary. Saturday 4th:
"Big queue at Orga" – that's Hungary into Yugoslavia.
"Many trucks again. 5½ kilometres. 16 hours 40 minutes."
Monday 6th: Yugo, tipped Skopje. Tuesday 7th: Yugoslavia, Bulgaria – I'm going empty to pick a load up. Wednesday 8th: loaded peppers at Plogde. Then Yugo that night.
Thursday 9th: Yugoslavia, Hungary, Czechoslovakian
border. Friday 10th: I've got into Germany. Saturday 11th:
out of Germany, into Belgium and France, and I've caught
the 22.45 Sealink from Calais to Dover. Then I had a 36-
hour break in Dover. Started from there Monday morning,
drove up to Lowestoft. Tipped there, and then to Great
Yarmouth empty, picked up a load at Bird's Eye and took
it to Birmingham . . .

'And then it goes on . . . Picked up a new trailer in
Kidderminster with a load of pharmaceuticals, caught the
15.30 Sealink from Dover to Calais. Friday 17th: tipped at
Compiègne – and then another Fransen driver brought my
trailer down to Compiègne, loaded with fresh meat, and

we swapped trailers, and I went on down to Sicily . . . And then it carries on . . . and carries on . . . I got back on the 30th April, had a night at home, then I went back out to Sicily . . .'

How many people had the spiritual security of knowing their own lives in such rhythmic detail – of such weblike support within space and time? I had already come to appreciate the intensive modulation of delicacy and foresight you needed to drive a big rig. Now I was starting to see how the long-distance men carried their lives around with them, a kind of caravan of memory – and to appreciate properly the extent to which such men weren't, and couldn't be, off-the-wall mavericks who floated with the tide. Instead they were tidy men with accountants' brains – mapping their present, their future and their past. They calculated distances constantly to ensure their fuel would last them until the next place where they could fill up; counted hours – 100 kilometres is an hour and a half's driving, Tony reckoned – so they stayed within their tachograph limits and were sure of reaching a safe place to park up every night; kept an internal sense of the datelines they'd be crossing so they could use the extra hour when they gained it – Tony left his dashboard clock on English time throughout; and they knew their load in minute detail, checking forms against manifests against invoices, translating kilograms on one into pallets on another, into boxes and cases on a third and individual bottles and barrels on a fourth, so as to get it safely through borders. They were like long-distance runners: all they knew was the distance ahead, and the goal at the end; safe within the race they could negotiate everything else as only potential hindrances or assistances. It was time to move again. Tony wiped the mugs dry with kitchen paper – we got through rolls of the stuff – and inserted them back into our cardboard box of provisions, wedging them next to the packet of tea bags. He carefully wrapped the teaspoons in kitchen paper and laid them alongside the knives and forks – also rolled up as though serviette-enclosed for a restaurant buffet – in the Tupperware cutlery box, and that slotted into the cardboard box too.

The Silver Knight rolled on. Doubly cushioned on our air suspension – one system between the cab and the road, another buoying up our seats – I felt as though the Strato would sail through wherever it went. Everyone gave way to it. Everyone doffed their hat to it. It was like an aristocrat with guaranteed passage. Crowds wilted apart before us: they required a regally idle wave in passing. A Lada was being jacked up at the roadside with a tree bough under the front axle. An antique motorbike wavered along in front of us, a strange bulbous slug-shape balanced across the sidecar. As we drew level and could look over at the goggled and tense driver we could see that the passenger was holding the sidecar roof blister in his arms like a bloated baby. Russian trucks were laid up all the way along the side of the road – we could have stopped every ten minutes to give them assistance. Russian truckers did not have Seddon–Atkinson Stratos: the domestic drivers had to put up with little old-fashioned ZILs, still in state-owned light blue – humpy, snouty, bonneted jobs with tiny cramped cabs, gear-levers like fence-posts and a steering-wheel up under your chin. You craned through the brow-low windscreen and drove it with a hunch back, a cricked neck and your elbows in your ribs. The cold weather and the bumpy roads were starting to find them out. There were drivers giving us the double thumbs-down – flat battery – or drawing their hands downwards around an invisible loop – tyres – or hammering the air with a fist, which seemed to suggest more radical mechanical failure. Another Lada crept by us: in the caked mud along the doorsills where you'd put a go-fast stripe a finger had written MERCEDES-BENZ. Tony was doing some forward calculations. 'So we'll be in Moscow tonight' – this was Wednesday. 'If we can tip our load by the end of Friday . . . which means we need to get the Savoy off first tomorrow . . . tip the beer and wine so I can get at the frozen compartment . . . and then if we can do the other two' – he called the ice-cream parlour Basket Robbins – 'the next day . . . then there can't be a back load until Monday – which means we can have the weekend in Moscow for some sightseeing!' Sounded fine to me.

A Renault fridge with an English number-plate went by the other way. Tony recognized the waving driver – Alan Bremner, another erstwhile colleague of his from Middle East days. Now pulling for Kepstowe's, Bremner was an owner–driver who'd been driven off the Middle East run by the cowboys, said Tony – the fly-by-nights who bought knackered second-hand trucks, which they ran on red diesel all the way through Europe until they were caught, didn't pay their road tax, and did the job for a song until they got stranded with an engine blow-up in Bulgaria. Russia hadn't gone that way yet, but sooner or later, everyone reckoned, the cowboys would move in and undercut sharply the £4,000 or so it cost to do a Moscow run properly – Istanbul was going for around £2,300 these days. The only potential restraint was an EC proposal to abolish red diesel altogether: that would capsize the knife-edge, seat-of-the-pants economics of the cowboy. But there were other threats, too. 'Those Hungarians' – Tony pointed to one of the ubiquitous yellow and blue Hungarocamion trucks that we'd been seeing all the way here – 'they're taking fifty per cent of the work from our trucks.' Hungaro-camion was the state-owned haulage company, a huge operation with over fifteen hundred smart vehicles. They double-manned all the way, did the job quickly and for catastrophically low rates to build up their share of the market, and they were pricing British truckers out of business. Sometimes, said Tony, they did go too far in their attempt to loss-lead. 'They sent six lorries across to Dover with half a ton of frozen peas between them – just to get into England to pick up a return load. The customs sent them all back on the next boat and told them to put it all on one truck.'

Darkness fell around five. When an oncoming vehicle's headlights were suddenly blacked out Tony braked. Ahead of us was a coach trundling along at forty with no lights at all, front or back. We overtook it: it was full of schoolkids. We swerved out again to avoid two cyclists, no lights or reflectors, standing chatting at the edge of the road.

We drove into the outskirts of Moscow at the end of the evening rush hour. The memory is more like one of approaching a great city from the air: after two days of travelling through nowhere, suspended between distant conurbations, we came out of unlit, unstructured dark to behold the sky lit orange by street-lights and illuminated windows. After such a distance, seeming to float across the earth with only trees and flat fields to sign our way, here we had at last touched down to human pace – traffic nosing along either side of us in low gear, pedestrians scurrying across the road at traffic lights. From here on in we were just taxiing. Perhaps it was also our means of transport, and more so the banal load, but Moscow never seemed mysterious, exotic, even on first entry. Sometimes when you arrive in a great city for the first time you don't want it to be other than sensual chaos, a thrilling disorientation, Shangri-La. But to drive there all the way, and in from the very edge – past the giant concrete walls of apartment blocks, the parades of shops, the trolleybuses full of homeward-bound commuters – with food and drink to oil wheels somewhere in Moscow's midst, was to feel a tiny part of it, because you had brought something for it.

Chapter Five

There were two places to park a truck in Moscow. The Turks and the Eastern Europeans favoured a huge yard on the western approach road. Dirty brown and grey artics spilled out into side roads and along the sides of the main carriageway – there must have been three hundred of them parked up. Unlike the neat acreage of railway wagons confined to a marshalling yard, trucks could go anywhere, and tip themselves in a giant litter over a neighbourhood. We headed on into the centre, past the bigger of the two Pizza Huts, towards the Moskva River. The western trucks made for the Sovincentre, a showpiece development financed by Armand Hammer, made up of the swish new Mez Hotel and a trade centre where all the major western companies had their Moscow representative offices. There was a Kepstowe's tilt at the riverside already: we parked behind him, and headed into the Sovincentre to look for a bite to eat.

Inside, we gazed up around us at a towering marble atrium, glass-sided lifts, fountains playing out of brass fixtures, expensive perfume shops. Out of a two-bunk caravan, across the road, and into richer environs just like Geneva. The glittery ground-floor brasserie was full of suavely dressed westerners and murmured chat, so we wandered up to the next floor.

'There's a bar,' I said to Tony. It was the Red Lion. Here was the destination for most of that beer we'd brought out from England.

Before I'd left the UK a friend of mine had said to me, for some reason, 'Ah – the Red Lion! That's apparently quite a legendary place!' I'd travelled out with eager intimations of some basement dive down a side street that opened late and stayed open the latest – the kind of place where people read airmail copies of *The Times* and talked about the pit closures as though they were just down the road, where Kim Philby's name would be scrawled on the walls of the bogs and washed-up expats would be sagging over the bar, insanely drunk on vodka. A seething stew; an embattled outpost: a Russian Coach and Horses. I hadn't bothered to check.

Inside, all was discreet quiet. Our feet padded audibly across the thick carpet. Décor was bog-standard Great British Revivalist – the full works. Flock wallpaper, red velvet curtains, brass curtain-rails, button-upholstered seats, little creamy hat-shaped lampshades and, just to complete that warm cosy glow of your homely local, framed prints of Queen Victoria and a red London B-type bus on the walls. Mid-nineteen-eighties antique; a departure-lounge bar in a marbled mall: a teensy islet of Arndale Centre England abroad. Someone had gone to great lengths to get it just so. It was 8.00 p.m: half a dozen in for the evening.

Bad news may infect the teller, or so Shakespeare says. Had he taken a 38-ton truck a long distance he would also have discovered that the reverse is not true. Good news does not exalt him. Journey's end and the handing over of the torch: a mournful and cadaverous barman, sunken eyes and long irritated pulls at his cigarette, mildly uninterested to hear what we'd got for him. But then he hadn't anywhere – he was just selling what he was given. We got 275 barrels out in the truck: with 72 pints in each th was nearly *20,000 pints* on board. We didn't get a single free one out of this guy. Instead, a choice of – well, we knew what the selection was. Two pints of bitter, please. He didn't tilt the glass as he poured the beer out, so by the time he'd overfilled it with foam a few times and scraped the top off with a large spatula he was probably using up a pint and a half for each order. Ten dollars. Two thousand miles to drink the stuff we'd had in the back all the way, for three and a half quid a pint.

A German in a double-breasted pinstripe was buying a round of Skols. The bill for a trayful came to more than 50 Deutschmarks. He handed over his American Express card. 'What is this bitter?' He peered over at our John Smith's. 'Is that Guinness and lager?' I bought a Mars Bar, checked the wrapper: made in Veghel, Holland.

A silver-haired man in a yachting club sweatshirt was sitting up at the bar scrutinizing the *International Herald Tribune*.

'We just brought the beer out from England,' I said. Someone was going to know about it.

He glanced up over his half-spectacles. 'That's Russia for you.' His accent was clipped, Scandinavian. 'Everything comes in, nothing goes out,' he remarked severely, and returned to his paper.

It took us one drink, probably encouraged by the flock wallpaper and the presence of Queen Victoria, to settle into the English custom of several more, and by eleven o'clock we'd spent thirty quid just on knocking back pints of John Smith's. Then we went back to the truck and ate some of Tony's Mr Kipling fruit tarts.

By daybreak I was wearing my wool-enhanced thermals, my thick red thermal socks, my double-thickness wool sweater, my gloves and woolly hat, had my coat and blanket over my sleeping bag, and I was still cold.

'Night heater's packed up,' mumbled Tony. The night heater was supposed to come on about an hour before we got up, as well as warming the cab up before you went to bed – you could keep it on all night, but then you woke up a dried-out mummy with the paper eye of Keith Douglas's 'Vergissmeinichts' and it was mid-morning before you could blow your nose. Outside, the Moskva River was half-frozen over. Tony was pensive and alarmed: a truck cab in the Russian winter with no night heater – we'd have to keep the engine running all night to give us some stuffy heat. Otherwise this would be a cold trip from now on.

We had a map to tell us how to get to the Savoy. It had been drawn on the back of an envelope by the regular Moscow driver, Dave Danks. We'd arranged to meet Fransen's Moscow agent there. It was very simple, according to Tony: straight on past the Pizza Hut, left at the Kremlin, a quick left-and-left again, and there you go. I was getting used to the intuitive aboriginal-songlines method of truck drivers' directions to each other. Fine for the open road – Danks's directions had found us the Minsk overnight – but hopeless for central Moscow.

I had a grand sightseeing tour of Moscow; Tony had an exhausting hour of coaxing a 50-foot-long, right-hand-drive, articulated truck through the speeding traffic of a strange city – the black ZIL Party limos pulling out from the kerb without signal, the tipper lorries carrying rubble away from the dozens of city-centre building projects, the bumping over tram tracks, the bridges too low for the truck to get under.

'Poxy fuckin' place,' Tony thought it was. 'Never been anywhere like it. Can't fuckin' turn left.' A couple of times he got out to ask the way, in classic Brit-abroad pidgin-English: 'Me Eengleesh? *You* show *me* – yes? – way to *Savoy Ho-tel* – mm?' Tony had been doing long-distance for eighteen years, been everywhere, without benefit of languages. He said he knew 'Kirche' meant cherries, because he'd picked them up in Poland so often. The elderly Russian women he asked, the traffic police, all pointed politely in different directions. It was as we passed the *second* Pizza Hut on our way down towards the Lubianka that I realised where Danks's envelope scrawlings had started out from.

Andreas the agent was waiting for us – a lugubrious careworn man who smoked his cigarettes in three or four intense and meticulous pulls. If sighs were exhaling your cares, he seemed to be reversing them to suck in new woe. Tony backed us into the loading bay to start unloading the wine, and I had three-quarters of an hour to go sightseeing. First, though, it took some persuading the scruffy supplic ant messenger, once again, bringing the valuable load – to get let inside the Savoy to use the Men's room. Right here a piss underneath the trailer was not an option. I could see there was no chance of pushing my luck and stopping at the opulently rococo bar, all golds and emerald satin, for a British-trucked Luminarc glass of British-trucked Beaujolais, but at least I got as far as some very swanky bogs. It struck me for the first time then how a truck driver was in most respects a stereotypical business traveller, once he'd arrived in the big city. He was the same accidental tourist as the company executive, seeing a capital city from the vantage point of its hotels, the interior of a moving vehicle, its commercial districts. The difference was that the trucker came from the wrong side of the tracks. While making the life of the executive possible, he was himself excluded as the pariah, the one who looks longingly through the window at the illicit opulence inside.

I wandered through the lunchtime crowds up to Red Square. It was very cold – already I had the side flaps of my Cossack hat down in full spaniel-configuration. Street vendors were selling ice-cream from big ice-filled boxes – ice-cream is a year-round delicacy in Russia: in the days of central planning it was seized upon as a useful way of dealing with the overproduction of milk. While Russian beer was almost a contradiction in terms – 'Mm . . . might be interesting from a journalist's point of view . . .' Andreas suggested in extreme doubt – and John Smith's and Guinness therefore blazing a new trail as much as Pizza Hut, Baskin Robbins were only finessing a time-honoured tradition. Outside Lenin's tomb they were changing the guard. The Japanese tourists in jostled audience pressed their flashbulbs, the teenage soldiers in their greatcoats stomped and goose-stepped to and fro, and as they stared ahead at us I caught one of them, unmasked amongst the melodramatic redundancy of it all, suppressing a wry smile. But already it was time to turn back across Red Square to join the truck again. It was to be my only sight of tourist Moscow.

The Savoy's beer kegs were to go to a cold store on the outskirts. Sergei, the hotel's warehouse manager, hitched a ride to show us the way. We'd sampled the Red Lion, I said, thank you very much – but where did he, a Muscovite, go, if he went out for a meal?

He didn't earn much money, he said.

But if he did go out anywhere, I persisted, where would it be?

'When I go out,' Sergei said, '. . . I like to go to McDonald's.'

At the dank, stinking 'Big Refrigerator' cold store, a strong smell of putrefying meat in the air, the warehouse-man who forklifted off the Savoy's kegs had a boil on his neck the size of a small apple. It was dark by the time we'd dropped Sergei off, collected our authorized customs papers, and got back to the Sovincentre. Two drops: a whole day.

In the Red Lion that evening we had six pints of John Smith's each, and a microwaved pub meal. One sprout, two baby carrots, a little dab of potato purée crisped at the edges, and a frazzled gammon steak. It arrived on the bar about a minute after you placed your order, though it was cold by the time the barman had finished scraping the foam off his pints before bringing it to you. Ten quid. We'd brought the next consignment so that they could continue with this hale English tradition.

At the next table sat a German couple, a mid-thirties man hunched inside his charcoal suit, raincoat folded at his side, with an immaculate and haughty young woman who dabbed at her shiny lipstick. The man's imploring eyes – he was starting to pouch beneath them – shone like a cow's with tremulous nervousness. The boss and his PA on a naughty business trip? They sat alternately cooing and minutely billing or in icy silence. Every ten minutes she would toss her head away from him and his face would set more tightly bovine. A jazz duo – they'd been in the previous night, too – played deferential, anodyne lines on sax and keyboards. The keyboards man wore a tank-top and a tie and looked about to fall asleep. The sax player sat down to pick at a guitar and gaze about him as though in a park deckchair. In between sets they padded silently in and out. I wished we'd brought Ian Gillan and his guitars and drums and pool table. I'd never been in such a deep, quiet, underwater place.

'So . . . if we can get the Red Lion off in the morning' – Tony was thinking out loud – 'and Basket Robbins in the afternoon . . . and all the paperwork done . . . and we make an early start first thing Saturday morning . . . we can be back in Poland Monday!'

Leaving Moscow that soon? What about our weekend of sightseeing as our reward to ourselves for being so efficient?

'I'm worried about the weather,' Tony said. 'We're getting snow already. When that night heater packed up this morning – I don't fancy a weekend here in the truck running the engine all night.'

'But don't you want to look around Moscow?'

Tony said he'd seen the Kremlin – I suppose on the strict rules of evidence, as we'd swung past the Lubianka on the look-out for the Savoy, he had – and he'd be back. 'The rule is, when you can go, go. Keep going forward, keep driving. Whenever you have the chance to get ahead of yourself, take it. You never know what you're going to meet the next day. That's my rule.'

So we were already on our way – back, for me; ahead, for Tony. At least when you were a truck driver you never had to leave anywhere. You were always on the way to somewhere else.

'What's the longest you've been holed up anywhere, Tony?'

'Turkey. When I was working for a company down in Folkestone, they had a phone call – he was a good customer of theirs – saying he had a load of mozzarella cheese up in Scotland, Glasgow, like, to go to Istanbul, for the Pizza

Hut. This was the beginning of November. Bonfire night. So I'm flying up there the next morning, picking up seventeen tons of cheese, and down to Dover.

'I got down to Istanbul – did quite well: six or seven days. Park up at the TIR park and get a taxi down to the address I've been given. Walk into this office: hello, Pizza Hut, I'm Tony Meddings from Folkestone – got a load of cheese for you.

'The guy says, yes, well, this is the right place. There's only one problem. We haven't built it yet. He showed me the telex. It said, "November 4. Wait for shipping details." But Scotland never waited.

'Well, then the guy had to get an import licence – it takes two weeks in Turkey – and then find a cold store to take all this cheese. I sat there for thirty-five days in the end. One of the worst jobs I've ever done: something that normally takes two and a half weeks to do. Left Bonfire night, got home Christmas Eve. But every time I go back there now – well, they know me – all the pizzas are free. I was there last December, taking the American bases' meat for Fransen's – this was after four years. Still got a free pizza.'

We drifted into conversation with a couple of Swedes – by now I was too far gone to remember anything of it afterwards except that they liked the beer here better than back home – and then, again dozens of dollars lighter, rolled outside to the Silver Knight. I rummaged among the sheaf of travel documents on the dashboard and fished out the Red Lion's beer invoice, Tony poked away at his pocket calculator, resting it on the steering-wheel hub, and we worked it all out. Two hundred and seventy-five kegs ... £11,902 ... 72 pints in a keg ... so the *fugg'n Re'Lion ... buysissbeerat ... sixypencerpint – sixy pence! Sixy fu'n pence*

– '*nwe driveallaway frEngland s'nemfuggers 'ncharge fu'n freep-ounfiffy 'ndunno whereallermoney's – cerny not givin wus 'nissa fu'n disgrace.*

In the morning I gazed at myself in the mirror in the Sovincentre bogs, and a red-eyed tousled ruffian who'd spent the last few nights unwashed under a hedge stared back. I got another can of Coke out of the vending machine in the foyer and had that for breakfast with another Dutch Mars Bar. In front of us a Dutchman had dropped his trailer on its legs – probably gone off to find some fuel for his unit. Now we'd gone and parked in front of it – and a French artic had squeezed in behind us – and the Dutchman was pulling up in his unit to pick his trailer up. We sat there with our morning cuppa waiting for Andreas to arrive to supervise the Red Lion tipping. The Dutchman's truck was a limited edition Iveco Turbostar in navy blue – beautiful rakish thing: side panels and aerofoil, turquoise high-backed seats, coffee percolator on the dashboard. The guy had to jackknife in to get under the trailer – the space was hardly longer than the unit. In and out he went, wrestling the wheel on full lock both ways, jumping in and out of the cab to check his clearance, leaning out with the door open. It took him about ten minutes. Hands clasped together on his steering-wheel hub, Tony watched with idle interest. I thought, this is the kind of thing – first thing in the morning, before you can even start the day's work – that ages you. Tony said, 'He's not very good, is he?'

We spent Friday morning in Moscow on a building site. Next door to the Mez Hotel an extension was being built to the Sovincentre, doubling the size of the complex: the Red Lion's loading bay was between the two. It was a bitter morning. Wispy snowflecks swirled in the air; my

last two fun-sized Snickers Bars – English variety – were
not enough calories to ward off the freeze. By mid-morning
the load was off and Andreas back from the customs office
with the TIR carnet cleared.

'This was unloaded good and quick,' I said – I was
bone-chilled and grateful.

Andreas rubbed his fingertips together. 'By paying
people much money.'

The Baskin Robbins cold store was across town in
Moscow's northern district, next to the city's television
tower, a teetering pinnacle like a cavalryman's lance stood
on end, whose tip was lost in the fog. Beside the cold store
a sign announced an empty building plot as the site of
Baskin Robbins's new ice-cream-making plant. In time,
therefore, these truck deliveries all the way from England
would cease as the American business made its own
American ice-cream for Russia in Moscow, not in Reading.
A queue of Russian trucks was jockeying to get in the
narrow gates – one bonneted ZIL had to be hand-cranked,
a back-breaking wrench, to get it to start. The gateway
was barely wider than the Silver Knight; once inside, Tony
had to nose the truck between box-vans, army trucks, piles
of pallets, and round the blind corner of a wall end. Other
trucks inside the compound were themselves inching out
of loading bays, swinging in, pulling back to let someone
else through, or trying to nudge in front of another to get
unloaded first. The Silver Knight, two and a half times as
long as any of the ZILs, was a Queen Mary among
randomly floating icebergs. Andreas and the Baskin Robbins rep appointed themselves traffic policemen, but eventually we realized it was no good: until a couple of these
ZILs moved there'd never be enough room for us to get
to our loading bay. A teenaged army kid curled up asleep

on the seat of his ZIL was woken up by his officer with a lot of rapping on the window, and treated to ten minutes of bleary terrified reversing practice to get his truck out of a postage-stamp space to make way for us. This then left him completely blocking the route out of the yard for all the ZILs who wanted to get away. The air was filled with horn blasts and angry hollers. More jockeying and wheel-wrestling to unlock the jigsaw puzzle enough to let them out, and they caroomed past us, nearly taking the end of the trailer off.

Out came the ice-cream, the Very Berry and the Raspberry Ripple, and the fridge parts, and the plastic spoons from Plastico, Mitcham Road, Croydon. I was glad my home town was sending a token of its identity all the way to Moscow. A beefy ruddy-faced man in a ripped old sheepskin drove the forklift, a roll-up as small as a match piercing his lips. When the load was off Tony ran out the temperature-control print-out from the Thermo-King freezer unit on the trailer – a comprehensive record of the computer-controlled temperature within the fridge compartment since loading in England – folded and rolled it and secreted it away for return to base at Kidderminster. Groups of tattered, lumpy women coming off shift stopped to stare at the Silver Knight and chatter to each other.

Then we sat for two hours at a customs post out on a squalid industrial estate while the Baskin Robbins representative got customs clearance for his import. Behind us an enormous power station poured steam into the air from its chimneys. Ahead were colossal blue and white blocks of flats, L-shaped and eighteen storeys high: there must have been a dozen of them. Andreas was jumping out of the cab every half an hour to smoke a cigarette in three pulls. If the customs house didn't get around to clearing our invoice and collecting the 25 per cent import duty before end of business today we'd be here the weekend anyway. 'This customs house is a partnership between a very stupid Russian,' said Andreas, 'and a very stupid Dutch company. All they want is money.' Battered Russian trucks bumped in and out of an oily cinder yard alongside, throaty engines gargling and tootling squirts of black exhaust. It was dark again before we dropped Andreas off at a Metro station.

At the revolving-door entrance to the Sovincentre – Tony needed to phone Kidderminster to report the load tipped – I got stopped by a commissionaire making no secret of his distaste for the raggle-taggle starveling trying to gain entrance to Citizen Kane's marbled hall. There was no return load for us here – so we were to leave in the morning and head for Poland as quickly as possible, where Fransen's would try and have something ready for us to collect. A Kepstowe's Volvo box had pulled up at the riverside behind us, and the young driver, same age as me, was heading where we'd come from with a towel under his arm. We followed him into a luxurious health centre: the hedge-dwelling urchin could have had a shower all the time he was here. The Kepstowe's guy, a New Zealander, had just got back from delivering a consignment of medicines to Crosnagaya, north of Moscow: the roads up there had been bad, he said. 'Trailer was going all over the place.' But in his tennis shirt logostyled 'Kepstowe's' he looked like a fresh-faced sports shop assistant whose day's work had been selling a pair of trainers. He was confident and worldly and unreflective in his job. ' "Boshing" Pete, one of our guys,' he said, 'went all the way to Perm. He had a bit of fun with that one.' Actually Perm wasn't so far: Sverdlovsk was further, and Novosibirsk much further still. The psychotically clean and possessive Barry had done the Sverdlovsk run: on his return, apparently, he'd reported that he'd made his Russian soldier-escort sleep in his seat every night – even though he had two bunks in his cab – and hadn't made him so much as a cup of tea the whole way.

The New Zealander said he usually did the Eastern Europe exhibition runs – taking out display furniture for trade exhibitions – but now that season had finished he was coming to Moscow. 'This'll all stop for the winter,' he said, 'and then next year it'll be first one all the way to Vladivostok!' I was beginning to dislike this guy for being so young and clean and relaxed and smugly in charge of the world – or maybe for just reminding me I was English. Beside him Tony seemed, for the first time, hesitant, humble, even stumbling. He'd obviously never heard of Tony. Tony asked him about the new border crossing into Poland the Russians had opened at Grodno, a couple of hundred kilometres north of Brest. The New Zealander shrugged. 'It was great when it first opened. But the last time we went through we were there for three days and two nights, and by the end we were just about ready to burn the fucking Polish side down.'

Did the Kepstowe's guy fancy a drink later?

He shook his head. 'I've got an appointment with a young lady,' he said. 'I don't know what'll happen – I might get kicked out.'

The Kepstowe's truck parked here when we'd first arrived hadn't had anyone in its cab at night, said Tony.

'No, I think he's got a girl here. Most of them do. It gives you some incentive to get here.'

We hadn't properly introduced ourselves until now. It came out that I was doing the travel writing. 'Ah! You're

Penguin Books?' said the New Zealander. 'Yeah, we saw your notice. I think if you'd said you had blonde hair and big tits you'd have had everyone queueing up to take you.'

On our way out he said we should try the Continental Restaurant in the Sovincentre — pay in roubles, so dead cheap. 'They usually put on a pretty good floor show. Who knows' — he became an egregious game-show-host — 'you might just fix yourselves up with a couple-a-girls . . .'

But we ended up at our local just the same. We'd gone back to the Silver Knight, glowing and mellow, to spruce up before heading out on the town. When I'd tried to shut my passenger door, it had thudded dully. By the time Tony had spent an hour and a half freezing his hands blue trying to mend the jammed lock (eventually we had to wire the door shut; for the entire return journey I had to climb in and out of the cab through the driver's side) and we had watched a little Lada draw up at the Kepstowe's truck, the New Zealander retrieve his clothes from the cab, and his date drive him away, it was too late, too cold, and we were too fucked off to mess around finding somewhere new.

The Red Lion. At least we had the chance of a valedictory drink to our very own corner of Moscow that was forever England, whose survival we'd come all this way to assist. A man buying some beers at the bar turned out to be an affable British Telecom engineer from Leamington Spa, out here to advise the Russians — now I noticed the neat little BT piper logo on his jumper — on their new satellite international telephone service. The same solitary young Englishman sat in the far corner, as he had done the previous two nights, having a few beers and parrying Tony's attempts to draw him out on where he came from to end up in here every evening. He didn't talk to anyone;

no one talked to him; he gazed about him as if daring you to remind him of his solitude, and by mid-evening he'd disappeared. The jazz duo padded in. The microwaved food arrived in seconds, half-cold as usual.

'Tony, who was this guy Andrew Wilson-Young I've been hearing about? Driver who pitched camp on some British Embassy lawn?'

'Oh, *Andrew*. Well, he was a legend even in his own time. Andrew Wilson-Young. He was a chicken farmer from Carlisle – very well-educated, talked with a plum in his mouth – and he's in the *Guinness Book of Records* for one single hen laying the most eggs in a year. He used to say he played them classical music.

'But he used to pull for Astrans – done the Middle East for years and years. He was one of the longest on it, like. And he holds the record still – nobody'll beat it – for six days and so many hours all the way down to Qatar. He was an insomniac, never slept, used to run night and day, night and day, all the time. You'd meet him in Istanbul on your way down when he was coming back – and then when you were coming out of the Middle East he'd pass you again, and he'd already got all the way home and then come back out again.

'He never used to carry a cooker. I don't think he knew how to operate one. He lived on yoghurts, soups, and tins of this chicken in white sauce. When he opened his trailer box there'd be just soups on one side, and chicken in white sauce on the other. Many a time he used to say, "I hate decisions . . ." He'd open the tins and eat it all cold. I can't remember if he ever had a cup of tea or coffee – because he never had time to do it, like. It was always Cokes and things.

'This was his reputation: he was very fit for his age –

muscular bloke in his fifties – and he'd have shorts on, and green wellingtons. It could be temperatures of a hundred plus, and there'd be him in his green wellingtons.'

And his finest hour?

'Well, he went to Kuwait once, had this load of dry freight. The customs post for dry freight, you had to park your lorry and go to a hotel and wait for the paperwork. But not Andrew. He went round to the British Embassy and pitched his tent in the grounds. "I'm a British citizen!" he kept saying. "I'm a British citizen!" They had to give in at the finish, because he was right in his way, like. He was there for three days – and in the morning they'd bring him tea and biscuits to his tent . . .

'He used to turn up at borders – didn't matter where, all the way down to the Middle East. Kapik, Sovagazu, Ramptka going into Jordan: everybody knew him. "Oh, Andrew's here." There'd be a big queue of everyone trying to get into this one little cubbyhole to do their customs papers and passports, and Andrew – he was six-foot three – he used to wave his passport in the air and call out, "Excuse me, I'm British." Used to fly through all the borders.'

But one day, said Tony, Andrew Wilson-Young had checked into a hospital in Jeddah complaining of stomach pains, thinking it was probably his appendix. An exploratory operation had revealed cancer, and he'd been discharged with six weeks to live. 'And five weeks and four days later, he died.'

And that, all of a sudden – nobody could believe it – was that. The thought came to me – I couldn't suppress it – that, even in his dying, Andrew Wilson-Young had managed to get there three days sooner than he was supposed to.

'He was a good person to talk to,' Tony mused. 'That's if you could get him to stop.'

At the next table two young guys in T-shirts were getting blind, shitfaced drunk. Every half an hour the two girls with them, a brunette and a blonde, would put their coats on in ostentatious outrage at this sloppy boozing and flounce out. Five minutes later they'd return to get the men to buy them another drink. This place felt like the end of our stay in Moscow – I was not even going to get to eat our own Very Berry ice-cream in Moscow's Baskin Robbins parlour. But the Red Lion had felt like the end the first night here: not somewhere that was new, but an institution that was winding down. Not the face of the future, but an exhausted, obsolete place. Why go all this way to export old Britain to new Russia: why try and get Russia to catch up to that? To complete the entropy perhaps a future Fransen's trip could bring out a few old ladies with string shopping bags to sit around getting tight on gins, and a scattering of ratlike Brylcreemed men in gabardine raincoats cradling half o' Guinness and a *Sporting Life* all evening.

The jazz duo had padded out. The brunette was smacking and cuffing the drunk with a moustache round the head. The other guy was trying to paw and grope the blonde. Eventually both girls got up and left for good. The moustachioed guy hauled himself upright as if out of thick mud and staggered away. His mate sat on, slumped asleep, head bowed. The barmen were draping drip cloths over the pumps and switching out the lights. In the half light a girl had appeared, sitting up at the bar, smoking. I hadn't seen her walk in. Her golden-brown hair! It glowed satin, iridescent, the finest and smoothest tresses I had ever seen (but it was time to go: we were already leaving

Moscow); they were all you could see of her as she sat over her drink, alcoved by the dark – falling past her waist, live, tingling copper.

Chapter Six

It was still dark on Saturday when, grumpy and morose, we drove out of Moscow. In less than an hour a dusty snow was falling fast, and when we stopped to fill up with fuel on the edge of the forest it had become a blizzard. A few minutes down the road a solitary headscarfed woman stood in a lay-by, the white flakes shaken around as in a snow-scene ornament, beside a pig's head on a table. The roadsign read 'Brest 875'. We were aiming for Minsk tonight, but if the weather got too bad we could wait it out at Smolensk. When the snow abated for a while we saw an army truck already being hauled out of a ditch on the far side of the road.

Danks would be through this soon, said Tony: he was due out any day with the British Embassy run – 'a month's shopping at Tesco's,' as he put it. Toothbrushes, baked beans, bottles of Scotch, corn pads – there'd be everything you'd need for living, except the Snickers Bars. Fransen's did that job all the year round, with similar runs to Bucharest and Budapest. The beer run, like ours, was a winter contract: the kegs only needed to travel in a temperature-controlled trailer when there was a risk of the beer freezing. The fridge, perversely, was to keep them warm enough; in the summer a firm like Kepstowe's could undercut the job by loading them in a tilt. Away across the fields a man was walking along a snow-covered railway line.

Beer delivery, low-tech work, was the kind of job a cowboy could muscle in on: going international, an owner–driver could get half his fee up front, in cash, as running money, and then the balance, by law, within seven days once he'd presented his stamped CMR back in England. On the domestic scene some of the haulage industry's biggest customers, I'd already heard, only paid their bills twice a year, and up to six months' credit wasn't something you were in a position to give when you had a monthly HP liability of several hundred pounds on your truck. You were more likely to be spending half your running money before you even got on the boat at Dover. And the further away you were from home, the greater the opportunity for the trucker's favourite occupation: *ducking and diving*. (Tony was the only driver I met who didn't enunciate the words with head weaving crafty and defensive on his shoulders.) The red-diesel wheeze in Europe was straightforward enough, and likewise black market diesel in the former eastern bloc – so cheap, if you paid dollars or Deutsch-marks for it, that you could easily charge it back to the company at double what you paid for it and pocket the difference. But further out meant far-out: 'You might buy a spare wheel off another driver,' said Tony. 'He needs to raise some cash in a hurry so you get it for fifty quid – and you know it's worth a hundred and forty when you sell it on. I've done it myself. He gets back to England and tells the company he had it nicked.'

Some of the grosser black market dodges could end you up in an East European prison if you got caught. But the only time Tony had ever found himself in jail was an altogether improbable tale. 'Defacing the King's currency,' he recalled. With several other truckers – Britons and Germans – he'd been laid up in Greece waiting for a back load, and they were passing the time one evening playing cards in a bar. The card game had got boisterous, and Tony, disgusted at losing with a good hand, had paid up by tossing some scrumpled Greek bank notes across the table at the winner. But a draught from the doorway had caught the notes in mid-trajectory – and blown them in the fire. The next thing everybody knew, the police were in the bar, and Tony and his mates had to spend two days in the cells before the case was dismissed.

But although a lot of people were starting to run the odd truck to Russia, as Fransen's Sales Manager Andrew Southall had told me, one of the biggest deterrents to the cowboys for the time being, restricting their chances of driving down the going rate as they had done with the Istanbul run, was the lack of lucrative back loads. Tony and I were running out empty, destined for Poland in the hope of reloading there. On Tony's Kiev trip, his previous time in Russia, there had only been offal from a slaughter-house in Brest to take as far as Paris. The best Fransen's could hope for was a load of Russian-made domestic freezers, or some haphazard dry-freight business acting as removal vans for the growing trade in exporting Russia's antiques and vintage pianos to the West. 'The problem,' as Andrew Southall had put it, 'is that the country's flat broke. On a Russian trip you're not pinging the cash till.'

It was the middle of the day, and the first of several Saturday weddings was on the road: a line of Ladas and Moskvitchs festooned with coloured bunting and balloons. The groom wore a white shirt decorated with a big black cross, the bride yards of white; the fields and verges were white; the whole party huddled around a small roadside shrine to some fallen relative who couldn't join the festivity.

'What's your favourite city? Out of all the places you've been to?'

'Istanbul,' came the immediate answer: the Blue Mosque, the food, always fresh vegetables and fresh meat, freshly cooked . . . But Tony's answer tailed off – he'd obviously been going there so often he was too familiar with it to articulate his own fascination.

'Well,' I tried, 'where do other drivers tend to go when they get there?'

'Oh, there's a big new Galleria just on the outskirts. Everyone goes there. It's got everything – roller-skating, ten-pin bowling . . . and on the top floor there's every kind of restaurant – Pizza Hut, Kentucky Fried Chicken . . .'

The snow was thick around us again, and we were bumping along at 30 miles an hour over a hard-packed road – in Russia they put sand down, not grit or salt, and it wasn't helping much. A plodding horse towed along two men on a low sledge. We reached the turn-off to the Smolensk motel at two-thirty: the snow was driving and heavy now, but with several hours of daylight in hand Tony decided we'd press on for Minsk. On the hills we were now overtaking the Ladas, their thin tyres skating about underneath their ponderous water-tank bodies. A big tractor was hauling an orange tipper out of a ditch. In places the snow had narrowed the dual carriageway to a single sanded lane for both directions; soon, all traffic from the other direction had disappeared – so the weather was only worse where we were going. In a lay-by on the opposite side of the road a Kepstowe's Volvo and a blue Sovtrans artic were parked up. The Russian driver had his arm thrust out of the cab, signalling for us to turn around.

'Sod that,' Tony muttered. 'It's too deep over there. That snow's a couple of feet thick.' We ground on. It was still nearly two hundred and fifty kilometres to Minsk. Snow was drifting across the road from the open fields. There was nowhere to stop by the roadside. At this speed it would take us another three and a half hours to reach safe parking for the night.

By five o'clock we had outrun the last of the snow-ploughs and gritters, and the thick snow under us was compacted into ruts that rattled the whole truck. Within an hour it was dark. Tony was peering into the wing mirror on my side, switching the nearside indicator light on to illuminate in flashes the side of the trailer: the constant bumping was shaking the wheel mudguards out of their mountings. One was already protruding nearly a foot. We'd have to stop so Tony could knock them back in. Soon it was a regular routine: gingerly nose the Silver Knight to a halt, half on and half off the narrow track through the snow, jump down into the whirling white and fetch the fucking things a good kick. After the first time I'd have just flung them over a hedge, but it wasn't my truck. We pulled over once more, Tony trying to slew the truck's bulk safely out of the path of anyone looming up on us from behind out of the snow. When he hauled himself back into his seat and put the Silver Knight in gear to move off there was a weak slipping of wheels.

'Shit,' Tony exclaimed quietly.

Tried again: the Silver Knight, featherbedded in exactly the kind of soft bolstered snow we'd avoided joining the Kepstowe's guy in, wouldn't budge. It took three goes, and a long contemplation of the prospect of a snowbound sojourn nowhere near Minsk with some teabags and a packet of Hob-nobs, before the Silver Knight decided to ease itself out into the road again. We juddered on across the white snowscape – there was hardly another vehicle on the road. The truck seemed to stumble and race for a purchase on the fresh snow. Tony shook his head to himself: 'This is crazy' – but it was still, it seemed to me, the safest thing to do.

We didn't hit the outskirts of Minsk until eight-thirty, the city bypass road cleared black and slick by all the traffic. Out of the worst of the snowstorm, tonight's end of the road just round the corner, we were coasting round an exhilarating bend at 70 kilometres an hour when, suddenly, a flashing blue light appeared in the mirror. *Speeding*. After that journey. They'd caught Tony on the red-eye. The officer wanted us to go with him to the police station, wanted Tony to sign all sorts of forms. It was looking like a long haul. But Tony played the dumb foreigner, no speekee any language at all, dunno what you're on about, mate – English, right? – and scrambled back into the cab after the officer had closed all his files and notebooks and pocketed a hundred-rouble fine for himself: satisfactory for both sides. We arrived at the Minsk motel having been on the road for thirteen hours. Tony had driven the last leg eight and a half hours non-stop.

Under tachograph regulations, of course – governing all truck work within EC countries – spending that long at the wheel without a break is far outside the law. Four and a half hours is the most you can drive in one stretch: then you must take at least forty minutes' break. A tacho disc recording a trip like ours, with no extenuating circumstances, would land the driver with a fine of several thousand pounds. The spy-in-the-cab – which records every speeding excess as well as time violations – is to stop exactly the kind of exhausting marathon drive we had just done. Outside the EC, of course, tachographs aren't recognized, and most owner–drivers, as soon as they cross the German border, will just drive like the clappers. Fransen's drivers, however, wherever they went, were expected to drive 'legal' all the way – and in any case, for a journey like ours, the regulations permit the driver to exceed his normal quota of hours if it is the lesser evil against, say, stopping in an unsafe place.

But toiling through the snow to get to Minsk also brought home to me the essential flaw of the tachograph. (I met several drivers who, with oblivious felicity, mispronounced it 'tachograft'.) It didn't eliminate the dangerous risks a truck driver might take with his stamina and the 38-ton leviathan he had control of – it just altered the reasons for taking them. Truck drivers had destinations to get to, and a tightly timed schedule from the customer for getting there. You divided out your journey with staging-posts to help you keep up with the clock and complete the trip within the time you had: stringing them together in $4\frac{1}{2}$-hour segments made no difference to the number of miles you had to cover and the average speed you had to maintain. Indeed, knowing you'd lost an hour before you'd even got into Belgium because the ferry was late docking, and then you only had four and a half hours to get to that truckstop at Duisburg where you could have a shower and buy some fuel . . . At the very least the tachograph system, it seemed to me, only encouraged a driver to drive always to the legal limit of his hours, and at worst it made what should have been a paced, graduated long-distance run into a succession of adrenalin-pumped sprints.

The ferocious French lorry-drivers' revolt a few months before I'd set out for Moscow – when they'd blocked the motorways in convoys, emptied the supermarkets of food, and quickly brought the country to a standstill – had been principally fomented by new French laws further finessing this Catch-22. Not only were EC truckers already required to watch their hours: now the French government was also introducing heavy fines for drivers caught speeding. The Frenchmen had rebelled. You can't have it both ways, their roadblocks and barricades were saying. More and more industry worked to just-in-time orders for goods and wanted them delivered yesterday – and the truckers were the ones sent on their way with the terrifying deadlines. If they missed them, they lost their jobs. If they were to get their loads there on time *and* drive legal hours, they had to speed. Eventually the French government decided to pass some laws on the employers instead.

That night we ate in the Minsk motel restaurant, a huge ballroom with a hundred tables and linen napkins and black-clad servers. There was chicken on the menu – 'Only chicken,' the waiter apologized firmly. 'Only Chicken Kiev.' The puny fried drumsticks came with greasy slices of fried potato and a pile of limp beige cabbage, and as much white bread as you could eat. For dessert there was 'only ice-cream', and for topping 'only jam'. The brusque frankness was touching. On stage at the far end of the hall a grungy band crashed away at huge volume. It was a busy night: the room babbled with conversation. The serving staff dished up this poor meal with an edgy deference that knew the presentation dwarfed the fare. The thousands of roubles the bill totalled for both of us, including our beers, cost me about three quid. It was a sad, warm, honest place, with barely the materials to keep the whole big show going. It was a far better meal than any at the Red Lion.

Sunday morning was a 4½-hour drive to Brest. At daybreak we had got out of the cab to find the motel islanded and silent amidst a sheet of snow. I jumped down into a drift up to my knees. 'I shan't stop now till I get to the border,' Tony said as we overtook four Iranian Mercedes tilts. 'If you stop for forty-five minutes that's ten trucks can go past you.' This dogged convoy, apparently, was a common ploy of Iranian drivers: all grind along nose-to-tail on the last leg before a difficult border, and with luck no trucks behind you would be able to get past to gain an earlier place in the queue. Then, as swiftly as the blizzard had come upon us outside Moscow, the snow disappeared on the way to Brest. A thin sunlight pushed through the clouds. An old woman walked her white calf along the hard shoulder. A brown cow grazed the grass on the central reservation. Empty and light, the Silver Knight now hit all the raised motorway bridges with a gigantic crash; a couple of times we were thrown up in our seats as the whole truck momentarily took to the air.

Off the motorway on to the narrow lane to the border crossing, and all of a sudden there was the queue – stretched back along the levee between the scratched, muddy fields a good two and a half kilometres. One o'clock in the afternoon: truck after truck lined up on a country road, the wind gusting across the levee, spitting a fine rain against the windscreen. To either side of the road the fields were strewn with truckers' rubbish: drinks cans, fag packets, paper bags. Tony switched the engine off. All was quiet. We settled down for a long wait.

I jumped down from the Silver Knight and slithered down the levee to take a pee in the field. Most truckers just stood by the side of their trailer and watered the tarmac underneath. If it was a grimy old heap you were driving you'd actually piss up the mudguards. In the middle of the night you'd stand on the step and piss out of the open door. Out here there was no one in a stripy shirt and a Welcome Break baseball cap polishing wash-taps and squeegeeing the floor once an hour. But when you knew that truckers were going to have to share this stretch of road – each for hours, days at a time – around the clock you sought out more distant facilities. Neither was there, in any case, brimming anticipation fired up by the prospect of the customs compound up the road: the friend of mine who once coined the name, 'The Cloaca-room', has obviously been there in his dreams. But I was lucky: throughout the trip I managed to avoid the real indignity. Here, where I was standing with my back to the wind, trying not to spray myself, amongst the tumbleweeds of old newspaper and the rusting cans and the dog-ends and trampled mud, was where it would have had to be. Never mind the lack of washbasins and hot water and soap to maintain hygiene afterwards: this is the real definition, if you're in sod-this-for-a-game-of-soldiers mood, of the trucker's lot: the spread-axle by the roadside in front of a captive audience.

Tony opened his diary, and when he got to today's page looked over at me. The 15th of November. 'Today, it's the eighteenth anniversary of my first continental trip.' Eighteen years ago he'd left England for the first time, never having been abroad in his life, and driven all the way to Saudi Arabia. He fished in his wallet and handed me a floppy folded-up newspaper cutting from 1979. Quiffed and extravagantly side-burned, Tony stood in front of an artic with his children. As a reward for his service on the Middle East run, reported the local paper – there and back every six weeks for five years – Spiers and Hartwell had lent him an artic to take the kids to Spain in. Now Tony was punching at his calculator: more life-accountancy. 'And since I've had this new motor ... which was eighteen weeks ago ... I've done an average of ... two hundred and ninety-three miles every day.' That one long road: always married to somewhere in the world: a present that always connected you to your past, however far back you looked: a good thing to celebrate with anniversaries, even if you were the only one there to do it.

Tony wedged his feet up inside his steering-wheel and opened a fat paperback thriller called *USSA*, about the former Soviet Union being taken over, following a brief superpower war, by America. I clicked his tape of *Tammy Wynette, Queen of Country* into my Walkman. A procession of hawkers, their pushbikes propped up against the trailer, were tapping on my window with their wares. Champagne, vodka – a man with a filthy rasping cough; a tin of instant coffee; brandy – 'Napoleon? *Franzozisch*?' – a woman mournfully holding up a few coins – 'Franc? Mark?' Tammy gulped her way through 'D.I.V.O.R.C.E.' I was trying not to laugh out loud. Country and western, I thought to myself, is truckers' music because it's straight-ahead music: no irony, no humour, no scepticism – and because its comfortable lachrymosity makes it only a music for solitude, not loneliness. It makes being alone sound pretty.

But now she was singing 'Please Come to Boston'. At a stroke, after half-a-dozen variations on that parodically cracking voice, here was a song she sang with simple, young passion. There was no irony, no double-take, but it went out to a real man somewhere.

> I said I won't come to Denver,
> But you come home to me.
> *Ramblin' boy won't you settle down . . . ?*

I stared through the windscreen. I thought, a trucker looks

straight ahead – because there is nowhere else to look. For me this was the journey home. For Tony it was driving onward. There was only ever onward. You didn't need a sense of irony, because you didn't look to the side of you, and you didn't look back. How could you, when instead you could drive on? I hadn't come very far, but I knew already that, if I found myself behind a big wheel, I'd do it that way too.

Outside my window a genial, bespectacled man in a denim jacket was unwrapping a white cloth and coyly offering a large silver-bladed cleaver for my inspection.

The light faded at five. In four hours we had moved forward half a kilometre. A man cycled past holding up a can of beer. Tony said, 'The local off-licence.' By six it was dark. A handful of gold rings were waved at the window.

The Tammy Wynette tape had finished: I started on the cassettes I'd brought with me. Steve Earle: one of my favourite albums – *Guitar Town*, a wistful and yearning collection of New Country songs to a twanging twelve-string guitar.

> Some day I'm finally gonna let go,
> 'Cos I know there's a better way.
> And I don't know what's over that rainbow,
> But I'm gonna get outta here so-ome day . . .

On a quiet, downbeat track called 'Down the Road', lightly strumming a mandolin, he sang of

> . . . when the darkness takes control.
> You'll start loo-kin' for a reason, To take your own self, on
>   down the road . . .

Ahead of us out of the darkness a snake of red lights was flickering on towards us. Engines were starting up again, too far off to hear. As the red chain wound nearer, trucks cleared their throats and blasted out pulses of exhaust cloud. Time to move forward a few more lorry-lengths and then, until an hour or so's time, watch the red chain extinguish itself, two links at a time, switch off and hear the silence return, and see nothing but know of a mile of trucks ahead, as quiet as the night.

I listened to Anson Funderburgh and the Rockets, a Texas bar-band I'd caught twice in London playing at Highbury Corner, just up the road from where I lived. The kind that's on the road all the time, three hundred gigs a year, singing for its supper every night – a jaunty, jogging blues band with one of the most charismatic front men I'd ever seen: Sam Myers, a nearly blind black man from Jackson, Mississippi. I closed my eyes and imagined him creeping on stage in a three-piece suit buttoned up to the nines, his fingers waving in the air lightly like sea anemones until they touched his waiting microphone. But once anchored behind the mike he'd extract cigarette after cigarette in slow motion from a silver case, between puffs honk out tripping, bouncy harp on the Marine Bands he kept in his leather harmonica holster slung over his shoulder – and, bearish and stock-still as Pavarotti, he'd roar out the vocals through a halo of smoke.

> *Hold* that train, conductor . . .
> *Pleeease* don't let that engineer start.
> Well I wanna ride your train this evening,
> Just to ea-ea-ease, my aching hear-eart . . .

Three Russian cattle lorries shuddered past us. Trucks that jumped the queue at borders risked having a rock lobbed through their windscreens, but drivers with livestock on board were exempted anyway – international regulations forbade animals to be held up for days at borders.

I played the Blues Band, I played B.B. King. 'That's our life, the light that brightly shone,' sang Paul Jones on the grave and rueful number that closed the Blues Band's *Fat City* album.

> Well it was such a long time coming.
> It's gonna be a long time gone . . .

'I'm movin' *on*,' declaimed B.B.: 'I'll see you somewhere down the line . . .' In that silent, becalmed capsule, limboed in the middle of nowhere, music coming into my ears like messages gathered from outer space, all songs seemed to be about travelling: putting the past behind you, keeping on going because you hadn't achieved what you wanted to, but not knowing why you were going this way. What else could prompt anyone to song? On the title track of B.B.'s wonderful *There's Always One More Time* album, an old Doc Pomus number that wound it to a close, B.B.'s guitar soared and picked its way out of his last crying vocals, soared and picked its way through its blues, straining to get nearer to what it wanted to say, exquisitely ever higher in search of that one necessary phrase, which he never found because each one took him further.

By eleven o'clock that night we were one shunt away from the Russian border compound, a cold cantilevered glow in the night like a small-town football ground. I was down to my last tape. In the final half hour before the engines came on and we drove into the floodlit arena I listened to Palestrina's *Missa Papae Marcelli*, and the only memory I have of the music is a visual one. I see those chill, chaste, spiralling, tumbling voices in the cool white cave of light ahead under the sky, and a white chain now snaking away to the invisible horizon when I peered back to where we'd come from, and night all around.

Chapter Seven

Cab control on the way back was a distinguished military gentleman with silver hair, steel-rimmed spectacles and greatcoat with epaulettes. I was ejected from the cab to stand and shiver by the trailer while he poked and peeked about: it was damn cold out there without my coat. Then it was my turn. The man had another covetous rummage in Tony's felt-pen box, and then took an interest in my Walkman. I mimed pleasurable groovin' rhythms, but he was going to have a listen for himself. He pressed the headset to his ear, fumbled the volume up to maximum and switched on. A tinny blast of Allegri's *Miserere* skeetered out at us. A nod of approval, and the Walkman was handed back with a distant, intrigued smile.

'He was only after my truck polisher,' Tony said as we strode over to the customs hall. 'Brand new polisher – I've only just bought it.' Stowed away in the hanging wardrobe behind my seat, it was the latest addition to Tony's housekeeping kit: an electric buffer to shine up the Silver Knight's paintwork. Its potential use to a Russian customs officer escaped me. After much jostling and queueing with a coachload of students, we discovered that Tony had to hand in a green ticket before any visas or paperwork could be sorted out. The green ticket was supposed to have been issued to confirm the cab control – by the unrequited lover of the truck polisher ... We searched all over the compound for him. I was posted to remain inside the hall for any glimpse of the steel spectacles. Tony stumped off outside again and exploded in through the swing doors of the hall every five or ten minutes going, 'Where the fock's that focker got to?' It wasn't until one in the morning that we spied him up in the balcony on his tea break, and got our green ticket.

Then an hour's wait in the compound to go over the inspection pit. Beside us a beaten-up roadtrain full of sand was being searched all over with prod wires and torches. When the guards had plumbed every square inch of the load, they turned it back. We hadn't seen them find anything, but now, after huddled conversations, much scuffing of the ground and standing around with hands in pockets, they were implacable. The driver threw his teddy in the air. He pleaded and remonstrated: after all that wait he was beside himself. The driver of a second sand-wagon pointed over to the grass verge behind their trucks, led him quietly over. The hysterical driver bent down: he'd even dropped his passport in the grass.

Just after two we were through the pit inspection. Fiercely barked commands for our exit visas from a gangling acne'd conscript in oversized peaked cap, the nimble extraction of a felt-tip marker pen from Tony's pen-pot – 'Is working? Good present? Good-bye' – and we crossed over into Poland. There, waiting for the Polish visa check, we watched the three Russian cattle lorries that had hurried past us all those hours earlier now being turned back into Russia. Steaming black and white cows stared through the trailers' slatted sides as they rumbled off. Tony said, 'Where's that focking idiot got to?' just as the customs man opened the cab door. At last we were driving out of the border post gates for the middle-of-the-night run back to Siedlce. The Silver Knight rolled through the tunnel of trees, Tammy Wynette sang,

> I'd like to see Jesus
> On the Midnight Special
> And hear him sing
> My favourite song . . .

and when we pulled in to the motel compound at four-thirty in the morning Tony said he was absolutely-fucking-bollocksed:

'Nineteen-seventy-nine was the biggest job,' Tony said. 'That was when I was still with Hartwell's. It was taking the parts to build a desalination plant down to Jelalabai in Dubai. A hundred loads in six weeks.' We were rolling across Poland – there hadn't been a load for us when Tony had rung Kidderminster from Siedlce, but there was one in Bremen. Now we had a day to transnavigate the whole of Poland and most of Germany to pick up twelve pallets of ice-cream by Tuesday afternoon, which we had to get to Eastleigh, outside Southampton, for 8.00 a.m. Friday. I was playing Tony's *Truckin' USA* tape, the guitars going *twanga-diddle-um-diddle*, *twanga-diddle-um-diddle*, and the rhythm ticking along like an engine. Monday morning: in all the cemeteries we passed every grave was bright with new floral displays.

'They sent me up to Glasgow to negotiate the deal, and I said we could do it. They needed the parts for building the plant delivered to a timetable. It meant fifteen days for each load to get down there. I did four trips, and I got the first truck down there in twelve days. We had air-conditioned cabs, so we used to drive a lot at night for the cool, and sleep during the day. Every load got there on time, and eventually we got all one hundred there with three days to spare.' Foggy, grey Warsaw slipped by in the fine rain. I registered the bare trees beyond the city thick with clods of mistletoe; already it was dark. Once again Poland had spooled past in a day: a whole country as a quick shuffle of snapshots.

'Silly little cars, them things,' said Tony as we bore down, *Duel*-like, on a tiny Polish Fiat 126 struggling along with a full load of passengers. 'We could almost go over the top of them in this.'

'What are those really big Renaults we see every so often? Big boxy things, twin headlights. I really like them.'

'The Magnum. I was in Italy over Christmas and we got twelve of us sitting in one of them.' It had a walk-through cab, he explained: the cab floor was raised above the height of the engine. 'We had one of them in the yard on demo. Too heavy for fridges – a six-axle was nine tons. This thing's only seven: that's two tons more on the payload. See, it's a mistake, making a heavy truck. These days people are trying for *more* horsepower and less weight. Fridge trailers used to carry only twenty-one pallets – the ones we've got now can take twenty-six. Even having alloy wheels on this thing saves half a ton. They're all electric, too, Magnums. Electric blinds, everything. You get a flat battery on the brat like we did, and you're buggered. Can't even get in them.'

Well, maybe they weren't a trucker's truck. But throughout our journey I noticed every one that passed us: beautiful square slabs of truck, tall as houses and yawing slowly like a plane – imagine having a two-seat executive motorway coach all to yourself, and knowing everyone could see it. It was the first European truck I'd seen that came near the aristocratic grandeur of the big American rigs. It was as big as it wanted to be, not as small as it could get away with. That's what my haulage firm would have had, and sod the HP payments.

'Jesus Christ,' said Tony. There was a queue of trucks ahead already, and we were still a good five miles from the Polish border. 'That'll take us days if we sit in that.' We were travelling empty – no load to be checked or import/export paperwork to do – so we decided to keep going down the side of the line. They should let us through: it just depended how irate were the guys who'd been sitting there all weekend. This backlog of several hundred trucks – all waiting for the shipping agents to clock on Monday morning – would take hours and hours and hours to clear. It was taking ages to drive past them. All the Russians, without TIR carnets, would probably be here till about Thursday. We had to stop a couple of times at drivers' roadblocks for Tony to shout '*Leer! Leer!*' and let a suspicious Russian trucker have a look in the back. But we got through with our windscreen intact and pulled up inside the compound next to an Irish roadtrain full of bleating sheep and lowing calves – the harsh, crazed crying echoed under the concrete canopies.

Suddenly I felt a peaky weariness at all this: tired of driving all day and half the night against the clock: the chaos of the border posts, the drumming of big lorries all around you, the glaring fluorescent lights, the booming concrete echoes ... Imagine hacking this all the time, several times a week, every week. Even after Brest I'd been thinking that it would be good, an interesting experience, to have to spend two, three days in a border queue. But tonight, 11.00 p.m. already, I was very glad to overshoot that interminable dusty queue and sail straight through.

We woke up at six at the Tankstelle fifty kilometres from Berlin, to find a note tucked under the wiper blades: 'Tony. Knock us up and say hello before you go. Phil.' The maroon Volvo Globetrotter parked alongside us with the curtains drawn had PHIL HORTON TRANSPORT LONDON above the windscreen. Phil Horton joined us in the filling-station kiosk for some coffee and bleary conversation, a grizzled Liverpudlian with two days' grey growth and a languid, wry way with words. He and Tony had worked together for the Folkestone haulier years back, and they'd both been on the Middle East run at the same time. For some years Phil had lived in Holland and driven a Dutch-registered truck: now he was based in south-west London and in business on his own. It was many months since he'd bumped into Tony: 'I've got two of these Globetrotters – bought them on snatchback for a good price. Tipped in Poznan yesterday: I've got this contract with the Polish mafia – well, they're not the mafia. Supplying a big super-market chain.' Phil and his wife – she was still asleep in the truck: didn't drive, but came along for the ride – hadn't been home for three months. They did four trips a month from Germany to Poland, and they'd been going non-stop since August. It had been a good year for them, he said.

Tony pointed at his nice new Silver Knight, and they exchanged the glances that said, 'OK, *flash*.'

'I'd heard you had it,' said Phil, 'here and there on life's road.' He proffered Tony his pack of cigarettes.

Tony shook his head. 'Can't afford it.'

Phil looked at me. 'Listen to him.' He fingered Tony's green tartan jacket. 'He's looking like a country gent these days.' He took a long pull. 'You know, I'm getting a bit sick of this. All this queuing. It took me *six hours* to get through that border empty.'

I went and bought myself a hazelnut Mars Bar in the filling station shop, checked the wrapper – more important than eating it: in this part of the world they came from Hagenau in France, near Strasbourg – and it was time to hit the road. We were going to meet up again for breakfast at Helmstedt services.

Driving with Phil was an exception for Tony. Usually, he said, he preferred to drive on his own and keep himself to himself. There were only a chosen few he'd ride with between places. Just the other side of Berlin a hundred ducks flew above the motorway against the early morning sun, a huge rippling V. The roadside around Magdeburg was littered with the wheel-less shells of old Trabants. We passed the abandoned East German border post – big empty canopied bays, empty watch towers, no-man's land still screened by concrete walls. 'It used to be daylight here all the time,' said Tony. 'And in those days, once you were through into the old DDR, you ran on to cobbles – even on the main roads.' Rattling to a stop in a lay-by where they hadn't yet been tarmacked over gave me a good idea of what a boneshaking way it must have been – especially in the days before air suspension – to take a truck across a whole country. Here, for once, a whole theatre of trucker's border fatigue had been miraculously taken out.

Waiting for our wursts and mustard at the Helmstedt services Phil Horton studied his held-out hand. 'I'm shaking,' he said. 'I only had half an hour's sleep last night.' When we sat down with our late breakfasts he said again, 'I'm getting *tired* of this stuff. All the traffic, all the queuing . . . I got through this border once with cigarettes on board' – his eyes brightened – 'by filling out a CMR saying I had fresh fish in my fridge. Lobsters, prawns, the lot. Felt a bit bad about that,' he added, with a rueful laugh. 'I'm trying to get the Mars contract to Jordan,' he told Tony. 'Dutch company. The Middle East . . . empty roads . . . no hassle. In the Middle East you can lose a day and go to the beach.

'I used to be a seaman,' he said. 'The people who make the best truckers are probably those who make the best seamen – guys from the north-east coast, Scotland, or, dare I say it, like me. Scousers. The worst are the guys who just go to Italy and back all the time – usually southerners. You find they whinge all the time. Can't hack the time away from home. This job . . .' Phil thought: '. . . it's closest to, say, a farmer's. To be able to handle the loneliness, the . . . *bareness* of the life . . .'

'I was telling Graham about Andrew,' said Tony.

'Andrew,' Phil mused, lighting another cigarette. 'I was in Bahrain with him once. He said to me, "I say, old boy – would you take me to the airport? I'm flying home for Christmas." He was wearing his green wellies, those old khaki army shorts flapping round his knees – absolutely *filthy* – and a T-shirt. Concorde was due in – he was going back on that. I said, "Andrew, it'll hardly be the weather for that back in England." He says, "Oh, no worries. Daddy'll send someone to pick me up in the Roller . . ." And when we got to the airport the woman on check-in thought it was *me* who was flying.'

But Phil had his reservations about Andrew Wilson-Young. 'Wrote a truck off every year – it wasn't ever his money. That's not clever.' Which reminded him of the big story of the road he'd picked up last week as he'd been coming through Poland. It had been one of the Dutch companies. 'Did you hear about it? They sent one of their

drivers to Moscow and he smashed the truck badly –
totalled it. So they sent him out again with another driver
and a new Merc, and he smashed that too, head-on with
another Russian truck near the Poland-German border.
They're both bad, still in hospital, and the Russians too.'
Dutch drivers, Tony explained, got paid by the kilometre.
It was why, although Holland had the stiffest driving test,
its truckers also had lots of accidents – driving against the
clock to get as far as they could.

'I saw their boss out there,' Phil said. 'He'd come out
with a wrecker to go into Russia to pick the first truck up,
and by the time he got across into Poland he got the telex
about the second one. He was going crazy – two trucks
written off in a week, and the same driver! How are the
insurance going to look at that?'

It was time to be going. 'We'll be tipping at Eastleigh
first thing Friday,' said Tony. 'They'll have us booked in
for eight in the morning.'

Phil raised his eyebrows. 'They'll give you an exact
time? Ah, *logistics*! *Logistics* – that's the word we've got to
use these days. You should paint it on the side of your cab
like Exxel do.'

'Graham didn't notice it was an English motor right
next to him when he got up,' said Tony.

'Didn't you see the Clanger hanging in the window?'

I joined Phil and Susan in their Volvo for a few miles.
After the bareness of the Silver Knight their cab was a
cluttered living-room. I suppose the rich wine-red uphol-
stery would have come with the truck, just like the Strato's
antiseptic greys and pale blues, but it still gave a close,
cosy feel. Along the dashboard and the shelf above the
windscreen sat little fluffy toys and ornaments, the sort of
random collectibles from holidays and gifts that build

up to crowd a mantelpiece. There was a long line of cassettes, there were cans of fizzy drink. One person in a flat buys slightly too few possessions for it: you notice the lack of plants, pictures, scatter cushions; two people acquire too much: the furniture is huddled together amidst a double helping of favourite trinkets. Tony's show-cab was a bachelor flat; here was a married couple's home. When the ceaseless nomadism was the point, the burrs didn't catch you and stick – and who would they be for, anyway? Phil and Susan's Volvo glowed 'This is where we are': could you fit a tiny WELCOME mat to the cab step?

I jumped out just outside Bremen; Tony and Phil shook hands, and we left them to drive on into Bremen's industrial area to drop their trailer for loading with the next consignment for Poland; we were bound for Schwanewede, a village north of the city.

Just as, all the way to Moscow, Tony had been telling me how he was planning to be tipped by Friday so we'd have the weekend free for sightseeing, so all the way back through Russia and Poland he'd been saying how he was looking forward to getting back into Germany – Germany meant a decent meal and a good shower wherever you stopped. Now, Tuesday, having busted his arse to get back through the snow to Minsk, then to get through the Russian border and out the other side to Siedlce, he was talking about driving on till ten tonight after we'd loaded this afternoon so we could get into Holland. So if all Germany means is a good shower and a meal, but you end up overshooting even that, I wondered, what's in it for you? I was the tourist, of course, only along for the ride, but I was feeling stroppy and superior and in a mood to play devil's advocate. 'All you're doing, Tony,' I declared, 'driving like crazy, trying all the time to get ahead of yourself, is to leave yourself open to getting sent out again before the end of the week. I bet you,' I concluded in triumph, 'if we reach Eastleigh on Friday morning you'll be turned round and back out on the ferry Friday night. They can see you coming.'

Tony shrugged. The customer paid his wages, he said. He didn't want to be one of the three million. 'I believe, when you've got a job, you give it your all. I've done all this' – he meant all the arse-busting – 'for myself.' I didn't understand what he meant until later in the day.

As for me, it was a growing sensation: the journey was speeding up. This was driving away from enjoying yourself, driving away from taking stock, from ever catching your breath. It was like always overshooting the runway of your life: overshooting every future goal you set yourself. It was something like the culture shock of air travel – the passage of a few hours and suddenly you're the other side of the world. Just as the narrator of V.S. Naipaul's novel *A Bend in the River* flies in to London from Africa and tells of standing in the Gloucester Road and finding all his African bus tickets still in his pocket, so we were talking about being in Holland tonight and I felt like I'd only just brushed the Minsk snow off my boots. Trucking made you sick of queuing at borders, and traffic jams, and customs forms – but it also kept you a moving target. It saved you from being sick of other things.

Warncke Eiskrem at Schwanewede was set amongst undulating pasture, black and white Friesian cows in the pleasantly hedged fields. While the forklift loaded twelve pallets of Sainsbury's Fiorella block ice-cream into the trailer – these were the larger Euro-pallets, and with them we'd be half full – Tony jumped from one foot to the other. 'All the T-forms and customs stuff were ready in the office. Now I can do another 3 hours 20 minutes' driving today – and then tomorrow I can do a 10-hour day – because I save them up for special occasions – and that means we've got thirteen hours to get to Calais – so we should be on a boat tomorrow night!' I had never seen him so animated: the prospect of another breakneck day-and-a-half against the clock made him gleeful and fulfilled.

I wandered off into the yard to get a photo of the Silver Knight in Bremen. By now the slush and sludge thrown up off the Minsk road had sprayed iron-grey plumes along the white sides of the trailer. Tony was itching to find a truck wash – company policy, in any case, was for clean white trucks, the correct clinical image for fridge work, but to me at last the Silver Knight was telling everyone it'd been a long way. The foreman from the building site next door, where they were extending the factory, wandered over to take a look.

'That truck wants a good wash and polish before you take a picture of it.'

'We've just been to Russia. There was a lot of snow.'

'And did you take ice-cream *there*?'

'Yes,' I said.

Tony, who had meanwhile phoned Kidderminster, was looking grimly thrilled. 'We're not going to be on the ferry tomorrow night.' We had to go on to Ardhuis in Belgium for one more pallet. Then into France for six more pallets. Then three drops in England: first at Lympne, near Folkestone; then at Smarden, near Maidstone; and then on to Eastleigh with the ice-cream for Sainsbury's – which the cold store now wanted before the end of Thursday! Into the cab, ten to four on Tuesday afternoon, and head for Norddorf on the German border. The challenge! It was the getting it there – I realized now: a trucker was

just like any traveller, like St Augustine, like Robert Louis
Stevenson – like all the people through the ages who had
said it was better to travel than to arrive. Never mind the
destination itself: the end was the means, the challenge in
being thrown a new curve ball at every turn and managing
to grab hold of it and pitch it back. You lived through the
monotony of motorway days and the frustration of border
queues for this kind of challenge: to shoot at a constantly
moving target. No one would know about all this except
Tony – the only way anyone else could would be if he
fucked up. I understood now what Tony had meant about
doing all this for himself.

Three hours negotiating rush-hour jams and contraflows
bypassing Bremen – we passed Phil and Susan coming the
other way in their Globetrotter – and torrential rain in
south-western Germany got us to the Norddorf truckstop
for the night. There in the clamorous truckers' restaurant
we spent the evening chatting to a genial Dutch driver,
Coo. Like Phil Horton, he'd started out as a merchant
seaman, been all round the world, but got fed up with
being away from home for three months at a time. Truck
ing from Holland to Germany and back was good for his
family life – 'now I get home every weekend.' There was
no adventure for him in truck driving – fetching up at
ports in Sierra Leone and Argentina and Iceland or wherever in his seafaring days had obviously seen to that. 'Oh,
I'd go to Moscow,' he agreed when I asked him, '– if the
money was right. They'd have to pay me more money.'
When I asked him what his favourite music was for the
open road he said emphatically, 'Country music – especially
for driving at night' – but only because 'I want something
relaxing. I don't want any fast rock and roll.' He'd been to
America and spent a couple of weeks driving with a

Florida trucker friend of his — admired the in-cab videos, walk-in wardrobes, even waterbeds, the American truckers had kitted their cabs out with ('They're like cowboys with their horses') — but what had struck him most was the number of hours they had to drive over there, tougher even than in Europe, to make their trucks pay. Trucking these days, from his account — he wasn't happy about it but it gave him a secure job — was no longer anything like tramp steamers on wheels, but rather a finely tuned science. Phil Horton had told me a story — at the time I thought it was apocryphal — about stopping in a lay-by to share a tea-break with a couple of Dutch truckers who had fax machines in their cabs. 'After we'd been there a while,' he said, 'the fax machine starts up, and out comes this message from the boss. "Why are you stopped here? Please proceed to destination."' Exactly, said Coo. 'Soon my company will be installing satellite links to all our cabs. Then they'll know exactly where you are every minute of the day and night. You'll have no freedom at all. Already I have to drive for more than the hours I'm allowed on my tachograph — I just pay the fine.' But he was philosophical rather than angry: for him trucking was a modern-world job, not a way of life.

'Right, you've had your lie-in,' said Tony. It was 4.00 a.m.

'I think I'll get a paper-round when I get back.'

By early morning we were in Belgium. This was regular Fransen territory. We passed the pork-rind processing factory — Fransen's would truck them over from Portsmouth. 'You have to dump them in the yard,' Tony said, 'and while you're doing it hundreds of seagulls flock overhead and shit all over you. One of the other drivers, George, carries a brolly.'

We were at Ardhuis at eleven: a small, scruffy town, a big new frozen-foods warehouse, windowless and silent, and flat fields of green vegetables all around. A pallet of frozen courgettes on board, it was on to the French customs post at Poperinghe to clear the Ardhuis documents. We were traversing Western Front country, D-Day landings country: little islands of white gravestones were scattered both sides of the road. But this blustery prairie under a cloudy sky, where so much history had been buried and tilled, soon came to seem numinously crowded. All around us this empty land was what we were carrying: this horizon-distant vegetable patch was growing all the produce that lorries like ours were traversing countries to transport. My attention switched from one side of the road to the other, from the middle distance to the nearest field, from one shade of green to another. All kinds of things were growing along the way – Tony and I competed with each other to point them out. Here were piles of sugar beets – near Calais we were to hit the heavy sweet smell of the processing plant; over there were Brussels sprouts; here orchards of fruit trees; there in the distance – potatoes? carrots? This land was too busy growing to have room for anything else: it was a factory at ground level. Accustomed to think of the Country and the City as a binary opposition, of green fields as an escape from grey streets, of earth built-on or earth untouched, I had never seen an agricultural landscape in this way before: live, dynamic – and it took a 38-ton silver truck to show me. Those placid Friesian cows across the road from the German ice-cream factory: only now I saw the connection – that the factory hadn't been installed there in defiance of their green field, but in need of it. I'd set out on this trucking travel as an exploration of an industrial landscape. I'd associated a

450-horsepower Seddon–Atkinson Strato artic with trading estates and motorway services and engine grease and mechanics in overalls – as if all that was some separate, self-contained world. Now, as the Silver Knight rumbled through small French villages, across green fields, the sky low and boiling, the wind tugging at the hedgerows, it seemed the most – the word fits if you say it without thinking, and it still does if you do – *natural* thing.

On past the pâté factory where Fransen's regularly called – Tony had been there on the trip before this one; past the sunflower margarine factory – fifty loads a week from Belgium to England, making up the whole of Safeway's and Tesco's weekly supplies; past the factory near Ghent that made the bonding agent used in windscreen lamination – it had to be transported under refrigeration; past the Breda cheese plant. A quick stop at the Poperinghe customs, and then on to the Oncle Demaret bakery at Lens, near Lille, for the final pick-up: 180 cartons of frozen part-baked baguettes destined for Lincoln's Patisserie in Eastbourne, and another 3,780 kilograms on the load. A phone call to Kidderminster to confirm that we were full, and the news that, because we'd made such good time in all our loadings, the last tipping at Eastleigh had been brought forward. It was now two-thirty in Lens, France. We were due at Southampton, the first two loads already tipped, at four o'clock tomorrow! That swelling feeling returned – that the faster you were running the quicker the ground came up to hit you. Each time you made a crazy deadline it only qualified you to be given an even tighter one. Quicken your pace, and the winning-post only recedes. Five to three: the *Fantasia* was sailing from Calais at seven.

Chapter Eight

On the parking apron at the Calais quayside a white Fransen's Strato drove over to us. This was Dave Danks, the regular Russia driver – we'd got his run this time because his visa renewal had been delayed. Now he was on his way out to Hanover with a load of pharmaceuticals. Danks wanted to hear how we'd got on, and we had time before our boat sailed, so he took us for a coffee in the ferry terminal café.

'Those mudguards,' he said, listening to the tale of the Tiller Girl high-kicks in the blizzard: 'you want to *pull* the fockers off and *throw* them in some ditch.' Danks was a dour, wiry Brummie, his face finely lined, a cadaverous leanness. He said, 'I had both door locks go on mine in Russia,' when he heard about the frozen-hands messing-about in Moscow. 'Had to go all the way there and back climbing through the window.' Then he told us the story of a driver with one of Fransen's main competitors who'd killed a woman motorist in Russia. 'The police kept him in a hotel for a month while they sorted it out – and their drivers all speak Russian. The managing director had to fly out in the end.' Danks counted off on his fingers. 'It cost them a new Lada, a video, and a burial for the old woman. But her folks didn't care about her. They were more worried about the six pigs that had been in the boot.'

Back on the quay more Fransen's drivers were pulling up, tapping on each other's windows, leaning against cab doors to exchange stories. Chris Smith, a young university graduate, was on his way back from Italy with a load of kiwi-fruits for Spalding in Lincolnshire. John Coombs was due in Harlow first thing in the morning. The Professor – this was a different Professor to the ragamuffin drop-out of Pete from Yeovil's acquaintance – had been in Lille earlier today, collecting bread, like us, and was en route for Gillingham on the Medway. Danks was pulling away in his Strato, waving goodbye, bound for Germany, and we were on the return leg from Russia and heading for Kent and Hampshire. The quayside had filled up with trucks waiting to go on the ferry: dozens and dozens. I watched the ship dock: all of a sudden dozens more lorries were rolling up the loading ramp on to the shore, artic after artic and, where a minute before I could hear the squalling of hundreds of seagulls thronging the far end of the quay, now all was roar and and racing engines as one after another after another the outward-bound trucks accelerated away on to the Continent. Now trailers without units were being towed off the boat by port authority tractors. A British unit would have pulled them as far as Dover; here they'd be dropped back on their legs to await collection by a European haulier. The whole quay was alive with heavy movement. All these truck journeys sewing Europe together – those dozens and dozens of drivers fanning out off the boat to start on their long hauls through Europe; all our dozens and dozens of journeys – half a dozen guys from just one small Midlands firm in one country intersecting on just one ferry crossing on one particular evening – converging from all over Europe for the last leg over in Britain. All you could see, all there was room for in the scene, was trucks.

The Professor joined us in the *Fantasia*'s restaurant. No poncy waiter service here to hold appetites up: this was the truckers' favourite ferry. Seven quid each, serve yourself, and eat as much as you like. He sat down next to me with his first helping, a plate of vegetarian lasagne. A few mouthfuls soon revealed a large rump steak hidden underneath.

Chris Smith gazed at the Professor's plate with interest. 'That looks like my kind of vegetarian lasagne.'

'I haven't eaten for twenty-two hours,' said the Professor without irony. It sounded as though this had not been an unfortunate consequence of his road schedule: he'd been saving up for this. The Professor had a thick, brindled grey beard; his conversation was pedantic, innocently enthusiastic. Meet him at a party and, with his brown and white check shirt and his corduroy trousers and his hushed voice, you would have imagined him a head librarian. He was telling Chris Smith about the tapes he'd been listening to on this trip. He'd finished John Le Carré reading his own books – *Tinker, Tailor, Soldier, Spy* and *The Russia House* – and now, he said, he was working his way through the complete recorded repertoire of the cellist Jacqueline du Pré. He went off to the servery and came back with a second plateful of vegetarian lasagne, surmounting a second rump steak. 'You know' – the Professor turned to me (by now Tony, his meal long eaten, had shaken out his copy of the *Sun* and was engrossed in the sports pages) – 'I've been listening to everything I can get my hands on by Charlie Parker. And I think, there's more expression in, oh, just one middle eight than in' – he gestured helplessly with his hands – 'the entire world of pop music.' The second plate of lasagne and rump steak emptied, the Professor went off for chocolate fudge cake, a giant slice, with ice-cream. 'I found a complete set of the *National Geographic* for 1954 the other day,' he resumed to Chris Smith. 'I'm gradually working my way through those.' He came back again with a cappuccino. He listened to tapes along the way, he said to me, because 'otherwise you end up *thinking*. And that's . . .' – his face went pensive and puzzled – '. . . a bad thing . . .' The Professor finished off his meal with a second cappuccino.

'Heart of gold,' said one of the Professor's colleagues to me afterwards. 'The kind of guy,' said another trucker, 'if he's got to be in Warrington at eight in the morning, he'd go via central London to look up a rare book in the British Library.' 'He's got a dozen tapes of train noises he listens to,' said another. 'Just train noises – whistling when they go in a fuckin' tunnel.' But the best story concerned the Professor's artistic aspirations. He always took his paintbox along on a trip – in case the sunset over the mountains somewhere in Italy required him to stop and capture it in watercolour. One day he'd driven his truck on to the ferry at Felixstowe and was waiting for the boat to leave when he noticed the light falling particularly fine across the cliffs. He nipped back ashore, set up his easel on the quayside, and was still engrossed when the ferry sailed.

'So, do you think you'd like to be a trucker?' asked Chris Smith that night – we were in the Wheelhouse at Dover, the big restaurant and bar for drivers who were overnighting or waiting for customs clearance in the port compound.

I'd been wandering up and down the lines of trucks parked up for the night: acres of them, hundreds of them, all colours under the floodlights. From Truckworld to Calais to Dover, it was one of the grandest sights of all, mysterious in its scale. The potential energy of all that weight, all that horsepower, waiting to shiver into a momentum, to start rolling! At night time it was like coming upon elephants sleeping on their feet. 'Yes,' I said to Chris, 'but I'd be no good at it. That feeling of getting up in the early hours every day and hitting the ground running . . . I'd be distracted by everything. I'd never get there in time. The Professor's got the right idea. I'd be like the Professor. I'd do it his way.'

Chris bade us goodbye – he had to be away before dawn to get up to Lincolnshire. Once tipped, he'd probably be sent on into Norfolk to reload in Fakenham with cannelloni and lasagne for Mannheim and Dortmund. Italian food for Germany being transported not from Italy, but all the way from East Anglia. I was getting used to this coals-to-Newcastle trade. Ice-cream from England to Russia on the way out; ice-cream from Germany to England on the way back. Frozen sprouts from England to Russia on the way out; frozen courgettes from Belgium to England on the way back. Danish Skol lager, brewed under licence in England, to Russia, together with wines already trucked back to England from France and Germany so they could then be trucked out again. Centuries ago the tea clippers sailed to Britain from the China Seas: if you wanted tea then that was where it came from and that's how it arrived. Now, if the right truck could be in the right place for the right price, you could get anything from anywhere.

In the morning we met a guy bringing in shoes to Northampton – centre of Britain's shoemaking industry – all the way from Romania. Steve Griffiths came from Evesham like Tony: in his mid-thirties, he had his own Volvo F10 and pulled for R & J on eastern European work. At this early hour – it was still only seven – he was quite clear about Romania.

'Fuckin' *shit*.'

Some good border queues?

'Three days.' He looked down his nose at me. 'Time to write a fuckin' book.'

'And read it,' said Tony.

'I want to get out of it,' said Steve. 'I want to *retire*.'

That Thursday morning the countryside between Dover and Folkestone glowed in the morning sun. We tipped Eastbourne's French bread at Lympne – the lorry to take it on to the South Coast was due at the cold store almost as soon as we'd finished unloading. Around Folkestone the main road ducked under and round the massive earthworks and bridge construction and tunnel mouths and railway tracks for the Channel Tunnel. The work was remodelling a whole landscape, creating new hills and valleys and cuttings – all these hacked grass embankments and raw bites of red earth clearing room for a vast emerging theatre of industrial movement past which the Silver Knight sidled like an ant. Earlier I would have been appalled at the savage assault on this gentle downland, but this morning I was only excited. All the travelling, by goods, trucks, trains, people, courgettes, lasagnes, John Smith's bitter, muscle relaxants, windscreen laminates – all the new redefining patterns that Britain and Europe would be threaded with!

We drove through Kent, up the M20, then branched off into Ashford – past the new Sainsbury's superstore – and into the winding, wooded lanes of the Garden of England, amongst the rolling fields of dainty grazing sheep, the neat rows of hop-poles, the orchards of apple trees, the brown ploughed fields. Here, even in this bucolic prospect, as much as on the dull plain of France and Belgium, the land unravelled and interlocked as one boundless productive network, energized and alive. Everything, it seemed, in fact and in fancy, was feeding everything else. Never again could I see such a landscape as inert, passive, reassuringly indifferent. It had far too much work to do.

Smarden, where the courgettes were destined, was a pretty little village with a thirteenth-century pub, thatched and weather-boarded cottages and oast houses. The Silver Knight crept through narrow tunnels of trees to the cold store. While Tony saw to the unloading I wandered across the yard. In a byre behind the last warehouse two extravagantly horned buffalo stared back at me. To their right a lioness stretched out drowsily in a wire-netting enclosure. 'It's just the farmer's hobby,' the warehouse manager said. 'There's kangaroos over the back.' The buffalo shifted minutely in their stall, silent and shy. Tony swung the Silver Knight round and I jumped back in.

I'd won my bet. He'd rung Kidderminster. After we'd tipped at Eastleigh he was being turned back to Dover for the night boat. A pick-up in Belgium the next morning, and then he was due back in the UK again on Saturday morning for drops at Gravesend and Milton Keynes. Then next Tuesday he'd be setting out for Moscow again. But by now it was the Silver Knight that was flagging. Tony had been having trouble building up the air pressure in the transmission since we'd arrived at Calais – until it was at full you couldn't get the gears in. Our seats weren't rising any more on their air suspension. Any humpback bridges or potholes we were hitting with a crash. The trailer mudguards were falling off. One of the doors was broken. Russia's concrete motorway bridges on the Brest road had probably hammered the air suspension bags until they'd found a tiny leak. So if the Silver Knight was going to make it to Belgium and back – let alone another bashing on the road to Russia – it needed to be patched up today, so we had the Seddon–Atkinson dealership in Southampton added to our itinerary.

We left behind the beautiful sylvan garden of Kent, and motorways took us to Novacold, the big refrigerated depot outside Southampton, in a couple of hours. A queue of artics; another loading bay on another industrial estate; a brief crashing and thumping of forklifts and pallets in the back of the trailer, Sainsbury's Fiorella ice-cream had been safely delivered from Germany, and my round trip with the Silver Knight was just about over. Dover to Eastleigh via Moscow – twenty miles short of 4,000 miles. The Seddon garage fixed the Silver Knight's air leaks enough for the next trip, and we drove over to the Parkway station to drop me for the train to Waterloo. It was dark now, and lit up along the side of the motorway approach road was the sweeping frontage of the new Southampton Superstore Plaza: the glittering windows of a giant Marks & Spencer; acres of Sainsbury's. It rolled on and on beside us, illuminating the night more brightly than the airport the other side of the station. I stuffed my Cossack hat into my bag, jumped down from the Silver Knight, and watched its tail lights merge with the jockeying scatter of red in the distance as Tony rejoined the motorway east. Affixed to one of the lamp-posts where I crossed the road was a yellow A A sign: ADDITIONAL SUPERSTORE CAR PARK.

Part Two

WEST

Chapter Nine

On the subway platform at Times Square and 42nd Street station someone was singing Otis Redding. You could hear the huge crying voice, tearing the air with its passion, echoing along the connecting tunnels long before you reached the trains. Down on the platform a black man was bent over his guitar, the sweat shining on his jutting, ridged brow, lost in the sorrow of his song. 'I've got dreams . . . dreams!' he sang, in great gasps of grief. It filled the station, sobbed to the ceiling. When he finished, the Sunday evening crowd gathered round him burst into applause.

'Ladies and gentlemen,' he announced quietly, 'my name is Brother Ritton' – the dollar bills dropped into his guitar case – 'and I'm here to sing you the soul songs of the sixties, the songs of Wilson Pickett, Sam and Dave, and Sam Cooke . . .' – and then he gave us a wounded, moaning version of 'Will You Still Love Me Tomorrow?' Those guys' own records aside, I had never heard such fevered, beseeching singing. The trains banged in and out around him; I missed four hearing him sing.

Pavarotti was also singing that night, an enormous open-air concert in Central Park, and several hundred thousand New Yorkers had been streaming in through the park gates that afternoon as I'd made my way down the

Upper West Side towards Times Square. New York: the more time I spend there the more its tiny insularity astonishes me – that it sucks all these people in to crowd together in the sultry heat and the traffic fumes, when there's all that space for thousands of miles to the west. That evening a Jerry Lewis comedy special on the television had parodied the Pavarotti event by having a corpulent evening-dressed Italian – back to the camera – sing an emotional pre-park concert for Jerry and his friends in their own living-room. (Even the pet labrador was permitted a tear dabbed from its eye.) But that was what the evening felt like. New York looked to itself. Brother Ritton's voice, on the other hand, cried out from a wide, raw America beyond, a big bare world. I was going west tomorrow.

Pete of Yeovil had sown the idea way back on the road to Dover. Ride the American rigs: in his dreams, as he ground off on the arduous haul to Turkey, they were all that his life was not. The indestructible Kenworth, a Harley-Davidson of trucks, with a wide road and a distant horizon to itself: that night I'd gone to see for myself.

I met Dick Hudson at – where else? – Truckworld, where he had a 1973 Kenworth cabover unit for sale. He picked them up second-hand from a dealer in Baltimore, drove them across to the eastern seaboard and put them on a boat for Liverpool docks. That night the comedian in the smoky bar was so midnight blue we went out to sit in the Kenworth to chat. Seventies' vintage Kenworths like this were still upholstered in leather – seats, door panels, quilted and studded across the ceiling; the dashboard looked to be a genuine veneer as on a Bentley. A walk-in wardrobe, a fridge: it didn't matter that the cab itself was low and cramped compared to the Globetrotter height of the Fransen's Silver Knight – Tony had only two thin bunks behind his seat; the Kenworth had a small flat. No good me having a go at taking this chrome-hubbed and -smoke-stacked specimen round the truck park: no synchromesh on any of the gears. Hudson was a cherubic ringer for Richard Branson, and his colleague Paul had the biggest German shepherd I'd ever seen. 'It's not anyone who can drive one of these,' was Hudson's sweet advice. 'It's a *man's* truck.'

But Hudson had done all sorts of things that not anyone could or would have done. He'd made his first Middle East trip – to Iran – at the age of twenty-one. 'It was *horrendous*,' he recalled for me with ingenuous bemusement, 'the coldest winter in history' – and as soon as he got out there his haulier went broke, leaving him stranded in Tehran with no money. 'So I started running trucks intern-ally in Iran to get together enough money to come back – and then I began buying trucks off guys who were abandon-ing them out there. It was very rough in those days: the recession was driving a lot of truckers to try coming out to Tehran.' Like his boss, they went bust, and Hudson added their camions to his fleet. Did that for eight months, and then further on up the road – a spell in a Yugoslavian jail being just one intermediate incident, suddenly and capri-ciously terminated one weekend by a jailer in a good mood about attending his brother's wedding – he found himself in the Bahamas, to meet up with his brother, who'd given up his job as Travel Editor of *Playboy* in order to sail boats round the West Indies. Through a Laker Airways steward-ess who was having an affair with the skipper of his brother's boat, Hudson got the use of her room in the Nassau Hilton as a place to stay; one night in the hotel bar a bloke with a Brummie accent, trying to bum a drink off him with a tale of having sailed his yacht across the Atlantic and arriving penniless, turned out to be Graeme Edge of the Moody Blues, who told Hudson imperiously to write to Edwin Shirley's, who did all their trucking, and tell them to give him a job, or the Moody Blues would never use them again. In the end it took two years for Hudson to wend his way back from the West Indies, but he gave it a go as a joke just the same, and the next day found himself taking a Nazareth tour into Europe.

Then it had been Deep Purple tours, including a bit-part during the gigs following the lead singer with the spotlight, 'trying out the girls for the band' – he spread his hands helplessly – Simply Red tours, New Order, the Smiths, fond memories of inundations of champagne on Murray Head tours, all of which led to work taking a few American bands around Europe, and *they'd* said: you should get some of *our* trucks over here . . . Next time he was over in the States he'd taken the plunge, bought a Kenworth Aerodyne, used it as a camper and toured around in it for a few weeks, and when he shipped it to the UK he got £18,000 for it. 'It's the guys with the cowboy boots and baseball hats who want to buy them,' he said – and they'd kept buying them. Earlier that day, as we'd tried to find a sanitary stopping-place for a cup of coffee, Pete of Yeovil had been telling me about the days-long border queues, the non-existent facilities, the currency hassles – all in a day's work for the Continental trucker in Europe . . . We gazed out through the Kenworth's windscreen at the night-time scene of ERFs and Ford Cargos and DAFs and Volvos, lined up with curtains drawn for the night beneath the dwarfing, steaming monolith of West Thurrock Power Station. 'Here,' said Dick Hudson, 'a truck driver is a necessary evil. Over there you're respected as the hub of industry.' A Kenworth at Truckworld: that was news from elsewhere.

Even so, the trucks that Dick Hudson brought in weren't absolutely the real thing. They were *cabovers*. British road regulations mandated a maximum truck length, including the unit, of fifty feet: to pull the longest possible trailer, therefore, you needed the shortest possible tractor. Put the engine under the cab floor and, though you sacrificed some handling stability and had to settle for the looks of a box-on-wheels, you solved the problem. But the Americans didn't build many cabovers: the States was large enough to accommodate the biggest rig – you could leave the engine under a coffin-like hood in front of you and drive something that looked like an oversize vintage Bentley. 'Those Kenworths you'll find over here,' the marketing director of one UK truck manufacturer had sniffed to me: 'you'll only see them sitting by the roadside converted into wreckers, with naked ladies painted all over them . . .' But there was one place that flouted all the customs and regulations of British trucking – where guys drove the 'conventional' American rigs, with Caterpillar engines under the hood, and they drove them for very short distances at a time, and at *a hundred miles an hour* . . . I went to Brands Hatch, for some truck racing.

In Europe the sport is huge: the German Truck Grand Prix at the Nurburgring attracts 150,000 spectators. Mercedes-Benz runs a Research and Development facility in Switzerland dedicated to racing trucks, which has managed, through fuel injection, turbo-charging and methanol mixtures, to unleash speeds of 150 miles an hour in a production cabover. (Braking systems capable of stopping an 8-ton unit at such a speed on tight curves like the

Druids hairpin at Brands are some way behind in their development, however, so racing regulations permit a maximum speed of 100 miles an hour.) Take the top European drivers. The Swede Slim Borgudd, a professional rally driver, was also once a session driver for Abba. The German Gerd Körber, young and groovy beneath long permed locks, bids to be a Barry Sheene of the big rigs. MAN and Volvo and Mercedes take their truck racing very seriously, which is why their trucks tend to beat the pants off most of ours when they come over to the UK, because we don't.

Truck racing in Britain started off about ten years ago as a bit of a laugh for hauliers on their day off. Fleets would keep one spare unit for the mechanics to tinker with and hot up when they had a spare minute, and when Christian Salvesen or the works team from ERF had their day out at Donington Park it would be a bit of corporate PR and a lot of fun. It was how Richard Walker, the European champion in Group Three (for a certain weight range), had started out; I met him in the pits at Brands on practice day. A bluff, rosy-cheeked guy, he still ran the family haulage business in Nottinghamshire; in the past he'd done some rally driving, and then one day he'd heard about a truck racing meet at Donington up the road. 'So I took out each of the makes we then had in the fleet and swung them around the country lanes as fast as I could – a Volvo, a Scania and a Leyland Powertrain. The Powertrain was *very* quick, and it was also the cheapest if I smashed it up, so I entered in that.'

Nowadays, one of only two British guys who'd stayed in the top rank of the sport, he drove for the Lucas team – oil companies sponsored most of the race meetings and the top teams, Q8 supporting Körber, Mobil Borgudd – and we had a cup of tea in the team trailer, pulled by a beautiful coffin-bonneted Kenworth W924. The 'early, magic years' of the sport had gone, said Walker – now there were around a dozen full-time professionals. But there was no homicidal rivalry yet between race teams – they'd lend each other parts in the pits – and certainly no petulant Formula One egomania afflicting any of the drivers. Walker was still 'last to arrive, first to leave' at meetings – putting in the full week's work at the haulage business beforehand, and getting back after the weekend's competition to pitch in again on Monday morning.

Until 1989 he'd raced a superb Kenworth conventional, decked out in black and white and plenty of chrome – but then he'd written it off at Zolder in Austria. Now he drove a Volvo–White Aero, a droop-snouted product of the increasing multinational agglomeration of the truck business. White, a solid workhorse American make, had been bought by the US automotive giant GMC, which had in turn affiliated with Volvo to give the Swedish manufacturer an entry into the huge American truck market. Borgudd drove a White, too, as did several of the British part-timers. The Christian Salvesen and ERF teams, of course, had long since pulled out. When your mechanics gave up their weekends to watch their prized works truck take a thorough spanking it wasn't much fun any more, and as the speeds crept up managements had also started to wonder if this was quite such a good advertisement for a road haulage industry too often stereotyped as juggernauts plummeting through ancient High Streets and terrifying old ladies at zebra crossings with their air brakes. But at the same time the word had been spreading further across Europe. Outside on the circuit, as we sat over our tea, a

Russian MAZ was sprinting down the straight – the team were based in Minsk, and this year competing for the first time at all major meetings. Another Russian truck, a ZIL, was being driven by the former British women's skiing international, Davina Galica.

In the early days 500 horsepower had been enough to win a race, but Walker's White had a 10-litre American Caterpillar engine uprated from the 350 horsepower you'd expect in this kind of road truck to 900 horsepower. The White's new Lucas Electronic Unit Injectors in the fuel system, added to some serious turbocharging, gave him an acceleration of 0 to 100 in 11 seconds. BP's Mercedes had an 18-litre engine and 1400 horsepower, but the Mercedes was a cabover, and lost some of its speed advantage on its inferior handling. Otherwise, truck-racing specifications required your unit to be a standard road machine even to the retention of the fifth-wheel coupling for a trailer – and a passenger seat.

Whatever you're driving, Walker had declared, 'circuit driving's circuit driving. Maybe this is like driving a classic racing car – a Bentley Le Monza. You know, an earlier version of Stirling Moss.' This Bentley Le Monza weighed six tons.

'Do you want a ride?' he said.

When he turned the ignition the White's engine fired into a savage, hunting throb. Crash helmets on, seatbelts strapped, and we were away onto the straight. A swelling surge of acceleration down towards Paddock Bend, and then hard braking and a thudding release as the turbo cut out. Down the hill from Paddock, the truck's momentum carrying you out over the left edge of the track, and foot down to propel you to the hairpin at Druids. Druids was the best bit: you hit it at a sailing sixty or seventy, and

the Volvo–White yaws round the 180-degree curve side-
on, the side window momentarily the windscreen – a
crablike hurtling that at first seems like a controlled skid,
but in fact those thick truck tyres are clawing round all the
way. Think of modern Formula One cars, with their
computer-controlled suspension maintaining the same hair-
line clearance of the ground all the way round the circuit,
the flat magnetized trajectory of a metal pond-skater, almost
as though they are easing *underneath* every tight bend.
Whereas the outsize classic car with the Lucas logo –
Walker drove it, it seemed to me, somewhat as, say,
Fangio would have driven his early racing car round
Donington, spinning the big bus-driver steering-wheel and
powersliding the unwieldy, deadweight machine against its
own gravity, tricking it into clinging on to a racetrack it
was always trying to come off. Along the last straight each
time Walker built the Volvo–White up to a brimming 100
miles an hour and again the wonder was in something so
heavy being privileged with such speed! When I got into
my little Polo hatchback that afternoon to drive back
round the M25, it felt as though I had climbed inside a
carpet sweeper.

   The two race days, bitter spring afternoons flung about
with flurries of rain, turned out to have something of the
atmosphere of a professional wrestling presentation. It was
exciting, larger than life, and undisguisably naff. At one of
the souvenir stalls I bought a hedgehog-burger fluffy toy
for my godson. A portentous race commentator tried to
talk up every race into a titanic clash between feared
combatants – but since there were only thirty or forty
trucks at the whole meeting, and half a dozen races each
day, the same drivers were competing against each other
several times in an afternoon. At just ten laps of the short

Indy Circuit at Brands – a mile round – these were hardly gruelling endurance tests erupting into frantic pit-stops for tyres and fuel. In between truck heats, less-than-epic contests between swarms of droning Citroën 2CVs further helped to unwind the tension. When the first rain came on the Saturday the Swede Göransson spun off at Druids: interviewed afterwards by a breathless announcer he admitted beatifically that his wipers had packed up and he couldn't see where he was going. Five years ago, you felt, this would have been allcomers for amateurs, everyone would have had those handpainted ERFs and Chevrolet Bruins, and they would have just got on with it. Now sponsorship was trying to make it into Formula One, but truck drivers, even the 100-mile-an-hour merchants, just couldn't play up to it. They knew they were just driving trucks.

But the sight of twenty 6-ton rigs doing the ton down the straight at Brands, the air around them acrid with sooty smoke, is still a brimming, literally momentous experience, and at the end of Sunday the final race of the meeting, the Lucas Truck Prix itself, delivered a crazy, elemental climax. The sky was iron: the forecast rain was long overdue: did drivers opt for wet tyres or gamble on dry and the downpour holding off a little longer? After six laps Göransson was leading in his red and white Volvo N10, and the commentator was convinced that the sodden clouds were about to drop any second. To me the fast-fading light still looked much more like the extravagant clouds of black smoke issuing from a dozen massive, fuel-drenched engines being throttled back for the Druids hairpin. Körber in his yellow Phoenix-MAN was challenging for second, and Borgudd's black and red White was holding off Richard Walker for third. The race leaders slewed out of Druids, just visible again in the roaring murk; now they're growling down the back straight.

The heavens open. By the time they're out of Druids this time round the track is dancing with rain. Joke Kallio, the Finn, steers his white Sisu into Paddock, keeps going on the sheet of water and rips the bonnet off a Detroit Boss as he spins. The chequered flag is frantically waving a premature end to the race. Göransson hurtles straight through the Paddock gravel track and hits the banking. Richard Walker has just managed to take Borgudd on the straight before the flag, and careers off.

'Do you find truck racing scary?' I'd asked him in practice.

He'd shaken his head. 'I find doing sixty nose-to-tail on the M25 much worse.'

Chapter Ten

The taxi-driver filled the cab. He spilled out over his seat like bread rising from the tin; he could barely get his arms around his chest to reach the wheel. We drove south out of Manchester, New Hampshire, and he asked me what I was doing in the States.

Writing a book about riding with long-distance truckers.

'Interesting,' he said in that distant tone that bespeaks anything but interest. His expression was fixed on the smooth road.

The Peterbilt was parked at the top of a cratered, scrubby acre of derelict land opposite a Burger King. At eight in the morning the sun was already high and hard and bright. 'It's kind of . . . *mauve*?' the dispatcher, Paul, had said with a hint of a smirk in his voice when I'd rung him the day before. 'It's a pretty truck . . .' It was a proper truck. Big square hood, twin chromium smokestacks, wing mirrors protruding on chromium frames to give a touch of biplane technology, chromium fenders, big silver plank of chromium exhaust, chromium silencers, chromium windscreen shade and chromium hubcaps. Mauve? It was more of a metallic magenta, a claret colour: a West Ham or an Aston Villa supporter would have recognized it – but over here, it was soon to be made clear, there would be no such consolatory affiliations. Behind the Pete stood a long low-boy trailer; together they made a truck a good seventy feet long.

Parked at right angles to the Pete was a big yellow Caterpillar digger: what we'd call, by the eponym of its most ubiquitous British manufacturer, a JCB; what the Americans call a loader. A blond-haired man in a boiler suit was regarding it with distracted concern and a big wrench. This was Keith Derscheid, an owner–driver who hauled exclusively under contract for Midwest Specialized Transportation of Rochester, Minnesota – their discreet light-blue diamond logo was on his cab doors. He'd be hauling this loader westwards to Sioux Falls, South Dakota, and I'd be accompanying him as far as Midwest's depot in Rochester, where I'd join another of their drivers to head for the west coast.

'We have a problem straight away, Graham,' Keith said. He'd been here an hour already, trying without success to detach the bucket from the scoop arm of the loader. The bucket was wider, though only by a few inches, than the Peterbilt's trailer: by taking it off and securing it on the step of the low-boy end-on, Keith could haul the digger as a normal load. But the bolts holding the bucket on were locked tight: he'd managed to get one side out, but the other was immovable. If the bucket wouldn't come off, Keith would have to travel as a wide load, which meant he'd need separate permits from every state we travelled through for permission to transit, restrictions to using certain roads only, and in some states no driving after dark. This was the end of June: Independence Day weekend was only a few days away, and if Keith didn't reach his destination before the holiday shutdown, when wide loads weren't allowed to travel at all, he'd not only end up becalmed at some truckstop for several days and late with his load, but he'd also miss the holiday at home with his wife and two boys. It was time for a joint effort.

Keith sat me in the driver's seat of the loader, showed me the scoop arm and bucket levers, and climbed out to pick up his wrench again. I manipulated the levers to waggle the bucket on the end of its arm, as you would to empty it of a load of earth; Keith was hoping that the extra flexing would loosen the bolt while he tugged at it with the wrench. It was fun for me, making the big yellow hopper nod and waggle with the slow deliberation of an elephant's head, but the bolt wouldn't budge. Keith climbed into the cab again. 'Ever driven one of these things before?'

I'd just been driving a new Buick Skylark with wine-coloured plush seats around the green mountains and chocolate-box villages of Vermont.

I put the digger into gear – the raised central cab gave you the sensation of riding a lurching, lolloping metal camel – and we growled down the hill to the plant hire company's workshop. The equipment auctioneers who'd sold this digger had just moved out from next door, and this Caterpillar was one of a few scattered across the wasteground that were the last to be collected. In the workshop the engineer took a large lump hammer to the jammed bolt, swung and connected with an earsplitting *clung! clung! clung!* He swung until he was panting, but the bolt was fixed as fast as ever. We were a WIDE LOAD. Keith went into Reception to phone Midwest to get them fixing up our state permits, and then we chugged back up the hill. I stood on the trailer step and beckoned Keith on, and he drove the digger up on to the low-boy.

'People say this is a Mary-Kay truck,' Keith called out as

he climbed around the loader with cables to lash it to the trailer deck. 'You know? Mary-Kay, the cosmetics firm – the woman who founded it, she drives around in a pink Cadillac.'

It looked mauve to me, I offered.

'Mmmm-auve?' Keith squinted hard at me. Whereas I pronounced it to rhyme with 'Hove', the American way was more like 'Mmmovv' – with an uneasy doubtful double-m. '*That's* what you'd call it?' I'd obviously been co-opted as a new witness in a very large inquiry.

I jumped down from taping over the loader's exhaust pipe to prevent an inward rush of air once we were moving spinning the turbo blades – without lubrication from a running engine they'd eventually disintegrate, and Keith would leave Sioux Falls with a bill for new ones. Keith gave me a peering-over-the-top-of-your-glasses look round the side of the cab and said, 'It's not *pink*.'

The middle of the morning already, and we hadn't moved. At the other end of the wasteground a white Freightliner was starting to roll, aboard its trailer a massive caterpillar-tracked excavator that sagged over each side and towered into the air. It bumped past us across the rutted sandy lot and pulled out to the right, then sharp back to the left, to swing the low-boy round and up on to the exit road. Even as the unit was easing up on to the tarmac the clearance between the bowed trailer and the sloping ground was down to inches; one more pull and there was a dull grating as the trailer grounded out and wedged itself on the edge of the road.

'Oh, now that's trouble,' said Keith in concern. 'Because he can't get that thing off now.' Something that heavy, and simply too big for the longest and widest road trailer: you could drive it on, but it would need to be winched or craned off. Imagine setting out on a thousand-mile haul and coming to grief before you even got *on* to the highway . . .

The rig fidgeted and wriggled and twisted and had another go: then the driver, a raddled fiftyish guy with leather skin and a barrel of a belly slung in front of him, had jumped out, passed his hand across his brow to wipe away the glistening sweat, and was fiddling with some buttons at the side of his unit to try and redistribute the weight between his axles. Back in the cab he roared the engine, and eventually got enough traction to ease the trailer off the road for long enough to let the whole truck sag backwards and off the hump. He pulled round in as tight a jackknife as he could manage, and this time the excavator, undulating minutely on its pliant low-boy, was hauled off and away up on the main road. I went over to Burger King and got us some brunch.

We sat under a shade tree out of the fierce sun – in the middle of the day the temperature was in the high eighties – to wait for the fax in the Reception to bring Keith his wide-load permits. New Hampshire and Connecticut came through quickly, but by one in the afternoon we were still waiting for Massachusetts and New York – New York were never on the ball, said Keith, always kept you waiting hours. I hadn't realized before to what extent the United States' traffic regulations were divided into a maze of state-by-state variations. You didn't have the customs checks and border posts and visa requirements and ferry sailings the European drivers had to negotiate, but here we were on my first American truck ride, half a day gone already, doing the same thing as them: waiting around.

This was Keith's third load of the week since he'd last been home. He'd come down from Portland, Maine, where he'd delivered a 3,000-gallon liquid oxygen tank to the Mercy Hospital for use in cryogenic research, and before that he'd hauled a big generator for an office block into downtown Boston – a terrible job manoeuvring the trailer around its clogged city streets. 'If I'd known there was going to be this problem with the loader,' he reflected ruefully, 'I'd have come down here last night – I only stayed over fifty miles up the road.'

Keith had grown up in Kenyon, Minnesota – still his home town, where his wife now worked as a production controller in a factory making plastic seats for fast-food restaurants. He'd always been driving: learnt working on a farm, and started on four-wheeler trucks – 'we call them "cars"' – taking sweetcorn from the farm to the local canning plant and sugar beet to the refinery, and then nine years ago he'd got his first 'over the road', or long-distance, job. After a couple of years the guy he'd been working for told Midwest to hire him, and already, after a spell driving his own Kenworth (truckers called them KWs), he was on his second truck. 'The modern design trucks,' he said – that white Freightliner had been an example – 'have the fared-in sides covering the fuel tanks, the aerodynamic hoods, the headlights fared in to the fender, plastic bumpers. But we don't want that. Owner–operators like me run the classic trucks. We want the Petes and the Kenworths with two chimneys, two air filters, the gas tank sticking out. Then it looks like mine – it says, *I ride my way*.' This mauve Pete – he'd bought it used a year ago – was now four years old, had 400,000 miles on the clock, but he reckoned it was still worth $45,000. (A new Pete or Kenworth classic would be $85,000, or you could get a new Freightliner for about $70,000.) 'In a year and a half's time, when this one's paid for,' Keith said, 'I can go into the KW or the Peterbilt dealer and spec a new truck from the bottom up. You can have whatever you want – they can even chrome up stuff inside the cab . . .' With this one he'd had to take what he was given: the previous owner had fitted bars over the window in the rear of the sleeper compartment, a minute modification judged sufficient by the CB fraternity to christen Keith's Pete 'The Jailhouse'.

The white Freightliner was towing its excavator back towards us. We strolled over to the driver, who was fiddling with the axle weight controls again and holding a scruffy chit of paper at arm's length. He'd been up to the weigh-station to check his total weight, since there was a bridge on the way to his destination in Omaha with a loading limit he had to be under. The weigh-station print-out showed he was overweight on two axles – but now he was prodding at his little pocket calculator as if it was going to bite back, and it was telling him that the individual loadings didn't add up to the overall weight he'd been given: by his sums it came in under. So he'd gone back to the weigh-station and asked them to do a second reading, and now he'd got a second set of figures that also didn't add up but still told him he was overweight, but on different axles. He didn't know what to do. It seemed clear to me that he'd hit a duff set of scales or an innumerate scales officer – but if he got stopped by a highway patrol-man the official documentation would show he was over-weight and compounding his felony by driving on regardless.

'These days you have to have your weight-shift controls outside the cab, where you have to get out to do it,' murmured Keith to me as we watched the guy trying to transfer some weight from his middle axles to the front of the truck. 'When they were in the cab a driver could shift air from axle to axle as he was going over a scale – you needed to baffle the sound so the weigh-man didn't hear the hiss, but it was a way of getting through a weigh-station overweight.'

The Freightliner driver was no nearer solving his problem – unsurprisingly, since he didn't know where the fault lay: if it was the weigh-man's mistake no amount of air-shifting would make any difference – so doubtful, bemused and ill at ease, he ground off again.

It was two in the afternoon, but down in Reception our Massachusetts wide-load permit had arrived at last. That left New York, but Keith was going to get it sent to a truckstop further on up the road.

'What kind of music do you like?' said the pert little girl running the front desk, who'd just been flirting on the phone with a supplier who'd offered to take her out in his Jaguar.

'Blu-*ues*,' I said.

'*Eeeeugh*. I like dance music.'

We were off. The Jailhouse had a splendidly sumptuous cab: a low ceiling and a low windscreen to look through – the space was in the studio flat behind the seats – but all plush fabric coverings and wood trim. With the square hump of hood out front between you and the road a peaked cap would have been sartorial decorum for driver and passenger. The Pete had a harder, firmer ride than the Silver Knight, but it was a reassuring resilience: if anything was going to give, it was not going to be this tough tourer. We followed Interstate 93 south over the state line into Massachusetts and then turned south-west outside Lawrence on to the 495 towards Hartford, Connecticut, and along the way Keith started off my *I Spy American Trucks* collection.

Those cream-coloured cabovers with an Arkansas address on the side were from the huge J.B. Hunt fleet — nearly 6,000 trucks, one of the biggest in the States and growing fast. Hunt was shaving haulage rates so low it was squeezing the traditionally Teamster-unionized fleets hard.

The J.B. Hunt vehicles were Internationals, or 'farm tractors', in trucker-speak — a delicately ironic comparison between this less-expensive make of truck and the agricultural equipment also manufactured by International Harvester.

Those bright orange cabovers — the Schneider fleet, 9,000 vehicles, another huge nationwide trunking company — were 'pumpkin trucks', and the depot where they all parked at night was 'the pumpkin patch'.

Freightliners were 'Freightshakers': a reminder of the era *before* their specification had been improved a few years ago to compete with Kenworth and Peterbilt, both of whom they were now outselling.

The coffee-coloured United Parcel Service fleet were 'Buster Browns', after the kids' shoes, because, I supposed, they looked like a shoe on wheels. Actually, they didn't, but it's a less pompously polysyllabic moniker.

Now we were underway Keith was relaxed and ebullient, his cherubic, clean-scrubbed face and blue eyes inscrutable behind aviator-style mirror shades. When a Kenworth reefer (an English trucker would have called it a fridge — the kind of trailer Tony and I took to Russia) hurtled past in the outside lane he said, 'Whoa — that guy's really hauling the mail!' Three hours out of New Hampshire, and hitting heavy traffic outside Waterbury, Connecticut, he peered round the tailback and said, 'We got disco lights up here. Must be something up.' Eventually we dawdled past a couple of compacts parked bumper-to-tailgate while the traffic cop took details of their minor prang. 'One little fender-bender,' exclaimed Keith, 'and everyone has to rubberneck!'

He switched the CB radio on to hear of any other traffic hold-ups ahead, and we drove on with a crackling, hissing wash of noise that randomly erupted into barks and bellows of conversation, to my ears all utterly indecipherable. The highway passed across a bridge above a tall gorge, and at the bottom, late afternoon sun glinting off the rapids, I could see fishermen standing in the rushing river. The furred voices became animated, and one stentorian proclamation dominated all the rest, but still I hadn't a clue.

'What'd he say?'

'He said, "THAT'S WHERE I SHOULD BE, NOT UP HERE ON THUH GAHD-DANG HIGHWAY WITH THESE IDJITS!"'

On the western fringe of Connecticut – the city sprawl of Hartford had given way to dense woodland enclosing the Interstate – we pulled into the Danbury truckstop, a pitted, muddy dustbowl of a place that brought back homely memories of moonscapes on the A2, and we ran into the white Freightliner driver again, still hauling the heavy burden of his huge excavator, now poring over his road atlas to check the wide-load route New York State was confining him to. He shook his head: 'Man, they're sending me on some skinny-ass roads . . .'

Keith went to check at the truckstop office for his New York permit. It had been an early start out of Manchester this morning, the Burger King brunch was already a long while ago, and I was starving hungry. I pulled out the first Snickers bar of my US trip – Hackettstown, New Jersey, they were trucked from in this part of the world. But I can only attribute the delusion that follows either to a calorie-deficient faintness or to a sudden sugar rush.

'Right!' Keith was striding back to the Jailhouse, angelically severe, and yanking the red WIDE LOAD flags out from either side of his front bumper. His eyes were wide in melodramatic inquiry: 'What other business gives you the chance to be a *criminal*?'

'Ya gonna bootleg it?' said the Freightliner guy, not looking up from his atlas.

'They had their chance,' Keith called. We only had to cross the corner of New York State, a distance of merely fifty miles, it would be dark by then – and anyway, even if the bureaucrats hadn't got any kind of schedule to keep, we had.

If you really wanted to wangle it, he confided to me, there was one tip he'd been given and never tried out: raise the scoop-arm of the loader as high as it'll go – when the bucket's off the trailer and hanging high in the air no traffic cop will be able to see whether it overhangs the sides of the trailer by an inch or two. However, the cop would then wonder why you were choosing to haul a loader with the aerodynamic profile of a rearing sauropod. This loader was only a fraction wider than the low-boy: it was certainly no obstruction to other traffic; in the gathering twilight no one would pick it up. I dropped into the closed-down restaurant to find the bathroom and slithered my way through a raucous, carousing, smoke-wreathed truckers' pow-wow lobbing up disjointed shouts of 'Who says I ain't got an ego!' and '. . . rowdiest fucken truckstop!' We pulled out of the dustbowl past a line of tippers – over here, said Keith, they were 'coal-buckets' – loaded to the gunwales with rubbish. The name may have been different, but tipper drivers over here were obviously still the untouchables of the trucking world. Trevor, my instructor at Roadtrain, had inveighed against their driving standards: because tipper drivers got paid on weight, they all tried to haul prodigious numbers of loads of rubble and hardcore by driving everywhere like the clappers. 'Not for me,' pronounced Keith, weighing in with his homily. 'Guys these days are hauling garbage out of New York City and taking it up to landfills round here. "Wha'd'you haul?" *Garbage*. "Howd'ya get rich?" *Haulin' garbage . . .*'

We crossed the Hudson River soon after seven, and there were deer visible in the twilight woods to the side of the road. Near Port Jervis a 'James Bond' special-edition Kenworth was one for the spotter's book – this black and white striped specification had been introduced years back as a one-off production run to tie-in with a bit of product placement in a Bond movie – and even at $128,000 they were so revered amongst American truckers that Kenworth were still making them. Already we were crossing into Pennsylvania, and the road was climbing. We crested the hill summit just before the Twin Rocks truckstop where we were going to stop for a meal, with a magnificent pink-striated sunset ahead of us, and a rolling plain of woods and farmland and twinkling lights below.

All the tables in American truckstops, I was to find, had built-in telephone handsets so that drivers could make credit-card calls to their families during or after dinner in peace and comfort rather than having to stand around queuing for a windy phone kiosk. While Keith spoke quietly to his wife in the Twin Rocks restaurant a wheezy bewhiskered old boy seated behind me told me, 'Cheer up,' as the matriarchal waitress came up to our table. He gestured to the menus stuffed under her arm and confided breathlessly, 'It's *Christmas*!'

The waitress fetched him a colossal swipe round the head with the menus and said with pleasant belligerence, 'He thinks he's funny.'

In the truck park as we walked back Keith pointed out a new green Kenworth — another 900-series model, the square-hooded classic truck equivalent of Keith's Peterbilt, but this one was also special. Kenworth had just introduced the option of an *extended hood*. He pointed at the side of the truck: between the back of the front wheel-arch and the cab door was an *extra seven inches*. It was a very important seven inches, for those in the know: it turned a classic truck into one that just went that little bit further to be just that little bit more classic. As a modification it didn't seem to me to have quite the charisma of the latest wheeze I'd been reading about in an English truck mag before flying out to New York: fixing neon-light tubes around the underside of your rig so that come nightfall your entire truck seemed to float through the dark in an unearthly pool of lime-green or lemon light. But Keith was in no doubt about the extended-hood Kenworths: 'They're for the guys with the *real* big egos!'

We drove on until one in the morning, until we'd reached the AmBest truckstop at Milton, 416 miles from where we'd set out in New Hampshire. The CB boomed into life just once after we'd pulled out of Twin Rocks. A loud bass voice was rumbling, 'Here, kitty kitty . . . Here, kitty kitty . . .' In response came frenzied shrieks of '*Miaow! Miaow!*' Even with a 63-inch-wide bed in the sleeper compartment of the Jailhouse (there were no bunks) there was room for me to curl up on the floor to sleep with Keith's dumbbells at my head and his cowboy boots at my feet.

Chapter Eleven

Keith had never been on a train. He'd never been on a plane. He'd never been abroad – at least, not outside the American continent, and his only foray beyond the United States had been a brief visit across the southern border to Tijuana in Mexico. He had two sons; he'd known his wife since they'd been teenagers; he was the same age as me. His wife had travelled with relatives for a while in Latin America – spent some time, indeed, in Sandinista Nicaragua. 'You know, Graham,' said Keith – we were hauling our yellow loader through a dairy-farming landscape of little farms, grain silos and fields sprinkled with black and white cows – 'when she came back from Nicaragua, what she told me about how things are down there, it made me realize that the kind of picture Ronald Reagan used to paint about it, it really isn't the whole truth. Not at all.'

You could easily do a comparison of the practical superiorities of the American trucking life even after a mere day on the road: the smooth, straight Interstate highways to take you everywhere; the beautiful thoroughbred chromium-plated roadster you drove; the palatial truck-stops you could stop over at . . . We'd been 'dinkin' about', as Keith put it, till eleven o'clock this morning, luxuriating under steaming showers in spotless private cubicles, ordering huge breakfasts of pancakes and hash browns and fruit and french toast and bacon and eggs-over-easy and the rest from the waitress service in the quiet and civilized restaurant, even deliberating for an age over which flavour of Snapple fruit punch to choose – or perhaps a jumbo bottle of Gatorade? – from the enormous refrigerated selection to swig along the way.

But the difference was also spiritual. For the Continental hauler in Europe, travel was antagonistic, disorientating, continual displacement – wherever you went you became a foreigner. Almost everywhere was abroad. Here in the States to take a truck 1,400 miles, as the Pete was going to clock up between Manchester, New Hampshire and Rochester, Minnesota – almost as far as London to Moscow – was affirmatory, protective. You never left home.

'I like to get all my ducks in a row first thing,' declared Keith, sleek and showered and smug as we strode back to the Jailhouse.

For the American trucker, foreign difficulties meant the local vagaries of vehicle regulations in states like California or New York. 'They're the two states that truckers dislike,' said Keith. New York meant taxes, and taxes, and taxes: they charged you a road tax for using the state's roads, a tax on fuel every time you purchased it within the state, and then another fuel tax based on how many miles you'd travelled within the state during the year, regardless of where you'd bought your diesel. California meant pernick-ety, hairsplitting checks on your vehicle and your docu-mentation, with any violations – even small things wrong with your truck or your paperwork – punishable by ardu-ous fines. Take your driving-hours record (the States didn't have a tachograph system: every day a driver filled in a sheet of graph paper in his Log Book, the line inching along horizontal for spells of driving, down for stationary periods of overnighting, meal-breaks or unloading). Run your Biro against the side of your road atlas cover down the wrong column in your Log Book – an easy mistake for a tired driver who's not exactly in the mood for late-night geometry homework – and, said Keith, 'you can get fined $1,500 for drawing a little line.' Connecticut, on the other hand, was the most eccentrically arcane, its road transport regulations enshrining a residually stern New England Puritanism. In Connecticut a truck-driver's sleeper cab was required to show the bed made up whenever the truck was on the road, with the pillow at the left-hand, driver's, side of the cab. And white sheets on the bed, if you please. Drivers were also mandated to wear hard-soled shoes at the wheel – 'I met a guy last week,' said Keith, 'who just got a ticket in Connecticut for wearing sneakers.'

Pennsylvania was spooling by: we were now virtually in the centre of this big state on Interstate 80, which would take us all the way across from its eastern to its western boundary. A big natural cutting enclosed us, the gold and green trees and the haze of purple flowers down its sides a sudden bloom of colour after the hours of plain green pasture we'd endured all morning. It was easy driving: never a roundabout, a stop light, or even a single-carriage-way – you just rumbled straight ahead at a uniform sixty, the big yellow loader jogging almost imperceptibly behind us in our wing mirrors. Yesterday we'd made over four hundred miles even with a start as late as two in the afternoon: if you wanted to take a chance on your Log Book and just ride as far as you could, there were huge distances to be devoured. Keith was sticking to the law: no more than nine hours' driving in a day – but in his early days on the road, well before he'd come to work for

Midwest, he'd twice done hauls of a thousand miles in twenty-four hours.

'The first time, I picked up a piece of mining equipment from Portland, Oregon, where these things were made – and it had to be in Louisville, Kentucky in forty-eight hours. That's 2,400 miles. It was a double-man job – they added five hundred bucks to the price for a second driver. I told them the other guy was waiting down the road at the motel or something. Well, I got through a snowstorm, and I got over the hills, but I didn't make it. I got to fifty miles away on the second night and I rang them and said, look, I'm out of hours, it's dark, I gotta stop. They said, OK, no problem, we'll see you in the morning. Next morning I unloaded it, and the bossman comes out and says, "Here, we've got a special belt buckle to give you for doing such a good job in the time. And here's one for the second driver – where do we find him?" I said, "Oh, uh . . . give it to me, uh . . . he's just come off shift after driving all night and he's sleeping in the cab right now . . ."'

And then the *second* time . . . 'The second time – I was still working for the other guy – I had a load in Portland, again, for Des Moines, Iowa, but it only filled half a trailer. Then this other agent offered me a second load and seven hundred bucks to take it to Iowa. But this was Friday now, and that wasn't till the Monday. So I said to my guy, well, it's only an hour and a half further on – should I do it? He was paying my rooms, and he said, yeah, take it, and get a room over the weekend. So I stayed in Portland over the weekend, and then Monday morning my dispatch man calls me up and says, "What are you doing? You should be in Des Moines!" It was a forklift I was delivering – quite a small one, but it was for one of the biggest construction companies in the States. Man, he put me through it – he said, "If you make our company lose a multi-million-dollar account . . .!" Well, he got me quite upset. So I set off for Des Moines – and when I got there Tuesday and rang him – after 1,750 miles in two days – he said I was too late, I'd missed the truck that was taking the forklift on, and now I'd have to go all the way to upstate New York with it! That was another 3,000 miles! Well, I got it there, but on the third morning, just rolling along, suddenly I saw this *big pink dragon* walk right across the road in front of me. I learned my lesson.'

These days, married with a family, and hauling special-ized loads all the time, there wasn't the opportunity for Keith to drive crazy distances even if he had the inclination. Today was the first of July: before we'd set out from Milton he'd totted up in his Log Book: in the month of June he'd done 10,351 miles. 'That's good – that's the kind of miles guys with normal loads would run, ten to twelve thousand. Oversize you don't do as many' – yesterday morning had been proof of that – 'normally it'd be about 8,000. Me, it's about seven – but I've got a life.' Out of the hundred-odd drivers who hauled for Midwest Specialized, some fleet employees, others owner–driver contractors like Keith, about forty were million-milers. When you got more than a million miles under your belt the company gave you a commemorative buckle to go on your belt.

Specialized work was slower than conventional haulage, then, but it was skilful work – as I'd seen with the Freightliner guy, the most literal embodiment of a ponder-ous responsibility. For guys like Keith, who, I could see, had a somewhat more decisive approach to his work, the rewards were also greater. June had been a good month for him because he'd started off with three huge hauls from the Caterpillar plant in Peoria, Illinois. These were parts for the biggest Cat digger ever made: whereas our JCB-lookalike was a mere 35,000 pounds, this leviathan, destined for open-cast mining work up in Michigan, weighed in at 365,000 pounds. Its tyres alone stood higher than the top of the Peterbilt's exhaust stack. Keith had made two trips carrying assorted components, and one with just the digger arms on board – 48,000 pounds just by themselves. Peoria to the Michigan mine was five hundred miles, and he was on two dollars a mile for each run – at that rate he could afford to run back empty to pick up the next lot. A dollar a mile average over all the time a trucker was at the wheel was still a good rate for an owner–driver: normally you'd aim to get ninety cents a mile and would settle for eighty. After all your expenses, however – your financing on the truck, your diesel, your taxes, your toll-road permits, your motels, your meals – you took home a lot less. This year guys like Keith would be hoping for about twenty-six cents a mile profit; last year had not been as good – it had been more like fifteen.

In front of us was a shiny silver tanker, the back end of the tank a burnished, bevelled stainless-steel looking glass. 'One day I want to get a photo of my truck reflected in the back of one of them,' mused Keith. 'That would be real neat.' A few spots of rain were falling: it was an overcast, humid morning. The little clapboard farms showed few signs of life – just the odd tractor tilling one of the fields on the valley floor. From the Interstate, Pennsylvania was a muted, widely uniform landscape. Keith pointed to a white semi-trailer with a red and green flash on it: Continental Freightways, another nationwide fleet: 'They're called "Cornflakes".'

Caterpillar diggers may have been made in Peoria, but

right now they were doing a lot of travelling back into the Midwest. Trucks followed trade, and trade followed money. In its own prosaic way, this mauve Peterbilt heading from New Hampshire towards South Dakota was mapping history as specifically as the battered truck carrying Steinbeck's Joad family out of the dustbowl depression in *The Grapes of Wrath*. Our yellow loader's westward odyssey traced the United States' recent economic reversal. Until a year or so ago New England had been the boom region in the States for both residential and business development. Then the property bubble had burst, and such a customarily prosperous place now had a faster growth of unemployment, more failed construction projects and bankrupt developers than anywhere else – and a lot of redundant diggers and earthmovers to be sold off by receivers and liquidators. Caterpillar dealers in Nebraska, Minnesota and the Dakotas could pick them up for $20,000 less than the price of a new one – and that was where guys like Keith came in. 'In the last couple of years I've hauled quite a few of these back home . . .'

Just before three we were entering Ohio and pulling off the Interstate into the Hubbard truckstop. 'The other thing I might do,' said Keith, manoeuvring the Pete to park up between a couple of Macks, 'when this truck is paid for – I might change my job. I want to help my two boys get into their sports – it's important for them to see their parents at every ball game . . .' So he was thinking about giving up over-the-road hauling, at least while his sons were going through their teenage school years: a fishing friend of his who ran a delivery fleet in Minneapolis, running goods from a factory forty miles out on the outskirts into the city, had offered him an $11-an-hour job (Teamster rates). You'd start at eight in the morning, you were guaranteed at least forty hours' work a week – and you were home by three or four in the afternoon. The custom Keith Derscheid Peterbilt 'spec'd from the bottom up' might never hit a highway. And soon Keith might never come near places like this. This was Truckworld. It was nowhere near the Dartford Tunnel.

There was a tyre depot, a truck wash, a state-permit point, a big tools shop, a Yak-Yak shack for in-cab sound systems, and a motel. There was a booth making you up your own glowing-pink number plate. There was a fake-Irish pub. Cowboy boots covered an entire wall of the gift shop – every possible leather and colour, from plain no-nonsense black to triple-hued, embossed and studded and buckled, and countless pairs in snakeskin. Shelves were heaped full of Long Haul Jeans – designed, explained the labels, specifically for a trucker's needs, with 'full-cut seat, full-cut thigh, and a longer rise'. 'Yup,' said Keith at my shoulder, 'for a *big ass*!' There was a movie cinema, the equal of many multiplex halls, down to the raked floor and tip-up seats. There were racks of truckers' T-shirts, emblazoned with slogans like:

IF YOU CAN'T RUN WITH THE BIG DOGS,
STAY ON THE PORCH

HARD TIMES DON'T LAST FOREVER.
TRUCKERS DO

TRUCKERS MAKE AMERICA GREAT

Others, pastiching the logo-style of the Hard Rock Café, advertised:

THE ROAD-KILL CAFÉ – *You Kill It, We Grill It*

– and on the back was the week's menu, from Monday's 'Everything scraped up from the weekend' to 'Poodles with noodles and road toad à la mode' for the middle of the week.

There were spinners in the foyer full of colour leaflets and booklets from haulage firms advertising for drivers and owner–drivers: such a standard of design and inviting aura of professionalism we in Britain would save for holiday brochures. Truckers would get a black-and-white set-to-fit ad in the Classifieds at the back of *Commercial Motor*. As for British truckers' accessories, there was no hard sell on heavy image when simple subsistence was so much more difficult: you needed a hot meal before a wide-brimmed hat, which was why the mail-order ads in the UK mags offered gadgets like the Sausage Hotter attachment (max. twelve sausages) for boiling up frankfurters inside your electric kettle.

We wandered into the restaurant. The salad bar was heaped with fresh strawberries, peaches and red and green melon; the buffet bar was laden with steaming trenchers of lasagne, meatballs in sauce, garlic bread. And moral advice was free and abundant. Never mind HAPPY CHRISTMAS YOU TRUCKERS: here in Ohio the truckers' restaurant, taking its cue from the defiant declarations on the T-shirts, had imbibed that passion for public sentence you saw graven in granite and marble at the entrance halls of American university campuses. But Truckworld had chosen not a single apophthegm to stand as its motto: this restaurant was festooned with moralism – placards of it hung from the ceiling in quantities as liberal as the fruit in the salad bar.

Some of these sayings seemed obscurely directed at the trucking fraternity. When Mark Twain had observed that

NOTHING SO NEEDS REFORMING AS
OTHER PEOPLE'S HABITS

was it subconsciously premonitory of those little Chrysler sub-compacts nipping out in front of truckers on the Interstate?

FEAR IS THE TAX THAT CONSCIENCE
PAYS TO GUILT (Zachary Taylor)

I couldn't quite unravel that one – but fear and tax and guilt undoubtedly went together, and especially in New York State.

THE VAGABOND WHEN RICH IS CALLED A
TOURIST (as someone called Paul Richard had
observed)

seemed to have nothing to do with anything.

I was most pleased of all to find Schopenhauer quoted above the Truckworld buffet bar. You piled your platter with lasagne underneath the words

INTELLECT IS INVISIBLE TO THE MAN
WHO HAS NONE

I look at them now and I think: *I could have come up with that*.

If Schopenhauer had had the chance to visit Truckworld at Hubbard he'd have seen that the Road Kill Café T-shirts said it better.

We were following Interstate 80 still: it had taken us all the way across Pennsylvania, and now it would carry us right through the top of Ohio and out into Illinois. There was little to see once we were back on the highway: it was a grey, drizzly afternoon, and I recall the Ohio countryside as more unvariegated, flat drab green punctuated by distant grey settlements. Just past Cleveland I pointed out a Kenworth's cab door that read

DON'T MIND THE HORSE – JUST LOAD THE WAGON

'I saw one once,' said Keith. 'There's a picture on the back of the truck of a guy holding his sides laughing. The slogan says, YOU WANT IT *WHEN?*'

On the radio Delbert McClinton and Tanya Tucker were singing,

> *Tell* me about it,
> Tell me about teardrops in the dark

– an exuberant, bouncy song;

> *Tell* me about it,
> Tell me all about your broken heart.

At least there was some good music to listen to. McClinton was one of my favourite rhythm and blues singers – a white man from Texas with a blaring horn-rich band, and hoarse husky soul voice, and a repertoire that ranged from country to roadhouse blues. I'd caught him in London on a rare visit the previous summer playing a two-hour blinder at the T & C 2 club in Islington; but here the easeful ardour with which the two of them sang to each other seemed truly made for miles and miles of open road.

After that the music went downhill: dum-diddle-iddle-um country that reached its nadir with a terrible hickey-hokey thing from someone called Alan Jackson, entitled 'A Lot about Livin' and a Little 'bout Love', whose twinklin' and grinnin' catchiness immediately inspired in me a lot about hatred and a little 'bout homicide. On every radio station we turned the dial to we tuned in just in time to catch the opening bars.

A sign at the roadside trailing the imminent turn-off for the Embleton truckstop read:

HOME OF AMERICA'S WORST APPLE PIE

'Keith, why do truckers all go for country music?'

I hadn't expected his answer. 'I think it's 'cause all these guys are playing every night, in the tour bus every day – you know, they have the same gruelling road schedule as we do. The Judds, people like them: some of the country singers even have their own CBs in their buses and talk to truckers along the way.'

It's also, of course, that country music has historically been the music of the poor white working-class in America. Blacks had the blues, and then Motown; trucking was part of the white blue-collar constituency that identified with the simple sweet sentiment of country music, from Hank Williams through to George Strait. It was only with guys like Keith that trucking had turned into an individualist profession – but though his cassette box contained stuff like the Vaughan Brothers and the Traveling Wilburys, I also found a lot of country. Country music spoke for Keith's situation because it was exactly what its name said: not urban music, not the music of the city, all trend and fad, and wired and neurotic and hip, but the music of the country – this vast, placid, gently undulating plain of farming and small discrete towns we'd been creeping across: towns like Keith's own, Kenyon, Minnesota (pop. 1,500). Phil Horton in Germany had said he thought good truckers had to be like farmers; Andrew Wilson-Young had been a farmer; Keith said he thought farmers made good truckers. Over here, in the thousands of miles of country stretching away to the west of New York, the unsophisticated, unchanging lilt of country music nudged and jogged along at the same unforced pace as the view from your cab window.

A roadsign announced, GET TICKET, *2 miles*.

Was this prior warning of a Smokey Bear up ahead waiting for some customers – or was there actually a small hamlet in Ohio called Get Ticket? Keith remembered a sign he'd seen once warning of CLIMAX, *1 mile*. 'You're thinking, *Whoa! Get at it, babe!* But it's a place!'

I put the Vaughan Brothers' cassette into the stereo; it hadn't got the supercharged ferocity of Stevie Ray Vaughan's live album – the quintessence of a man who, in brother Jimmie's words, 'never played it the same way once' – but it was better than *a-diddle-iddle-iddle-and-a-little-'bout-love*. 'I was driving through Wisconsin the night his helicopter crashed,' Keith was recalling. 'I was only about forty miles away from the amphitheatre where he was playing. Such a foggy night . . . such a sad thing . . .'

We drove out of Ohio that day and nearly as far as Chicago: it was 559 miles from where we'd set out in Milton, Pennsylvania, by the time we pulled up for the night some sixty-five miles short of the Windy City. I fell off my perch during the night drive through Indiana, and when I woke to find us pulling off the Indiana Turnpike into the South Bend City Services it was already one-thirty in the morning, and the fog hung silver-grey above our headlights.

'Remember,' the radio announcer was offering a 'Barbecue Tip' for the holiday weekend: 'If you drop a hot dog on the floor – *give it to your neighbour's kid* . . .' Keith's giant alarm clock had shaken us out into another foggy, dank morning, and we had a tight schedule to make if we were going to reach Rochester, Minnesota before the holiday restrictions on heavy traffic in Wisconsin shut us down – we had to be out of that state by four o'clock: after then heavy loads weren't allowed on the highway.

'I think I'd need a double Jack Daniels for breakfast if I had that alarm waking me up every morning,' I said. The crazed jangle had had me trembling on the brink of throwing my teddy in the air and bellowing a bleary 'Gooooooooooood morning Vietnam!' 'You should get a cassette alarm, Keith. I wake up every morning to George Thorogood – you know that blast of slide guitar at the start of "Bad to the Bone"?'

'You mean, *BADA-BADA-BA-DAB*? Yup!'

Dion got us away that morning with 'The Wanderer': 'We-ee-ell *I'm* the kinda guy . . .' *Here* was a good trucking song: that wide-stride loping beat. Country and western rhythms were mostly too finicking, tripping, dainty. You needed that broad piston thump, the seven-league-boots gait.

'That's a song that sounds good whoever does it,' said Keith.

Radio news reports had more details of the Mississippi River floods in Iowa. Twenty-five hundred acres had been inundated after levees had burst; sewage plants were overrun with the torrent of water and discharging raw effluent into the river. This year the rains in the Midwest just hadn't stopped, and it was still raining. Keith had been pointing out the terrible state of the crops in Indiana — fields of golden wheat, he said, a month behind. It was even worse here in Illinois: 'That corn should be four foot high by now — it went in so late around here, should have gone in three months earlier, around March.' The fields were flooded. 'It's the same up in Minnesota.'

As the fog disappeared from a bright, overcast morning the Interstate was filling up with holiday traffic. At the rest area just over the border in Wisconsin the truck-parking area was full up with Winnebagos, cars towing boats, trailers of camping gear. We were going to have to get ahead of all this Independence weekend traffic if our Cat loader was going to get to Sioux Falls on time. We passed another Midwest driver with a Cat aboard his loader — he'd picked up his from Aurora, southwest of Chicago.

On the radio some guy was singing a hieratic, overblown, operatic rendition of 'God Bless America'.

'Ah, now this always gets a shiver going down my spine,' exclaimed Keith. 'It makes you all — you know' — he punched the air self-consciously — 'it makes you think about your country. It makes you wanna put a flag up on top of your truck!'

It made me think of Oliver North getting all lachrymose and self-righteous, of Ronald Reagan giving some Republican convention a winsome wave. I said I couldn't imagine ever singing a song like that, or in that way, about Britain. 'To be *that* ... proud ... it'd be like saying, there's nothing wrong with the place, no way in which it could be made better.'

Keith was listening intently. 'You mean you're saying people should be more ... *humble*? That this song isn't humble?' He wasn't being mocking or sceptical. It turned out he agreed. Keith sometimes deputized for his wife at Sunday school – and the CB fraternity, of course, had fastened on this as a customarily exaggerated pretext for dubbing him The Deacon. He had no strident chauvinism in him, no fundamentalist bigotry, none of the stereotyped vices that an Englishman like me associated with such belligerent sloganizing. To me he seemed a forthright, innocently happy man, and 'God Bless America' was singing to him about his life. It wasn't asking, 'Are you happy with your government's foreign policy record?' or 'Do you think healthcare provision is just and equitable for the majority of American citizens?' Keith knew all about that. It was asking, 'Does your life work?' Compared with a British long-haul trucker in attritional combat with border posts and running-to-stand-still to make a living going Continental, here was a man whose trucking hadn't taken him from his family, for whom America started at Kenyon, Minnesota, and right now was taking him back there, and who could sing back a big yes.

The weather was improving, but as the sun came out it shone on the full devastation of the crops. 'See that corn-field?' Keith pointed. 'It was too wet to mow last fall, and it's too wet to mow now. The tractor'd just sink.'

'If it's only one field, why don't they just scythe it by hand?'

'Because this is America. No one does anything by hand.'

For the first time since we had set out the landscape was something to look at. Tobacco fields gave way to rolling woodland hills, then we detoured off the Interstate to avoid a big tailback, and rode the back road around the edge of Wisconsin's Bluff Region, past outcrops of rock and lush woodland. Back on the Interstate – it had become a perfect sunny day, pale puffy clouds full of glowing gold – an entire semi-truck had been stood up on its end and mounted in the ground as the entry sign for the Standard Truckstop.

At Grandma's Kitchen at New Lisbon, Wisconsin, a friendly family roadhouse, all the staff knew Keith, and spoke about him as though he were a prodigal son. One of the waitresses knelt down in front of our table and fixed me with a mock-apoplectic glare. 'When he was here last time, do – you – know – what – he – did? He was so greedy – he actually started *eating* the food *in* the buffet bar! I mean – we wondered if we should bring him a *chair* . . .'

The other waitress topped up our coffee. 'You know my daughter's just discovered marijuana?' she sang. 'I told her, just make sure you come back down to earth in time to start college.'

We were only seventy miles from Rochester, and now the road was climbing. The Mississippi River was swollen to the top of its dam as we crossed it into Minnesota, a chocolate-coloured sleekness that lapped around the leaves of the trees along its banks. All barge traffic on these upper reaches had been suspended, Keith said, because the currents were now too strong – and this had hit the local hauliers: usually there was a big trade in grain to be hauled to the barge terminals for sailing down river. The road followed the side of a plunging gorge that cut away westwards from the river, and took us up and up until we levelled out on a plateau of farmland. It was nearly six in the evening, Minnesota time, when the Jailhouse pulled into the Midwest depot in Rochester. Over the last few miles Keith tested me on all I'd learnt since Manchester.

'What do we call a car transporter?'

'Portable parking-lot.'

'Weigh-station?'

'The chicken coop. When you get your truck weighed you say, "I'm weighing my chickens."'

'Kansas City?'

'The Bright Lights.'

'Denver?'

'The Mile High.'

'How many seasons are there in the Midwest?'

'Only two. Winter and road construction.'

'And why don't the geese fly south in winter any more?'

'Because *J.B. Hunt says he can haul them cheaper.*'

Chapter Twelve

If you could choose where you hauled your loads, I'd asked Keith, where would it be?

'Oh, the north-west, without a doubt. Every time. There's always something new to see out there.'

That was where I was headed.

'Well, you'll *enjoy* it.'

Keith and I had shaken hands, and he'd gone back to Kenyon to spend the holiday, I'd stayed the night in Rochester, and now on Saturday morning I was having biscuits and gravy for breakfast in the truckstop on the city limits with Jack, the dispatcher, and Bill Means, the Mid-west driver I was going to ride with to the west coast. Oversize haulage like Keith did was one staple of Midwest's business; this run was another. Several times a week a Midwest truck, hauling a flatbed trailer like Bill's, collected chassis frame rails from the A.O. Smith steelworks in Milwaukee and drove them 2,100 miles to the Kenworth truck factory in Seattle. Jack had done nineteen years on the road for Midwest himself – he and Bill had worked together for five years delivering grain silos from De Kalb, Illinois, to farmers all over the USA and Canada. He showed me his million-mile buckle: he'd also had his 10-years' service free trip to Nashville (Midwest's proprietor was a keen country and western fan) and next year he was due for the 20 years' 'mystery tour' reward. Now, working in the Rochester office matching drivers to loads, he said he was 'finding out how big an asshole I was as a driver'.

Bill ran a 1984-vintage Kenworth: the classic tall-hood 900 model I'd only encountered before pulling Richard Walker's race trailer at Brands Hatch. It was, as Bill put it, 'kind of an . . . individualistic truck.' In the nine years since he'd bought it new he'd put 850,000 miles on it. Like Keith, he was an owner–driver, but he had his truck painted up in Midwest's dark blue livery. Apart from two years' national service in Vietnam, and three years out, working first in construction and then in the lumber industry, since the early sixties he'd been driving trucks. He reckoned that altogether it added up to about $2\frac{1}{2}$ million miles. In Vietnam he'd driven one of the munitions trucks ferrying ammunition from the supply ships at the coast up into the interior. 'It made you . . . cherish other people's lives,' he said. He was a small, slight man whose bright eyes had kind lines at their corners, but when we got on to the subject of the new President and his non-war record, Bill's voice could go hard and flat. 'If Clinton said he wanted us all to go and fight for our country again,' he said, 'I'd tell him, "I'll be there, but you're going in first in front of all of us."' For years Bill had hauled loads to every state, but for ten years now he'd been doing just this run: Milwaukee to Seattle, a 4,200-mile round trip, and he did it about thirty-three times every year, or about three times every month. It was what he wanted: he'd had enough of going all over the place; now, in middle age, he preferred the routine. 'The roads have got better,' he said. 'With the Interstates you can knock a day off the time the journey used to take. But what hasn't changed is the hours. These days I can put on seven hundred and fifty, eight hundred and fifty miles in a day, because these are better trucks, and easier to drive. It sounds a lot if you're not used to driving, or if you don't like driving, but on good roads for fifteen, sixteen hours it's kind of enjoyable. You just have to watch your Log Book, that's all.'

Our route lay north-west from Minneapolis-St Paul on Interstate 94 across Minnesota: we'd stay on 94 right through North Dakota, too, and then it would take us halfway into Montana. When we crossed the Mississippi it was up above the river-bank trees even here. 'We've had more rain this year than I can ever remember,' Bill said. 'I've never seen it that high.' The huge Rosemont oil refinery loomed behind Minneapolis, pipes, derricks and chimneys a tangle of Meccano above the trees at the outskirts.

'It used to be four days to get from Milwaukee to Seattle,' Bill said. 'If you loaded before noon on Tuesday it had to be there by the end of Friday. Any time after noon and you had another day. But now, over the last year or so, you've had this just-in-time system coming in. Sometimes we'll be given a load of frames Wednesday night, and it's got to be there Friday morning! We'll have to put two guys on it to get it there. Drives you bananas.'

What about Hillary? I inquired, since we'd raised the subject of the President.

'Just another lawyer.' As for their policies: 'You've got all this year of the woman, year of the dog, year of the cat, all that nonsense . . . If a kid puts his hand in the fire,' said Bill, searching for an analogy, 'you don't move the stove out of the house so he can't burn it.' He looked across and smiled: 'I guess guys like me tend to look at things a little simplistically . . .'

The timber industry – the economic foundation of the north-west – was another example of all that was wrong. In recent years, Bill said, it had contracted by two-thirds, not least as a result of pressure from environmentalists. Now Clinton had just signed an order further restricting logging, in order to protect the habitat of the spotted – Bill spat the word out – 'the *spudded* owl! Now, if you cut down some trees where the spotted owl's been nesting, it'll just go fly away and nest in a new one! But they're going to take away jobs from *six thousand* people.' Bill shook his head.

Heavy rain was falling; the heavy holiday traffic had backed up into a jam; we were reduced to a crawl. It was midday before we pulled into the Clearwater truckstop – in two and a half hours we'd only come fifty miles out of Minneapolis. Bill said he was hoping the other Midwest driver he usually ran frames to Seattle with, Earl Henry, would catch us up here. 'You'll find Earl's kind of a straight talker. He's right off the boat – that's what you'd say.'

Eventually, after we'd downed a couple of coffees in the truckers' section of the restaurant, and watched steaming, bedraggled families shuffle past in a long line towards the food counter, a burly, square-faced man in a sports shirt and shorts wandered over to us and sat down in distracted silence. 'An hour and a quarter to get out of Minneapolis,' he announced after a while to no one in particular. His face and arms were brown and weathered; his silver-grey hair was brushed forward in a spiky fringe. 'Everybody was drivin' like they worked for the government of Minnesota. No idea how to decide things for themselves.' Earl ordered a tuna melt, and Bill told him how I'd be riding with them all the way to Seattle.

Earl was unwrapping himself a toothpick, which he then clenched between his teeth like a pipe. He studied me for a moment, then drew himself up and said, 'Prepare yourself for six hundred miles of absolutely *nuthin'*!'

A guy with a shaggy grey moustache and an Alaska Highway baseball cap sat down at the next table and leant across to us. 'Couldn't believe it – Minnesota coop was closed this morning. I had my comic book all lined out for 'em . . .' When Bill introduced us and said I was over from England to write a book about trucks, the man leant on his elbows to take a pull of his cigarette. 'Well, you coulda had mine outta Minneapolis this morning.' He considered. 'Make sure you get to the Doll's House in daylight,' he told Bill and Earl, 'so he can take a look over and see what it's all about. You know, top of the pass just over into Idaho, and there's that little house right down in the bottom? I call it the Doll's House.' He inhaled again with narrowed eyes. 'I knew of a guy who went over once. The other truckers hear him come on the CB going, "Get the hell outta there, I've lost it!" Brakes had gone, went straight over the edge. So the other truckers stopped, thought they'd better go look for the body. Found him at the bottom, and the whole top of the cab had been ripped off to the bottom of the windshield. The guy was curled up around the shift lever' – he pulled his forearms up under his chin to suggest the foetal position – 'and he's shouting to himself, *"I'm gonna git outta this sonofabitch soon as she stops!"*

'Anyway, they took him to a restaurant down the road, and he was shaking so much the waitress had to give him a straw for his coffee. But he said afterwards, "When I came over the crest and went for my brakes, and I hadn't got any, I knew my only hope was to get right down on the floor."'

Now Bill told a story about a friend of his getting one back on another trucker generally acknowledged to have been a pain in the ass. This was in the days when the old cabovers, such as Bill's colleague drove, had gear levers you detached when you wanted to swing the cab off the chassis to get at the engine; the other guy, meanwhile, had one of the old-style 'headache-racks' – the board fixed at the front of a flatbed trailer to prevent a load shifting forward and crushing the driver's cab. In those days headache-racks were metal-barred affairs resembling a hospital bed-head. So Bill's friend and the pain-in-the-ass were both grinding up a hill you need all your momentum to get up with a full load – '. . . and this friend of mine pulls out to overtake. He detaches the shift, and as he comes alongside he leans out on the running-board and drags the shift along the bars of this guy's headache-rack. There's this *terrible* clatter, and the guy gets the fright of his life and pulls up thinking his engine's blowing up!'

'Course, that's what the old guys used to do, didn't they?' said the trucker in the baseball cap. 'Going up Highway 41, in those old 250-horsepower motors, they'd ride up hangin' out on the running-board. If it didn't make it, they were off.'

We left the guy in the baseball cap to the last leg of his run to Minneapolis – his base was Fargo, North Dakota, where we were heading – and not far out of Clearwater the rain stopped. Though the sun was nowhere to be seen the sky was bright blue, a clear, hard light on the rolling prairie of the Lakes region approaching Fergus Falls. The waving, rippling and dappling sheet of grass was punctuated with marshy hollows set about with trees. Here and there Bill pointed out for me a blue Harvester silo – these were the ones he and Jack had hauled all over the States.

They'd been an advanced new design, airtight and made of glass, enabling farmers to store hay or corn harvested wet without it rotting. But they'd been expensive to buy, hadn't sold enough, and now none were riding through America on the back of a truck.

A Kenworth classic passed us pulling a milk tanker trailer; on the back of the tank was painted UDDER EXPRESS.

'The best one I ever saw', said Bill, laughing already, '– you know those signs people put in the rear window of their car: BABY ON BOARD? Well, I passed this lumber truck once, and on the back it had, BOARDS ON, BABY!'

Lumber was almost always their return load on this route: door jambs, or maybe skirting boards, from Tacoma outside Seattle, to be hauled back into the Midwest for cities like Minneapolis, or Milwaukee, or Duluth.

The indicator on Earl's Kenworth was flashing in our wing mirror, so we turned off into a rest station. Earl got out of his cab carrying a cool box and walked over to a waste bin, his head turned to fix us with a gnomic regard. We went to watch him unloading distended and swollen cans of Diet Pepsi into the bin. He'd stocked up at Clearwater with a bunch of cans, he explained, dumped them in the cooler and switched it on. Thirty miles out of Clearwater they'd started to explode. 'I could hear them going off, *Psht! Psht!*' The cool box was switched to Heat. 'Reached in for a can of cold Pepsi and nearly burnt my hand.'

Bill and I stopped again at the Big Chief truckstop at Fergus Falls for a bite to eat – a poster on the wall inside advertised 'Transport for Christ'. Earl plumped himself down next to us, watched us filling our faces with BLTs, and demanded, 'Are we goin' to be doin' this all the way to Seattle?'

Past Fergus Falls the landscape flattened out to every horizon, a green prairie of wheat, barley and sugar beet as far distant as you could see. Riding with Keith I'd figured why truckers liked country music: now for the first time I felt it. Country wasn't a style or a sensibility or an aesthetic you adopted like a football team, any more than was the blues. It was music for this, for here: it was the music that belonged to you if here was where you found yourself. The tourists on vacation, on their way up to the Great Lakes, we'd lost a while back; now the road ahead, and the road coming towards us, were empty. Keith had told me how Midwest truckers hated going to the east coast – it was too busy, too full of traffic, and too many people were in too much of a hurry. Now Bill was making the same complaint. Out here, on the other hand, things could take their time. Out here, too, the music relaxed. Country had time to jog along, and when it wanted to sing you neurosis and crisis it had to contrive them by ingenious conceit. The arrow-straight flat road unrolled for mile after mile, after mile.

At Fargo, where we crossed into North Dakota, a big new highway interchange was under construction. A sign read, SIOUX FALLS 29A SOUTH. Caterpillar diggers nodded and reared to heap up embankments, nosed around in ditches. I thought of Keith's load: suddenly the landscape was giving a literal point to the 1,400-mile haul he and I had just shared. The tousled wasteland at Manchester, New Hampshire, where we'd started out; this dusty tangle of tyre tracks and modern Stonehenge of concrete flyover pillars that were remaking the face of the land; a mauve Peterbilt inching westwards across the map of the States was giving me an image to tie the two together: money leaving the east coast for the Midwest.

This was the only main road across North Dakota – straight across the middle, from three o'clock to nine o'clock – and I rode it with Earl. He had an almost-new Kenworth 900, though to look at it you'd have been exercised to identify any difference from Bill's or, indeed, from a model twenty years older. But Earl's had an extended hood. Under the bonnet were all kinds of fuel-control microprocessors, and Earl could set the cruise control option in the gearbox for 62 miles an hour on a highway like this, take his feet off the pedals, and slump down in his seat. Toothpick waggling in the side of his mouth, he could let the Kenworth drive him all the way across North Dakota.

His father had driven a petrol-engined Mack, and around 1959, 1960, when Earl had been about twelve, 'I went out on a trip with him. I thought that was *it*. I decided at that moment I wanted to drive a truck. Unfortunately,' Earl reflected, 'I never changed my mind since.' For fifteen years he'd driven a fleet truck between Iowa, Wisconsin and Minnesota, an International cabover that had been 'like driving across a ploughed field'. Then he'd decided to go on his own – 'and I've been in the zoo ever since.'

'What does that mean?'

'Thrashin' around.'

In some five months Earl had already put 72,000 miles on his new truck. Since he'd been doing this frame-rails run to Kenworth in Seattle for some years, he'd thought how appropriate it would be to have a new truck that had been made at the very plant whose chassis he helped to build several times a month. So he'd put his order in with the Minnesota KW dealer, and several months later proudly taken delivery of a new blue and white extended-hood 900. On the delivery docket he noticed against the chassis number the code letters SHQ.

'What does that mean?' he asked the dealer.

'Saint Helene, Quebec,' said the dealer.

Earl thought. 'That doesn't mean Seattle, does it?'

'No, Earl,' said the dealer, 'that doesn't mean Seattle.'

So Earl, to whom it had never occurred that his truck might be built anywhere other than Seattle, but who had never thought to check, was doing his Seattle run thirty-three times a year in his new Canadian-built truck.

An immensely long train of coal wagons was threading towards us along a single spindly line. There must have been 130 wagons – I lost count after a hundred had slid past. They were bringing coal from the biggest opencast mine in the world, said Earl – the Colstrip Mine in Montana, near Little Bighorn on the Indian reservation – all the way to a power station in Chicago. Since Valley City, fifty miles into North Dakota, the land had rolled up into grey-green foothills, then smoothed out again into fields flooded with big lakes, the odd duck pert on the water's surface. Near Jamestown there were buffalo in the fields. Ahead of us above the road towards Bismarck glowed a pearly evening sunshine, but black clouds were boiling to the north, and the radio was warning of a tornado alert. Before you set out from home, Bill had said, you always listened to the weather forecast for this part of the country. There were two routes from Wisconsin to Seattle: the alternative to ours was to head south along the bottom of Minnesota and then across South Dakota. If the forecast for around here was bad, you always headed south.

Three years ago Bill and Earl had come through here in

winter, with the temperature just below freezing. 'I'd been giving him shit all day about it,' said Earl. 'There's going to be an ice-storm, Bill, there's going to be an ice-storm . . .' It began to rain. The rain froze as soon as it hit the road. The two of them had just agreed over the CB that beyond the brow of the hill ahead they'd stop at the next rest-station and put chains on their wheels. Bill, who was leading, crested the brow, and saw the traffic on both carriageways backed up around an accident. He'd put his foot on the brakes, the truck had just slid onwards, and Earl had watched between his fingers as Bill had slid down the narrow gap between two lines of traffic and disaster.

We fuelled up at a gas station twenty miles short of Bismarck – the midway point across North Dakota, and the state capital – and a third Midwest truck caught us up: one of the younger drivers, Geoff, in one of the new-style Kenworths with the droop-nosed 'anteater' look – another last-minute consignment of frame rails.

And then, at nine in the evening, the weather turned wondrous.

The sun still gleamed high in the sky. The rain-slick road ahead – a shower must have swathed across the horizon, but we'd seen none – was a ribbon of silver. To the south the sky was striated with lilac; to the north it was palest blue. Swirls of coffee-coloured cloud barely cleared the tops of the wind-shrivelled trees.

'Lot o' wind in those clouds,' Earl said. 'It's like they're upside down? That's when they get mean. Could be rain, hail . . .'

But it didn't rain or hail. Instead, as we drove on, perfect white Himalayas of cloud piled up just above our heads. Whiffs of indigo, like sheep's wool caught on a fence, brushed against them. The sun seemed to irradiate them from underneath, as though the sun was in the land. Telegraph wires and electricity cables paralleled each other across the glowing emerald fields; the high sky was peach-haloed.

Through the window in an airliner's cabin you look down on the mountain ranges of white cloud from thousands and thousands of feet above. From that altitude their collision and motion is a slow, radiant battlefield. Now, as we tugged along this empty, horizon-distant ribbon of road, that weather-from-an-airplane was something you could almost reach out and touch. It was as though the heavens had sunk low like a stage curtain to brush the land, and at the same time as though you were seeing the very top of the sky – and if you could climb that wind-blasted tree you might poke your head out of the sky and look about in some blinding pure region too bright for earth.

Soon the light was fading. Along the railway track that paralleled the Interstate across North Dakota a line of trucks was travelling by train. It was my first sight of the newest mutation of the American trucking business. Under the Reagan administration the haulage industry had been deregulated, favouring the growth of low-cost, cheap-rate mega-fleets like the Schneider's and J.B. Hunt's – though the latter, in fact, was an example of the Arkansas business boom of the eighties under the governorship of future President Bill Clinton as well. Several million new trucks had come on to the highways, with the traditionally highly unionized trunking fleets taking the brunt of the competition. It was all in economy of scale: the huge Hunt and Schneider fleets were each running up over a million miles a day: even if they were only making a single cent a mile profit, said Earl, that was a lot of money.

Now the same principle was behind the trailer-train: trucks were hitching a ride on the railroad. J.B. Hunt had bought 16,000 wagons – flatbed cars that could each transport two semi-trailers – and now your load could go by road haulage, but on rails, from Seattle to Chicago in four or five days, for fifty cents a mile, or half the price of that trailer being hauled there behind a Kenworth rig.

'Why is J.B. Hunt getting more deliveries on time?' asked Earl – it was the latest joke of the road. 'Because he's puttin' them on trains.'

The setting sun was molten in the sky. Sweet Briar Lake to the north, liquid gold, then opalescent, glowed with the last rays. HOME ON THE RANGE, read a roadsign: a mile away. We ran past the oil town of Dickinson – the small nodding pump-jacks dotted across the prairie were now invisible, but here was a bigger rig lit up out of the night, and then a low huddle of light that was the town. Earl twiddled with his radio; his was an extra-powerful set he'd specified for his new Kenworth that enabled him to pick up plays on the BBC World Service, Russian stations, and all kinds of distant, spacy jabber. Snatches of life from who knew where came at us, undecipherable. Dickinson was gone behind us, the road was empty but for the three Midwest trucks in convoy, visible only by their red taillights and the silhouettes of their headache-racks against the indigo sky. We rode on like this until midnight, and by then we had reached Beach on the border with Montana, and come six hundred and eighty miles since Rochester.

Chapter Thirteen

'Montana,' said Earl, 'is seven hundred miles wide. It's a state you think you're never going to get through.' Today was the 4th of July, Independence Day. We were going to spend it driving across Montana. When we'd arrived at Beach for the night Earl had insisted I take his bed in the sleeper: it wasn't an offer, it was a command. 'This is my home,' he'd growled, 'and in my home *I'm* the boss.' He'd taken a couple of cushions, put his head down on his arms and, after a 15-hour working day, slept at the wheel. Now we were up again at six-thirty, a vast piled-high all-you-can-eat breakfast in the Flying J truckstop restaurant, and then away. The Flying J is the fastest growing truckstop chain. Owned by the Mormon Church, no less, they are springing up all over America, a wall map in the entrance of each flashing with little lights to mark new outposts, and colonizing the territory of the truckers' traditional choke-and-pukes with their sanitized, corporate homogeneity. But the breakfasts are colossal, the teapots pour the tea into the cup rather than all over the table, and the bogs aren't paddyfields. If such are the benefits of modern organized religion, make me its tele-evangelist. This one at Beach straddled the North Dakota–Montana border: from here we were going to drive all day and at the end of it still be in Montana. With Tony in Europe I had crossed Poland in less than a day, knocked off both Holland and Belgium before lunch.

Bill and Earl had swapped trucks for the morning. Bill hadn't had a chance to try out Earl's new KW before; they both wanted, I could see, to give themselves the pretext for a long CB conversation about trucks. Keith had been different. Keith was the young family man, who talked as we rode about his sons in school, their prowess at baseball, who wondered whether he should even be changing his career to be able to offer them the best support as they grew up – and who drove a Peterbilt simply because that was the particular make available at the local dealer's when he'd needed to buy. Keith knew about extended hoods, but he also knew about Stevie Ray Vaughan and George Thorogood, and he'd wanted me to tell him all about the situation in Northern Ireland, and discuss the Thatcher years, and explain the workings of the National Health Service.

Earl and Bill, by contrast, though fifteen to twenty years older, were both single – Earl unmarried, Bill divorced; they were both confirmed Kenworth disciples, and clicked their CBs on and off, on and off along the way, with intricate questions for each other about their own trucks or about new mechanical modifications becoming available on the newest KWs. Now that Bill had paid off his trailer as well as his unit he was thinking of trading in his 1984 900 next year for a new one. How was Earl's fuel-injection system working? he wanted to know: what miles-per-gallon figures was he getting? Earl wanted to know why the driver's seat in Bill's 1984 KW was more comfortable than in his, when his state-of-the-art effort had just cost him eleven hundred dollars but was 'like sittin' in a peach tree'. They talked about the mounting of fuel tanks, about windscreen shades, about wing-mirror brackets, about bug shields for the radiator grille. Earl wanted to know how much easier Bill found driving his new truck with the benefit of cruise control; Bill wanted to tell Earl how much quieter and smoother it was inside the cab, too. Earl confided to me how unimpressed he was, after all he'd been promised with this new Caterpillar engine and its advanced electronics, with the fuel consumption he was getting. Bill confided to me how hard Earl drove his trucks: flat out all the way. Earl changed down through the gears on his new KW with a teeth-jarring *graunch*, and said they'd be better once they'd been ground down a bit. They both speculated on what would be unveiled in a few weeks' time at Anaheim, Los Angeles, when the American truck industry held its big annual show. Do you think Kenworth will do a one-piece sleeper cab unit? Will they be able to get rid of the step between cab and sleeping space? What do you think of these Aerodyne sleepers with the skylight in the roof? Should Bill go for one of the new larger sleeper cabs – so long that the bed was 83 inches wide and went lengthways, and still left enough space for a desk opposite where you could do your paperwork? I got the impression that they passed the time like this asking each other these same questions on every trip – it was like Englishmen discussing great cricket matches and swapping *Wisden* statistics.

Why always a KW? I tried to get the two of them to do sales job for Kenworth on me. But neither could give me chapter and verse: they were far too close to their trucks. When you'd settled into driving and driving the same route for all those years, like Bill and Earl did, you'd gone beyond trying to prove anything. Neither was there any point, out here in the empty wide open, in cultishness.

Who was looking? KWs just went on and on and on for a million miles without flagging. All the fat-chewing by CB about this accessory and that design twist: it wasn't a flirting with change and a new image – it was a confirmation that you were sticking with what you knew, going for the same, only more so.

Up around here, in any case, it seemed that Kenworths were what you drove. When I discovered that Peterbilts were made down South, in Nashville, the 'Guitar Town', it figured. Peterbilts – not just Keith's but the others I'd seen along the way – were always that little bit more chromed up, just a little shinier, and usually painted up a lot brighter. I never saw a mauve Kenworth. About the Peterbilt there was a touch of the antique automobile, a louche luxuriance. A Kenworth was pure truck. Petes were made to have the sun glinting off the chrome, the azure-blue sky reflected in the hood, and the desert heat shimmering all around. Kenworths were for buffeting across a wind-raked North Dakota prairie under an iron sky. Peterbilts appealed to dreamy romantics like me who got their ideas about trucking from Steve Earle records. Kenworths, just like Earl and Bill, got on with the job and drove till it was done, and then drove some more: who ever thought to indulge in any whimsy shit? I'd have had a Pete, but what did I know?

Neither were Earl and Bill full of trucking stories – no tales of near disaster or of masochistically prodigious hauls or the strangeness of folks way out wherever. All that was many miles back in the past. Instead, Earl told me a joke about Hillary and Billary Clinton: he hadn't a lot more time than Bill for the prospect of new taxes on fuel and, in his blanket assumption, new taxes on most everything else, too. 'Hillary and Billary are takin' a ride around Little

Rock in the car, and Billary pulls in at a gas station to fill up. When he gets back in Hillary says to him, "You know, Billary, that pump jockey who just served you, I used to go out with him at school." "Well, there you go," says Billary. "Just think, if you'd have married him you'd have ended up with a pump jockey instead of the President of the United States." "Uh-uh, Billary," says Hillary. "If I'd married him, you'd have ended up as the pump jockey and *he*'d be President of the United States . . ."'

I asked Earl if he had any ambition to, say, drive a truck abroad. He'd recently spent a vacation with his girlfriend in Vermont which, I was slightly surprised to hear, he'd thought 'real pretty'. But the answer was still 'Nope. I get all the trouble I need goin' to Seattle without goin' anywhere to look for more.' For Bill and Earl over-the-road trucking was not the high of incessant new challenges; nor was it – as Keith had said to me – the simple satisfaction that 'my office window is different every morning'. Instead, Earl and Bill had found a singular compromise: a regular run that had the linear simplicity of a bus route, there and back, the guarantee of uninterrupted, continual demand for the goods they were hauling – but also a mileage sufficiently huge, and an elemental contingency, to prevent routine from ever becoming a drudgery.

Bill tried to put it into words for me. 'You see, when I'm leaving home . . . it's not like I'm leaving home. I'm just heading back by kind of a long way round . . .' These days, he said, he always looked forward to spending time at home. He was divorced from his wife, but he liked visiting his granddaughter when he got a few days back in Minnesota, and he took a big pride in doing his garden. Until recently he'd taken his German shepherd Chrissie with him in the truck on trips away, but now that age and rheumatic hips had made her less agile for jumping in and out, she stayed at home, something else to get back for.

Eastern Montana was rolling, humpy moorland – the foot-hills weathered and eroded to resemble spoil heaps. This was moose and elk country, though they'd most likely be further north than here. 'Out here you can't even find a baseball game to watch,' said Earl. 'In Montana *all* they're interested in is country and western music.' But Earl was also a keen golfer, and at least there were golf courses out here. There was a set of clubs stowed under the bunk in his Kenworth in case the chance arose, while waiting for a load, to play the course in a strange town. He'd played a lot down in Florida, and he'd played these pretty courses along the route in Montana, and there was a golf course awaiting in Seattle. At last, in the midst of a stretch of desolate moorland, a McDonald's sign loomed up to an-nounce our approach to the town of Glendive. I counted more oil wells; to the south lay a big open-cast mine. 'Lotta money round here,' said Earl: beyond those Monument Valley-like buttes and mesas I could see through my side window were reserves of gold, silver, phosphates.

The Interstate followed the Yellowstone River out of Glendive and westwards. Near Miles City we pulled up on to the top of an empty plateau, all evidence of man's mining of the elements behind us for the moment, and I watched a couple of turkey vultures circle above the turbid river. For the first time since Tony and I had taken our leave of Phil Horton outside Berlin I understood truly what he'd meant about a trucker having to be like a farmer. When Keith had said the same thing in reverse – that farmers made the best truckers – I'd taken it as his tip for the easiest way to learn to drive one at a young age.

Now I saw how over-the-road trucking wasn't simply another kind of outdoor, wide-open-space work. It was next to the land. Through your windscreen you trained your own time-lapse camera on the seasons. You watched the crops around you grow, learned how the landscape worked, saw human habitation scratch the surface, and build, and sometimes blow away again – and saw it all with 20/20 vision. You lived by the weather, you worked with the elements. This 70-foot Kenworth was clawing its way across the whole of Montana in the same scale as a tractor slowly puttering back and forth across a field.

We passed the Spotted Ass Ranch – donkeys grazed amongst the scrub, raised to mingle with flocks of sheep and cows to keep away predators like wolves and foxes. Ahead lay the snow-capped summit of Granite Peak, the 12,799-foot highest point in Montana. To the south-west were the deep green hills marking the rim of the Yellowstone National Park. Then we were among industrial sprawl again, winding through the 9-mile-long sweep of Billings. A Conoco oil refinery at one end of the city, a gas refinery at the other, Montana's biggest rail terminal in the connected suburb of Laurel, marshalling those mighty coal trains and snaking ribbons of boxcars, lumber wagons, car carriers and scrap-iron trucks that had snorted and rumbled past us. Trailer parks joined the industrial fringe to the tussocky grassland beyond. It was oil wealth that had expanded Billings – Earl said he'd watched the place grow over the years as he'd come through. In the downtown district three skyscrapers towered above the low clutter of the rest of Billings.

Why would the Sheraton Hotel want a skyscraper here when there's so much land around?

'Good question,' said Earl. The toothpick waggled. 'Give 'em something to talk about when it falls down in an earthquake.' The road climbed out of Billings, declined over the next hill, rose and fell again, clear sunshine driving out the torrential rain shower that had smashed over us at Laurel.

At the Park City truckstop beyond Billings I rejoined Bill. 'We come through here in the fall and you watch the snow gradually coming further down the peaks,' he said – now we were climbing out of a wide sunny valley up towards the mountain pass at Livingston where the Yellowstone River would leave us to run south into the National Park. 'Until we hit the winter and the snow's all over. Then you come through in the spring and you see the snow gradually going back up the mountains. You're very lucky, doing this route. You get to see . . . Mother Nature at her best.'

I asked Bill if he'd noticed big changes in the ten years he'd been coming this way. He shook his head. 'No . . . That's what's kinda nice about it out here. Stuff don't keep closin' in and closin' in.' To the south: the snow capped range he called the Beartooth Mountains. Ahead – the peaks illuminated by the sun shining through the low white cloud – more snowy mountains, Crazy Peak and Big Timber. At Livingston the Yellowstone River ducked under the Interstate one last time and disappeared down a canyon. A hailstorm splintered and smoked on the windscreen. Out here the trees were beginning to march down the slopes, until the steep walls of the Bozeman Pass were forested all the way down with evergreens and we gained the 5,000-foot summit to look down on to the town of Bozeman through a mist of heavy rain, while behind us lay the more distant snowy mountains of the Gallatin range.

Bozeman, then Belgrade, then out on to another vast plain, and back into sunlight, and blue sky broken with blobs of white cloud. The weather came in sudden peaks and towers of storm; the landscape every so often churned into forbidding masses; in between land and sky settled into wide empty troughs. On the Cardwell Pass outside Bozeman we had passed Bobby, another of Midwest's drivers. There was a brief boom of exclamation from the CB as Bobby's greeting crackled across the carriageway, and then she was gone again, on her way back towards the Midwest with a Caterpillar grader from Spokane.

Bill was talking about rules and regulations. The worst development recently had been state plans for random drug tests – any traffic cop would then be able to pull over a trucker and ask for a sample, and if you were unlucky it could happen every half a mile down the road. Bill didn't mind sending in a specimen to the state police once in a while to show he was clean, but this new proposal was a further insult to professional integrity, and the kind of interference in people's lives that only got in the way of doing your job. 'You see, trucks *move* this country,' he insisted. 'There ain't nothing – people turning on a faucet, the water comes through tubing hauled on a truck – that doesn't go this way. It's kind of a unique profession. There ain't many other classes of people – nurses, maybe – who, if they all took three days off, the country just wouldn't work. Lawyers . . . well, if they took three days off we'd all be better off. Government . . . if they all took a *month* off we'd be better off. Here, you're moving people's *needs*. We're bringing lumber back to Minnesota, which they haven't got . . . There's some kind of pride, contentment, I don't know. And it's the kind of job – anyone can jump in a truck and drive it – but to do the job, and bring up a family, and – well, you can't be any kind of dumbhead.' He was not going get out at a windy roadside and piss in a bottle for anyone.

At five that afternoon we came up over the Pipestone Pass and crossed the Continental Divide: so far, all the way from New Hampshire with Keith and on to here, the land and the rivers had drained the other way into the Atlantic Ocean. From now on we were following the water to the Pacific. A disused railway clung to the mountainside precipitously high above us – it had run up to one of the old mineworkings, so only wagons would have had the chance to trundle along it, but it reminded me now that there were other ways to travel, and as I traced the old line's passage right round the side of this valley, in places perhaps a hundred and fifty feet up, on a ledge scarcely wider than the buckled track, I thought, that's the way to see this landscape, not through the tiny shallow windscreen of a truck down here. The highway was descending steeply from the pass, and Butte lay before us in the plain. Until a few years ago the silver mine here was closed down following a union dispute, and Butte virtually a ghost town. Now, with the mine reopened, it was one of the richest towns, on per capita earnings, in the country. The entrepreneur who'd reopened the mine – who also owned the lion's share of the Burlington North Railroad we'd been running alongside – had recently sold a half-share in it for $50 million. Beside the town, half the mountainside had been clawed away – this was for the town's copper mine. Atop the mountain above us a white statue of Our Lady of the Rock – an image of the Virgin Mary paid for by the local community, and reflecting its considerable Irish Catholic ancestry – looked down over the dusky red and grey buildings. We rolled on past the sprawling railway

freight terminal on its western fringe, and soon the excava-
tions and plunderings of mining, the grassed-over spoil
heaps, the fading furrowed patterns of old marshalling
yards, had given way to close, rich forestry. By Beavertail
Hill we dropped down through a tremendous wooded
canyon.

'Gets so hot and dry round here in the summer,' said
Bill, 'you get heat lightning from the clouds, and a big fire
problem with the forests. I've seen it through this canyon
– like, spears of light, fingers coming down from the sky
ahead of you. Sometimes it gets so dry they even have to
stop logging – an iron chain dragged across a log can start
it off.'

Heat lightning, said Earl, when I next rejoined him, was
'kind of different. It's kind of soft, like a reflection off of
other things . . .'

It was seven before we reached Missoula, where the
industry was all forestry. A Peterbilt of the Montana
Cartage Company heaved along ahead of us piled high
with sawdust bound for the partition-board factory.
I looked down on the Smokejumper Centre where they
trained aerial firemen who parachuted in to tackle remote
forest fires. Next to a big sawmill was the big brown
teepee-construction of a kiln-oven for drying wood, and
next to that the towering heaps of sawdust at another mill.
We rode on along the elevated Interstate until all this was
behind us before we stopped for the night at the truckstop
on the far outskirts.

That night I sat in my motel room and read in my *Real
Guide to the USA* of the Irish cafés of Butte and its mining
museum and grim union traditions, of 'pretty, genteel
Bozeman', of Missoula's liberal, easygoing university quarter, with pangs of ruefulness, for we'd rolled on through

all of them and left them all behind. At the motel, indeed, you were completely stranded by the Interstate – no sidewalks and a hellishly busy highway if you wanted to walk even beyond the parking lot. Montana would have to wait till another time for a proper look. This was travel by truck, where you saw things only out of the corner of your eye. No point asking Bill or Earl about any of these towns, either – in all their years on the route they'd never explored any of them.

'When I used to bring Chrissie with me on trips,' Bill said, 'I'd stop by the side of the road and take her for a walk down by the river and stand and listen to the sounds . . . Sometimes you think it'd be nice to drive up some of the little side roads you see – not in a truck – and explore what's up there, but . . .' His thoughts had trailed off: neither he nor Earl rode this route in order to spend time in places where things kept closin' in, which meant even places like Butte and Bozeman. To them, it seemed to me, an Interstate which sailed above, through and beyond all these places on a big concrete viaduct, and kept you going until you were well past and out into the country again, was exactly the way to travel.

'Earl and I were in a motel room in Seattle a while back,' Bill said. We were on our way the next morning, on the last leg from Montana to the coast. 'There were no loads out, and when you're waiting around day after day you start getting a bit antsy. Earl was standing looking over the second floor balcony, and he said to me, "If I thought it would help, I'd jump off." I said, "Well, Earl, if you did and it didn't help we'd come down and pick y'up and take you up to the next floor . . ."'

Just a few miles down the road from the truckstop the

valley had already closed in with high walls of conifers –
'from here on it'll be really pretty,' said Bill, genuinely
enthusiastic. The mountain face ahead was spiked with
dead trunks: 'That was cleared last year by summer lightning.' Drifts of white cloud lay between the mountain
peaks, tugged down the valley low over the road like
smoke swirling from a fire. As the road climbed, the drifts
became more and more dense until we were in a heavy
mist. Bill pointed at the stipple of evergreen forest, green
firs and brown larch, behind the mist. 'Those are the kind
of trees where the spotted owl lives.' After a pause he said,
'That's the stuff that keeps roofs over people's heads.'
From St Regis, fifteen miles short of the border with
Idaho, the road climbed again and swung north; the Clark
Fork river, which had created this valley we were following, criss-crossed underneath the Interstate, and soon the
valley had narrowed to a tall defile. A final slow haul
brought us to the Idaho state line, Lookout Pass: the Fargo
trucker's Doll's House. We pulled into the lay-by for a
look, behind two tourists unpacking their camera from the
trunk of their car.

It turned out that this retired couple were from Minnesota, too, over here from St Paul for a couple of weeks'
touring the northwest after thirty years' absence. The last
time they'd come, said the softly spoken man, they'd
brought his mother. Back then the road had been so much
narrower and scarier, he said, that when they'd stopped
here and opened the door for her she'd crawled out on her
hands and knees.

His wife had a genial forthrightness. 'And where are you
guys from?' she demanded.

'Oh, we live out here,' said Bill. 'These are our mobile
homes.'

'They sent us out here the first time with these chassis frames,' said Earl, 'and told us to find Seattle.' The toothpick twirled and twitched. Occasionally he extracted it like a pipe for punctuation and emphasis. 'And we found Seattle, and the Kenworth factory managed to make 'em into trucks, and they drove the trucks back to the Midwest, and so they figured they'd give us another load of frames and see if we could get them to Kenworth's so they could make them into trucks too.'

'Uh-huh,' said the woman. 'Go anywhere for a dollar.'

'There's no bucks involved, ma'am,' said Earl.

'You do it *just* for the love of your job!' The woman's eyes had narrowed.

Bill and I left her and Earl to their deadpan joust and walked over to the edge of the cliff with her husband to take a look at the view below. The little Doll's House was way down, a matchbox amongst the tall carpet of trees. Puffs of cloud floated far beneath us: it looked as though scattered camp fires were smouldering down there. In front of us was a curving green wall of forested mountainside.

'You know, I can stand here any day and see anything,' said Bill. His voice, and Earl's fifty yards away, were the only sounds; the odd bird wafted up off the trees below like a piece of black ash. 'But I could stand at the top of that Sears Tower in Chicago and not see a damned thing.'

We rejoined Earl and the woman. She and her husband were going to Seattle like us. 'You should take a trip over to Mount Washington on that new floating bridge,' said Earl. 'The contractor wanted to build it one way, the civil engineer wanted to build it another. The contractor built it the civil engineer's way and it sank . . . I hear they just got it up again . . .'

'We're going to try again at going up the Space Needle,' the woman said. 'Last time we waited *six hours* in line and still didn't get up.'

'I'd be sure to take your own extension cord, ma'am,' offered Earl. The toothpick was beating irregular time like a miniature conductor's baton. 'I hear that elevator cord's wearin' out and it shorts out once in a while, and you get stuck halfway up . . .'

The woman turned to me. 'He's giving you this kinda stuff for your book?'

'I write down everything he tells me,' I confirmed with solemnity.

'Uh-huh. And don't print the half of it.'

We all shook hands, and it was time for us to move on. When the couple had walked back to the cliff edge for some last pictures I said to Earl, 'Did you give the lady some good tourist advice while we were looking at the view?'

Earl gave a sage nod. 'She knows I know what I'm talking about. She knows I got all my ducks in a row. May be missin' a few feathers, but they're *aaaaaaaall* in a row.'

We had only sixty miles to ride in Idaho – across its northern tip. The silver mining town of Wallace, with its new bone-white concrete flyover and dual carriageway, slicing straight through the middle of the town, offered an ugly monument to the ubiquity of the Interstate system. Until earlier in the year, said Bill, this had been 'the last stoplight on the Interstates' – but now Wallace had made way for the non-stop no-hold-up needs of America's road-based economy, and we rolled on through. Kellogg was another mining town, but quiet and empty, with the mine shut down for the last three years. Huge heaps of black tailings from the silver workings lined the highway; woodyards and lumber mills marked the remaining precarious mainstay of the economy. Outside the town Bill pointed out a tree-covered crag to the south. 'Over there there used to be an eagle nesting, and for six or seven years we used to come by and watch her rearing her young. But last year she moved away, over the other side of the valley. There's an osprey there now.'

The new section of Interstate, cutting walls raw and clean, the tarmac a satiny black, climbed up above Coeur d'Alene Lake and hovered across the water on two high bridges. At the summit of the climb, before the descent into the exclusive community of Coeur d'Alene, a road sign beseeched,

TRUCKERS, PLEASE, NO JAKE BRAKE FOR 3 MILES

The Jake Brake, manufactured by the Jacob company, was the engine brake you used to retard your speed descending a steep incline with a heavy load: it held back the revolutions of the engine with a thick, dogged roar. Coeur d'Alene resembled an expensive Swiss lakeside resort: its residents had not moved out here, the sign reminded you, to listen to trucks bellowing at each other up on the mountain like rutting stags.

We crossed into Washington State at Post Falls, a big grass-seed-growing town; at the Jacksons Seeds processing plant hundreds of semi-trailers were parked, waiting to take its grass seed out across the US. Bill switched on the radio: there was someone he wanted me to listen to. It was time for Rush Limbaugh.

Rush Limbaugh is, I later discovered, America's most popular media pundit. His talkback radio show, *America*

Held Hostage, claims five million listeners at any one time. His book of homespun wisdom was in the bestseller lists; so was the double cassette of its author reading it. Rush was warming up for the phone-in with some topical commentary.

'So tell me – where was the anti-war movement when the US Marines went into Somalia?' He left a pleased-with-itself silence so that dazed applause could burst out across the country.

Clinton, noted Rush, was telling us things are looking up for the economy because interest rates are low: 'When has your government ever told you that your quality of life is going to improve because you can now afford debt more easily?'

The President in his speech the previous night had pledged that *75 per cent of the new taxes would be paid by 6 per cent of the population* (in other words, the richest 6 per cent): 'There you are,' declaimed Rush. 'He said it. Is that fair? What have they done to be punished? That 75 per cent – it means you and me!'

Today, however, Rush was going to be aiming his scimitars of wisdom at the question of the American Dream. *Is* there still such a thing? What does it stand for *today*? '*Is – the – American – Dream – dead?*'

'This may sound clichéd, Rush,' gulped Guy, twenty-two, from Brooklyn, 'but I think . . . it is being given the *unbridled* opportunity to be the best you can possibly be . . .'

Rush took the point as an opening to inveigh against 'multi-culturalism', because that promoted equality, and was therefore at odds with people having unbridled opportunities. Did Guy, twenty-two, who was training to be a lawyer, want to earn a lot of money? 'I don't have a problem with people doing things for money,' added Rush. 'Everybody does things for money, and don't say Mother Teresa' – the voice hardened to a snarl – 'because she needs money too.'

At last Wendy, eighteen, from California, called to suggest, with quiet, polite admonition, that the reason no one was ringing Rush to say the American Dream was dead was because all Rush's listeners were likely to be educated and successful. Now came the best bit of all.

'Well, I'm, er, very flattered you should say that, Wendy –. because I hadn't thought of that, and I think that probably is the case . . .'

Well, unfortunately Rush didn't have a CB link in his studio. Imprisoned in our small rolling capsule, I was so enthralled and astonished by this swollen, smirking, stupid demagogue, and that this was going out (his commercial broke in) to some twenty million people every week, that all of a sudden we were already past Spokane. A few years ago I'd written a short story about Spokane – about someone who tells his friends he's just been to Spokane, and that's where things started going confusing and wrong. But no one knows what exactly happened, no one is quite sure if the guy has ever even been to Spokane. They don't know anything about Spokane: they've never been there. *I'd* never been there. *I* knew nothing about Spokane. All the way from Rochester I'd been looking forward to even a moving picture of Spokane. And there it was, already behind me in the wing mirror! I still know nothing of Spokane.

Now, as I recall Rush Limbaugh talking to America, and us in the Kenworth hauling our chassis frames across the state of Washington, I recall that an English Labour MP once described a knee-jerk right-wing populist on the

Conservative benches as 'living proof that a pig's bladder on a stick can be elected to Parliament'.

For the last miles to Seattle I rejoined Earl. We were going to stay over tonight at the truckstop on the western edge of the city, so we could go in first thing Monday morning to the Kenworth plant before the rush hour.

'Lotta ro-ollin' land out over here,' said Earl. Fields of wheat waved around us; dust swirled up off the fields; here and there a tiny farm in a little grove of trees dotted the empty prairie. Earl pointed northwards: once in a while he and Bill would be sent up there, to one of the small towns like Omak and Republic, to load lumber for the road home. Then he was reaching down under his seat, and brought up a gadget akin to a giant pair of nutcrackers. 'Wanna do some exercises?' This was how a sedentary trucker toned up at the wheel. With all my energy, squeezing hard, I could close this spring-loaded grip once or twice. The idea, Earl showed me, was to maintain your circulation, and build up your hand and forearm muscles, by flexing away, *scrunch scrunch scrunch*, for a hundred at a time. The nutcrackers were returned for me to start working on, and Earl showed me the other apparatus of his in-cab gym. Up, down, up, down, went the dumb-bell through 90 degrees while he steered with his other hand. Multiply by half the width of America, and back again: I could see Earl stayed quite fit sitting still.

Much of the hay grown in these vast fields was shipped out through the port of Seattle to countries like Japan for cattle feed. The big hay barns alongside the road were piled with bales in shades of gold through pea-green, which forklifts were unstacking and inserting into a long line of container semi-trailers. Soon the truck would be taking them off to the coast. Then six red combines in procession lumbered up the approach road beside us on their way to the pea fields: when they came back with their harvest, trucks would be on hand to haul them – as Keith had done in his early days – to canning plants down the road at Moses Lake, or at Pasco in the south of the state.

The final hundred miles of the journey were some of the most spectacularly elevated. We crossed the Columbia River after a slow, endlessly curling descent from the prairie, the sparkling pewter water opening out and blazing with sunlight as the road came down level, and then it was a 10-mile slow haul back up the other side to Ellensburg, and a rest-station at the top to pull in at and rest hot engines. Then up and over Elk Heights, a 2,800-foot summit, and down Indian John Hill the other side – suddenly the wheat prairie had shrunk as though sucked into a funnel, and we were amongst thick pine forest again. 'I was through here once in winter,' Earl said. 'There'd been some bad snow, I was coming down slowly with chains on, and there was this car in front gone over in the ditch, and a highway patrolman stopped by it. And I could see this truck coming down behind me real fast. So I hollered to him over the radio to slow down! And he came round the bend, and saw the car, and stood on his brakes, and he went right round in a circle three times, all the way down. I reckon he had a little fear in him afterwards . . .'

I said, 'I can't believe what that guy from Fargo was telling us – that someone could have gone over the edge back there at the Doll's House and survived.'

'Yep. Ninety-five per cent of the time if you stay inside the truck it'll save you. If you jump out it'll kill you by rollin' on you.'

The last pass to go over was the biggest of them all: Snoqualmie Pass. It was a vast valley – scars down the mountainside through the pine trees showed the winter runs for the ski resort of Snoqualmie. But here the Interstate, a new construction, doubling the width of the road, had ruined the valley. Two lanes hugged one wall of the pass, two hugged the other, and draped themselves all the way down its sides in buzzing, droning rivers of concrete. There was nowhere even to stop and have a look around you: nowhere at all simply to walk up the valley to perceive its scale from a humble pedestrian perspective. Snoqualmie had become solely a conduit for traffic like us – and the traffic had more important things to do than admire what remained of a phenomenal natural monument. I had to squint at it through the low, narrow TV screen of the Kenworth's windscreen.

Pacific Time: 3.51 – like Tony in Russia, Earl and Bill both stayed on home time to keep their Log Books correct, and I'd already lost track of what time it must be back in Minnesota, except that wherever we were away from it always appeared to involve getting up at the crack of dawn – and we were at the Seattle East truck stop. At the end of the holiday the place was packed: the only space for us across the road in the overspill parking area. Here was a reassuring British gravel pit to jounce across. Bill and Earl were not impressed, either by the potholes and the puddles, or by some of the scruffy old wagons their Kenworths were having to share them with.

'There are a number of terminologies for places like this,' Earl observed.

'A rat-trap,' pronounced Bill.

'A sophisticated-idiot-park,' declared Earl. 'You'll find a lot of rocket scientists around places like this,' he added. 'And none of the rockets'll fly.'

'What's a rocket scientist?'

Earl held his hand at knee-level. 'A guy about this big.'

'Who doesn't know how he got here,' added Bill.

I could not imagine Bill and Earl in the farmyard at Minsk.

I left them to have a crack at fixing Earl's eleven-hundred-dollar seat to cure it of the ergonomics of a peach tree – I could see they'd been itching to get down to some proper tinkering and boffinry – and checked out the truck-stop shop across the road. There I bought myself a Road Kill Café T-shirt – I found an improved variety featuring a cartoon of a flattened cat with a strip of tyre treads rolled across him – and also, a bonus, a set of Road Kill Bingo, 'An Educational Travel Game Providing Smiles For The Highway Miles'. You covered a square for every roadkill you spotted along the highway: there were squares reserved for squirrels, birds, tyres, shoes, cats, raccoons and rabbits, and special extra squares you could cover on the sight of an URK, or Unidentified Road Kill, when the remains were too mangled for identification. It came not with counters to cover each little drawing of a road kill, but small 'white square sheets (out of respect for the deceased)'. I forgot to check in the bookrack to see if they had the collected works of Heidegger.

Chapter Fourteen

That night I read about Guilt. *Wheels Alive* – I'd picked up a copy in the Seattle diner – is the free-sheet newspaper of the Association of Christian Truckers, founded by Chaplain Jim, who hauls his own mobile chapel, a converted semi-trailer christened 'Spirit of the Road', around the truckstops of America. For a donation of thirty dollars, a back-page ad announced, you could even receive *Wheels Alive* mudflaps for your truck that read JESUS CARRIES MY LOAD.

On its inside pages *Wheels Alive* had reprinted a profile the *Chicago Tribune* had done on founder Jim Keys in which he recounted how he'd nearly lost his truck when it had started to fishtail on an icy road in the Canadian Rockies. 'I just cried "Jesus!" And that trailer literally came back.' Then in 1968, testified his wife, 'The Lord told Jim to build a chapel in an 18-wheeler.' But though *Wheels Alive* proclaimed itself 'blessed' to pick up on this feature, it was less a panegyric than a wry demystification. There was obviously a fair amount of driving uphill for Chaplain Jim in his mission to evangelize ornery truckers. 'I've had a lot of smart-mouthed guys say to me, "Hah! If I go to hell, I'll be with a lot of buddies . . .!"'

But this issue ('Route 17, Trip 4') was still trying. OVERLOADED WITH GUILT, blazoned its front-cover headline: WEIGH-STATION AHEAD. The sermon itself was standard fundamentalist fare of homophobia, anti-abortion and morbid confession of sin, but I liked the accompanying illustration of a semi-trailer bannered along its whole side with big black extra-bold capitals like a Tautliner curtain: **GUILT**. I thought of Phil Horton sailing through Polish customs with a load of cigarettes manifested as fresh lobster; of Andrew Wilson-Young clumping on to Concorde in his green wellies; of Les Parker pocketing the surreptitious second teabag in the Truckworld cafeteria. I thought, *I* never met a guilty trucker.

In the morning, when I joined Earl and Bill in the diner before first light Earl said, 'I was going to look you up when I went jogging to see if you wanted to come with me.'

'Earl,' I said, 'I wouldn't have wanted to come jogging with you if it was three o'clock in the afternoon.'

At six-thirty we dropped off our first consignments of frames at the new Kenworth truck factory in Renton, near Seattle. Underneath all the tarpaulin they turned out to be just slabby, flanged girders: you set a pair of them down in parallel about eight feet apart, and you had the two mainstays of your chassis. But out of Earl's fifty pairs and Bill's forty-seven they only wanted three sets from each, and the rest were for the main plant opposite Boeing Field. But at Renton Earl and Bill had spied a new Kenworth unit over in the corner of the lot. This was the new, redesigned 900-series Aerodyne sleeper, due to be unveiled in a few weeks' time at the Anaheim truck show, and till then strictly under wraps. It had windows in the side walls of the sleeper, a skylight in the aerodynamically swept-back roof, a rakish striped paint job, and the whole construction one sleek unit rather than a sleeper-box bolted on to the back of a cab. As trucks went it seemed to me quite smart, but Bill was whistling in awe and appreciation. 'Boy, they sure made a cleaner-lookin' truck outta that,' he mused, half to himself. If he went ahead next year and traded in his Kenworth, one of these could be his . . . Here, at last, was the tangible embodiment of all the theoretical truck-building-by-CB he and Earl had been doing since Rochester. But it was only a distant, tantalizing glimpse: men with nylon coats and clipboards got very officious when we asked if we could take a closer look.

At the main Kenworth plant a few miles into Seattle we joined a line of trucks waiting to bring in bits of new trucks. An International pulling a Sleepeezee trailer was delivering mattresses for the beds in the sleeper cabs. An antique Kenworth had fibreglass hoods and sleeper-cab roofs. Stacked on pallets just inside the factory gates were crates of new engines. Cummins engines were painted black – they'd come over from Columbus, Indiana. Detroit Diesels were blue, delivered from Michigan. The yellow Caterpillar engines had travelled from Peoria, Illinois. Most component manufacture was situated around that part of the States – the north central industrial belt: which made it odd for Kenworth to be right out here on a limb on the western seaboard – although it provided for Kenworth trucks like ours to travel thousands and thousands of miles to furnish the parts to propagate the species.

It was a tight squeeze for Bill, who went in first – there was only room at the back of the plant for one semi at a time to unload its chassis rails – to slither the truck round between cab units waiting for wheels, chassis waiting for cabs, racks of tyres and radiators and fuel tanks. While the forklift took Bill's frame rails off we chatted to the delivery foreman, Al Cassidy, who'd been here at Kenworth's for twenty-six years; Bill had been coming for ten already, so they were solid friends who took up their chat where they'd left off the previous time. Bill's rails were not booked in to be used until the middle of the following week, but Earl's truck had the stock they needed for the remainder of this week's production, and Geoff, who was third in line, had one pair on his trailer that were going to be taken off for drilling and laying down as soon as they could get their hands on them. It was a tightly timed business, said Cassidy: last week a hitch in supply from the steelmaker in Milwaukee had come within ten minutes of shutting down the whole truck-assembly line. So they were bringing in a new firm to supply chassis frames − in Cleveland, Ohio, more than four hundred miles further east!

All the rails we'd brought were reserved for two Kenworth models, the 600 and the 800. The 600 was the popular 'anteater', like Geoff drove: the droop-snoop streamlined model that had revolutionized American truck design when it had been unveiled several years ago (though to a British eye it would suggest the lines of a 1950s Bedford, and a Russian might well see a distant shared ancestry with a bull-nosed ZIL). The 800 was a gawky hybrid: after all these miles I was starting to develop a forensic care about such things, and I'm afraid something that is neither a smooth anteater nor a defiantly boxy classic really should do better. These days 600s and 800s were the bread and butter of Kenworth's business: they could be sold in far greater numbers to fleet operations than the 900s could clock up in individual sales to owner−drivers like Bill and Earl.

'I been coming here for so long I'm like part of the

family,' said Bill as we climbed back into the cab, our goodbyes said and our load of frames handed over to Kenworth. 'That's what I was talking about the other day – you feel you're part of something. They depend on you and you depend on them.' Kenworth built thirty trucks a week here in Seattle: between them Bill and Earl had helped to put another hundred trucks on the road.

The more it sank in, the more it amazed me, once our assignment was over, to harmonize in my mind this just-in-time production schedule here at Kenworth with the journey we had made – and especially when you imagined it starting not in Rochester, Minnesota, where I'd joined Bill, but back in Cleveland, Ohio, where in future frames would be starting out from. It would have been as though I'd joined Keith back on the Thursday afternoon and we'd kept on riding until we got here more than a week later. Those thousands of miles: from the Iron Skillet restaurant and the dash back through the rain at the Petro truckstop in Toledo, Ohio – and on – the night mist in Indiana, 'God Bless America' sung for Independence weekend, the holiday jams outside Minneapolis, the exploding Coke cans of Fergus Falls, the sky tilting upside down over North Dakota, the Russian radio broadcasts burping and rustling out of Earl's radio around Dickinson by night, the oil and gas town of Billings, the snow-capped mountain prospect beyond Bozeman, the red-scarred and -scooped landscape around Butte, the St Paul couple at Lookout Pass, the eagle's lair past Kellogg, the Rush Limbaugh tirades that blotted out Spokane, the slow descent to the sunburst on the Columbus River, and the sophisticated-idiot-park at Seattle East. All that way at a steady 62 miles an hour or less, the sun coming up and hundreds of miles peeling by and eventually the sun going down again, and all the while

– it was like looking down the wrong end of the telescope
– Al Cassidy with his clipboard, twenty-six years at Kenworth, waiting for a Midwest Specialized truck to nose
into view at the factory gates a few feet away from his
yard, and sweating for his frame rails to show up just in
time to make the next truck out of them.

After breakfast in a transport café full of hollering and
violently disputatious construction workers – tempers were
trembling on the brink of blows – and a phone call back to
Rochester once it was late enough for them to be up, it
was time to say goodbye to Bill. Midwest had a load of
lumber waiting for him in Spokane to go back to Bayport,
Minnesota, near Minneapolis-St Paul: if he set off now he
could load before the day was out and be home by the
middle of the week. He bade us a characteristically quiet,
courteous farewell, and Earl and I drove off to find a motel.
Earl would probably end up loading down in Tacoma, but
it looked like there'd be nothing for him until tomorrow. I
was waiting to see if I was going to get a ride in a Mack
truck from the east coast across to California: together we
had a day or so to kill.

Having dropped the trailer at the motel, we drove off in
the unit to the Museum of Flight, parked it across two and
a half spaces, and Earl strolled in rapt fascination round
the prototype of the Lockheed SR71 'Blackbird' spyplane
– holder of the record for the fastest flights ever by
crossing the Atlantic in an hour and three-quarters, and
New York to LA in forty minutes.

'You say that over in Russia you have to hang about for
a whole day while some jerk decides to let you across the
border?' he asked me later. 'If you put us on the job we'd
end up shootin' a few people.'

In the afternoon we went to the driving range. There were a few raised eyebrows as the extended-hood Kenworth 900 pulled into the golf club car-park, but I doubted that any of these Toyota compact and Dodge Charger drivers would decide to push the point. Earl took a wood and an iron from the golf bag under his bed, we got a basket of balls from the clubhouse and found ourselves a free bay. Around us young women in jogging shorts and bobby-socks swiped away in a blind whirl, eager cowlicked teenage boys addressed their golfball as though it was a murder-ously serious exam, and elderly women decked out in all the accessories – tweed skirt, tasselled shoes, sun visor – spent hours rocking and fidgeting and shivering their shoulders before poking the ball a bobbling forty yards.

I, on the other hand, was with the long hitter. Earl Henry had once, he told me, played 120 holes of golf in a day in Milwaukee. He could hit a par-five green in two. He loosened up with a few 250-yard cracks, and then waited for a couple on bicycles to pedal past along the footpath beyond the range's 50-foot perimeter fence.

'Do they give you a prize if you hit it out of the range, Earl?'

'Nope. Usually they throw you out.' Earl put another ball on the mat – he didn't bother about teeing them up. 'Aim for the far corner of the fence,' he explained, 'and put a little draw on it.'

Sschwick! The ball was still rising as it cleared the top of the mesh.

The next day, with neither of our trips yet firmed up, we got Kenworth to give us a tour of its new Renton factory. Only opened at the end of May, this was the new state-of-the-art truck plant originally intended to supersede the

ramshackle environmental nightmare we'd delivered to in
Seattle. But between the first welcome from the burghers
of Renton to the idea of Kenworth joining them, and the
final design that had been given a go-ahead, things had
been scaled down. When the environmental implications of
having large trucks built in the midst of Renton had been
digested, Kenworth had ended up with a small plant.
Maximum production was set at twenty trucks a week:
Seattle was putting out thirty. If Kenworth went ahead and
decided to close Seattle, it would still need to build *another*
plant. There were limits to the late twentieth-century's
toleration of the heavy truck even in America.

We started our tour inside the doors where they'd
received our frame rails. This, said the plant manager
Gerry Warber, was the 'Oh-shit department'. 'These are
the rails that come in and the customer says, "Oh, actually
I wanted them drilled five feet further back", and you go,
"Oh, shit."' Oh-shit trucks were the exception that seemed
to prove the rule of a purpose-built fully coherent production line like this, where the rails came in at one door,
went right round the building on a single line having a
truck constructed upon them, and drove out the other
door at the end. Gerry Warber's dapper, bespectacled
appearance belied a beaming balefulness. He'd come to
Kenworth from Boeing, and a career in the production of
sleek, streamlined projectiles designed to slip the surly
bonds of earth and touch the face of God. 'So you've got
one of our 900s?' he demanded of Earl. He shook his head
at me. 'I had a go at steering one of them. Like driving a
fucken Patton tank!' A 900 was not an example of modern
aeronautical design. It was a Texas flat-top. It had the
aerodynamics of a Bristol Boxkite.

Gerry Warber couldn't believe how un-clued up

truckers were about performance, energy efficiency and aerodynamics. When he'd arrived at Kenworth truckers had been coming to him to complain about how much they were spending on diesel. 'I said to them: you're all driving round in these 900s – it's like driving a fucken snowplough! If you want better aerodynamics, *take something off the front*!'

So Kenworth had revolutionized the American truck business by launching the 600, the 'anteater': a tapered bonnet, headlamps and fuel tanks and fenders all smoothed and rounded and fared-in. This was Gerry Warber's kind of truck. But, at the same time, Kenworth's bread-and-butter business had always been the owner–driver. The guys like Earl, who hauled low, flat loads like frame rails across low, flat lands like North Dakota, didn't need to eradicate every tiny bit of wind resistance. And even if their loads *had* pulled hard, they'd still have wanted 900s just because they didn't look like the anteaters everyone else was driving. So Kenworth continued to build Texas flat-tops for people like Earl – but Warber didn't want you to be under any mystical illusion that you were buying your own original road warrior: 'You're just buying an 800 with a tall hood.'

It was the owner–drivers, it seemed to me, with their predilection for a truck customized in the myriad small ways that could confirm it as uniquely theirs, that made Warber's life exquisitely complicated. 'Kenworth keep adding new things to their range,' he admitted, serenely resigned. 'The latest is the integrated cab-and-sleeper that'll be unveiled in a couple weeks. But they don't take anything out! It means more shit all the time for us to be dealing with.' In 1976, for example, they'd built a special commemorative Bicentennial edition of just one hundred trucks.

'They told me, "Gerry, don't invest in any special tooling – we won't *ever* be building it again." We've been building the fucken thing for nearly twenty years!'

We'd reached the paint shop, where a royal blue anteater had just received a beautiful intricate striated flash along the side of the sleeper in gold and maroon. 'That's not a plastic *sticker*,' said Warber. 'That's *paint*.'

'You're talking eighteen hundred bucks for that kind of paint job,' said Earl.

Warber gazed at this extravagant commission with a mixture of pride at the execution and amazement at the folly. 'I wouldn't get us to paint the truck,' he said. 'I'd go to some tired old spaced-out hippie with an airbrush, go find yourself a cup of coffee and a doughnut and let him paint it up for you.'

American truckers, though, were more than happy to pay Kenworth to decorate their steeds as individualistically as a stained-glass window – a tradition that, more than anything, it turned out, had placed the restriction on the size of this new factory. The atmospheric emissions from the oil-based paints necessary for this kind of kaleido scope of colours invoked tough environmental restrictions: if Kenworth could move over to offering its customers a choice of, say, ten water-based paints, said Warber, and let the truck dealers do all the fiddly customizing stuff, they could have two shifts working here instead of one, speed up production to forty trucks a week, and shut down Seattle. Instead, he said, 'We're using *six thousand* different paints a year, all mixed by computer.' He nodded at Earl. 'If he wants 1947 Hudson Green on his new truck, he can have it. He just has to tell us what it is.'

'How far will you go to customize a truck for someone?'

'If we can do it, and it works, and it doesn't make us look silly, we'll put it in.'

'Well, is there anything you wouldn't do?'

Gerry Warber thought. 'We had a guy once, ordered a Kenworth and said to us, could you paint the hood in that red, white and blue stars-and-stripes pattern like Mack do? The managing director got to hear about it and told the guy to go fuck himself – if he wanted it like that, go buy a fucken Mack.'

Back at the motel a phone call confirmed that I had a ride in a Mack truck starting out north of Boston at the weekend. Earl had a load of lumber to pick up in Tacoma tomorrow for Rapid City, South Dakota, so it was time to part. We'd looked at aeroplanes together, gone golfing together, parked the Kenworth outside Seattle's most exclusive lakeside seafood restaurant where he'd treated me to a magnificent meal. We'd driven a complete circuit of the city sightseeing in the truck as though it had been an Avis super-compact, and we'd got here after 1,700 miles rolling westwards from Minnesota. The spiky, off-the-boat man from St Charles had turned out to be the most generous travelling companion you could have. I gave him a golf Log Book for him to record his long hitting on all the courses the Kenworth took him to in the future. The waggling toothpick was extracted for the customary, '*No-o-oo* problem.'

I flew back to Boston – six hours to do what had taken a week in the big rigs – and kicked my heels there for a couple of days while the next ride took shape. This was to be with a firm called Cargo Transportation, based in North Billerica, about thirty miles north of Boston. Before I left

Seattle, word had been that this would be a consignment of computer paper going to Los Angeles – due south-west down through Nebraska and Colorado. But this was 'LTL' haulage or 'Less-Than-a-Load' work where, instead of taking one big item like a Caterpillar loader or fifty sets of chassis rails, you filled up your truck like a parcel van with various part-loads for several destinations. As new loads came in to the depot all the time the allocations for each truck changed, and vehicles' routes were amended and re-amended from hour to hour in the run-up to departure. By the time I got to Boston the news had changed: California was for the moment off – instead there was now a truck going down to Laredo, on the Mexican border of Texas, with intermediate drops around Dallas. So it looked as if I'd be heading south instead into Virginia and down through the Carolinas and Georgia.

In the meantime I just had time for an evening at the House of Blues in Cambridge's Harvard Square to catch Jerome Geils and Magic Dick with their latest blues band. The House of Blues was a ghastly kitschy joint part-owned by Dan Aykroyd and done up like a baroque shrine in wearily extended homage to the religiose conceit of the Blues Brothers, but it was good to see Geils and the great harp player back in a small dive after all the years of bombastic stadium-rock. In middle age Jerome Geils had matured into a remarkable ringer for David Owen, and the razor-creased slacks and Hawaiian shirt confirmed that the days of supercharged rhythm-and-bluster like 'Hard Drivin' Man' had been long quitted for the minor roads. But Magic Dick, with a leonine mane and every limb, as always, faithfully black-clad in leather, still played, to the obligatory bawls of 'Yo, Dickhead', his harp classic, 'Whammer Jammer'. 'Or, as a lot of people prefer to call it,' he reminded us, in memory of the days when J. Geils Band in top gear were a runaway rig in the hammer lane, 'WHAIRMOARGH JAIRMOARGH . . .' I caught an hour of respectful and authentic Chicago blues covers, all of which Magic Dick sang with touchingly finicking enunciation, and all as well-groomed and carefully arranged as J. Geils's hair. A much better example if you were thinking of driving a large truck.

Chapter Fifteen

O'Malley was far from happy. He pointed a sausage of
a finger at the boss and waved a crumpled delivery
note at him and growled that next time George had fifteen
skips of fucken bags of cement to haul he could fucken
find somebody else because he'd had just about enough of
them shifting about all the fucken way back from Houston.
He took the two of us out into the yard where his lilac
Northern Star – a rugged Canadian make – stood ticking
amidst a swirl of dust, and kicked the front offside tyre.
Take a look, said the dismissive jerk of the head. We
looked. The outer edge of the tyre was halfway bald. New
tyre, said O'Malley: that was the load shifting about had
done that. Jack O'Malley had huge scarred forearms, a
bristling moustache and a medicine ball of a paunch. His
eyes glittered. He went and sat in the driver's rest room
and smoked hard. O'Malley, it was clear, was someone
who spoke only when he felt like it: when he did speak,
you knew he must really feel like it. I wasn't travelling
with O'Malley – he was one of Cargo's owner–driver
contractors, and he was already bound for Buffalo the next
night. O'Malley sat fierce, sombre and silent in his anger.
This was not the time to talk to O'Malley.

It was after lunch on the Saturday, and I was waiting for
my ride. Around two o'clock other drivers began to drift

in to find their trucks. Saturday was the big day at Cargo Transportation: all the loads had been accumulating during the week, routes had been worked out for delivering them, and now each vehicle had a full itinerary and only wanted a driver to take the wheel. A wasted, distracted, bare-to-the-waist man looked in. His arms were heavily tattooed, his hair hung in a ratty shoulder-length ponytail. If Willie Nelson lives to be a hundred and twenty, he will look like this man. It turned out he was just checking in to confirm he wasn't going to be needed today, and he disappeared again.

George, the boss, was a quietly spoken, slightly care-worn, courteous man – when I'd arrived he'd been the only one in the office and for a few moments, so retiring was his manner, I'd figured he must be the caretaker. The penny only dropped slowly that he owned this whole fleet. 'Ernie,' confided George about one of his drivers – to give me an instance of the sort of stuff he had to deal with – 'went to Lafayette, Indiana, last week. Should have gone to Lafayette, Tennessee. He thought it read IN on the invoice when it said TN . . .'

Arthur arrived, a vast, beefy black guy, garrulous and jovial, with a hollering voice. He had the expenses from his last trip to go over with the foreman, which led to an animated tale of the circumstances which had led to him having to buy a new wheel down South.

'Ea-easy, Arthur.' George gently rested his hands on Arthur's shoulders. 'We can hear you. You're in the office, not out in the yard.' But Arthur just had a big voice.

'Where've you been so far?' asked George. I told him about the run to Moscow, and New Hampshire to Seattle with Keith and Bill and Earl.

'And how far is it to Moscow, once you've gone over on the boat?'

About fourteen hundred miles, I said.

'Jeez,' said the foreman. 'That's Houston! Two days!'

I told George I'd equipped myself for America with a Road Kill Café T-shirt.

'Tim Brown,' said George, 'the guy you're going with, he eats *a lot*. He wouldn't even bother to grill it. He'd just scrape it up off the road and eat it right there.'

O'Malley sat on and smoked.

'He's a safe driver, Tim,' said George. 'Never had an accident. A little scary, sometimes, but safe. You want to get back there in the bunk and get some hours when you can, because you're gonna have to talk to him to keep him awake.'

Pinned up on the wall of the drivers' office was a photocopy of 'The Arkansas Prayer'. It started,

> Clinton is my shepherd,
> I shall soon want.
> He leadeth me beside closed factories . . .

And it ended,

> I'm glad I am American
> I'm glad I am free,
> But I wish I was a dog
> And Clinton was the tree.

A stocky guy in shades with a thick black beard showed up. This was Tim Brown – mid-thirties-ish, a strutting gait and another impressively rounded stomach. He'd only got back from Kansas City the day before, had rung in yesterday evening and been told there was nothing for him over the weekend. Good, he'd thought, and ripped it up at his friend's bar in Nashua, New Hampshire until the early hours. Then the phone had rung in the middle of the morning to say he *would* be needed after all. Where were we going?

California.

Via Laredo, Texas.

California: where they gave you huge fines for drawing the wrong line in your Log Book, and tickets for an unwashed trailer, and where you often holed up hanging around a truckstop for days, weeks, waiting for a decent back load.

A four-thousand-mile run: one of the longest continuous hauls you could do in the States. So I was going all the way across again – and via the Mexican border.

Tim Brown rubbed his eyes. 'How do I get through Arizona?'

'You buy your way through,' said George. Cargo's trailer fleet was registered in Maine, where the licences were cheaper. But states like Arizona objected to Maine undercutting them on trailer-plating business, and retaliated by refusing Maine reciprocal permit agreements, so we'd need to buy a special ticket on the border to let us through. 'You buy your way through New Mexico too.'

Mid-afternoon already: better be going. We stowed my bag in the back locker of the dark blue Mack and climbed in. Tim shook his head. 'California, man – that scares me.'

Another Cargo driver was pulling out of the yard just ahead of us. Neil was bound for Omaha, Nebraska, and had his daughter with him to drop off along the way at her grandparents' in Des Moines, Iowa. He came over the CB: 'Where you goin', Tim?'

'I think I'm goin' to Hell, but first I gotta go to Texas!'

*

'I'm an outlaw, man, a gipsy outlaw! I'm surprised they put me with you, man.' Tim talked fast, with much bustling gesticulation and a deafening shout of a laugh. 'They were going to put you with Ernie, but his parole don't extend beyond Mississippi.'

'Who was the guy who looked like a wasted Willie Nelson?'

'Ah, that's Don. Yeah, then they were going to put you with him, but he's sick right now.'

Tim had been driving for George for nearly nine years: 'I used to have my own truck, but I went flat broke, got divorced and it all went to shit.' He'd run a little 'sub shop' – a sandwich bar – in Nashua for a while, but he'd sold it when 'it got to be a pain in the balls'. Now he just drove – 'I'm homeless, man. When I go home I stay with my grandmother.' For a while he'd done a lot of deliveries for a company manufacturing waterbeds – hauled them all over the country. 'They offered me one' – he waved an arm at the monastic cell of his cab – 'but where the fuckamagonna put it?' With a late start like today we were looking to put on about four hundred miles tonight – just get as far as Pennsylvania. 'And then,' shouted Tim, 'we'll just ride, ride, ride!'

Our Mack was only four months old – George had paid half a million dollars for a fleet of six new trucks. Tim, as one of the senior drivers, had got one, and already clocked up 38,000 miles in his. Traditionally Macks, with their pugnacious bulldog mascot perched above the radiator, were America's workhorse trucks – the equivalent, if you like, of the British ERF, staple of tanker fleets and bread-and-butter motorway trunking work: 'A bit of a gaffer's truck,' as ERF's marketing manager had once put it to me, as the stereotype he'd had to overcome; 'you know, "I'd rather have a Scania, but the boss has given me this bloody ERF . . ."' Macks had been something similar: snouty and hulking, too often the first choice at the front of a coalbucket. Not pretty, not a style accessory: a brick shithouse on wheels. This CH600 wasn't as powerful as the Kenworths Bill and Earl drove – 350 horsepower would have to work quite hard to pull a full trailer up a big hill – but neither was it a snowplough. It had a streamlined hood, a deep wraparound windscreen, cruise control, and it was Mack's state-of-the-art.

We had four loads aboard our trailer. There were two drops around Dallas: one skip – a pallet in the UK – of advertising brochures to go to a print finisher, and some faulty computer monitors for return to the supplier down in Grapevine, Texas, just outside the Dallas–Fort Worth conurbation. Then there were four vertical swing pumps built by a firm in Lawrence, Massachusetts, to go to Santa Clara, Mexico, which we were taking as far as the Mexican border at Laredo where they'd be transhipped on to a Mexican truck. Mexico had suffered tornadoes a couple of weeks earlier: these pumps would be used to disperse sewage overflows or restore drinking water supplies: together they made up $171,000-worth of equipment. The Lawrence manufacturer, said Tim, was a good customer, 'because their loads have to go. Even if it's only half a load, they pay for the whole trailer. So Cargo makes its money by throwing all the other shit in on top.' And to take us all the way to California we had another consignment of NEC computer monitors for the Tatung warehouse in Long Beach.

'I like runnin' Texas,' Tim said. 'You can really lay down some miles there, really stretch your legs. There's no hills to pull. Nothin' about. You just *ride*.' Until a few

years ago he'd done East Coast to West Coast regularly –
Seattle in three days, California in three and a half, four, a
thousand miles a day. 'When I started working for this guy
that's all I used to do – Seattle and Los Angeles. Coast-to-
coast it's a 60-hour trip, so if you do four 15-hour days you
can still have eight hours' sleep every night. You just gotta
keep up with the programme.' California was the problem,
though – notorious for its paucity of good back loads to
the East Coast. This was the *rich* state, the consumer state:
it sucked in goods from the rest of America. Freight went
in: it didn't come out. All it had to send back was the
seasonal harvest of fruit, and some canned food, from its
produce growers. Truckers hated going to California –
they never knew when they'd get to leave. When I'd
ridden with Keith Derscheid he'd told me about the time
he'd had to sit around for over a week waiting for a back
load: that had been in California. It didn't sound very long
compared to the way days lost in European border queues
accumulated over a single trip – but this was antsy America.
The other place truckers hated going, however, with its
horrendous clogged traffic and mazy streets, was New
York City. So at least if you were prepared to take a New
York load you could put yourself at the head of the line to
get out of California. 'The only thing that saves my ass
loading back to the house is New York City,' said Tim. 'If
I see a load on the board sayin' New York City I say
"Yup! That's goin' on my wagon!"' But Tim hadn't done
Shaky – in CB-demotic California was the earthquake zone
– for four years. 'Now I'm too old. I thought, fuck all that
shit.'

We were riding the same route down towards Pennsylvania that I'd come with Keith a while back, down 495 and
290 to Worcester, Massachusetts, then Interstate 90 and

84 to Hartford, Connecticut – but then Keith had headed west, and we wanted south. Just because Tim hadn't been to Shaky for a while didn't mean he wasn't putting miles on. A fortnight ago he'd managed 4,400 miles in a week. 'I did Boston to San Antone and back in six days. I slept every night from midnight till the sun came up, but during the days, man, I was humpin' it. And as soon as I dropped my load I found another one a hundred miles away hauling trash bags. See, all the Chinese are movin' down to Texas and settin' up in business recycling plastics, all these food containers and things, and making them into trash bags, and then we haul them back up to the east coast. Got caught for speeding on the way, but this cop, he was kinda keen on us bringing the state business, so he even gives me directions to where the place is and lets me off with a warning! I got back from San Antone in two days – I was two days ahead of schedule. That pay check was a *real* good week!'

We hit the coast road at New Haven and followed it down towards Bridgeport and Stamford, and stopped for an early bite to eat with Neil and his daughter at the Milford Services at Bridge Haven. Tim told Neil how his daughter's dental brace was going to cost $1,200 – he also had a teenage son. His wife now had two children with her new husband, who was going to go halves with Tim on the dental bill. 'I was young,' he reflected. 'She was sixteen, I was twenty-one, just out of the services. I picked her out at a party, we spent a week at the Holiday Inn and I fell in love and I married her . . .'

'It happens,' said Neil.

By eight o'clock, the dusk starting to fade the New York skyline into a charcoal-etched silhouette, we were crossing the George Washington Bridge across the Hudson and passing through the top of Manhattan. In the tunnel on the approach to the bridge a hubcap came off a pick-up truck in front and bowled through the traffic towards us; the driver of a private hire bus in the next lane was smoking a colossal cigar. Neil was supposed to be following us – we were going to ride with him until Pennsylvania, when he cut off westwards, but we'd already lost him. Tim called up 'Cookie-Duster' – Neil's CB moniker; his own was 'Mr B.' – in vain. 'He's kinda slow,' said Tim. 'I like to ride wide open all the way. I don't like nobody on my front door . . .' We were due in Dallas Monday morning: that meant a thousand four, said Tim, to do today and tomorrow, and then two hundred to knock off on the morning we dropped.

On the radio Delbert McClinton and Tanya Tucker were singing their bouncy duet again about 'Teardrops in the Dark'.

'I like country music,' Tim said. 'Kenny Rogers, Willie Nelson, the new guys like Garth Brooks. I don't know – country music and driving seem to go together. Makes the miles slip down easier.'

The sun went down over New Jersey, and we drove into a deep pink sunset.

Sometimes, Bill had said to me, the miles just disappear, and sometimes you have to drive every single one of them. Today, despite the country music, felt like one of those times. Probably it was because we had no predetermined destination for tonight: we were just trying to get as far as possible. We weren't driving towards a winning tape: we were just driving away from where we'd started out. And also it felt as though we'd been bounced into this trip – you think you're going south to the Mexican border, and then you find you're going on from there and as far again.

Your mind takes a while to come up to speed. In *The Songlines*, Bruce Chatwin passes on the story of the white explorer who paid his African porters for a forced march: within sight of the final destination they suddenly sat down and refused all inducements to walk any further – saying they had to wait to give their souls a chance to catch up.

For the first time in the States, too, the ride felt unexalted, attritional: this wasn't a proud owner of a chromium steed allowing his services to be hired; this time it was a tired guy being catapulted out on to another long, long road – three times as far as a European slog to Moscow – and we were still at the start. You can sense the exact moment when the wind goes out of someone's sails. The truck rolls on at exactly the same speed, the hands still rest across the wheel-rim, the posture shifts not at all – but suddenly the tiredness has broken out like a sweat, and the gaze is directed so much further into the distance ahead.

'This is another good song,' Tim said. We listened in silence.

It was called 'A Thousand Miles from Nowhere'. Over that long-loping, seven-league-boots rhythm with which the best songs fell into perfect stride with the wheels eating up the highway, Dwight Yoakam sang a simple, rueful lament.

> I'm a thousand miles from nowhere
> Time don't matter to me
> 'Cause I'm a thousand miles from nowhere
> And there's no place I want to be . . .

A guitar engraved a crisp, pensive solo that soared slowly higher and higher, the reverb took Yoakam's voice out away into the distance – where was he singing from? – and he sang the words grave and solemn – he didn't need to put any sadness in them. In all the miles I rode I heard plenty of songs too many times, but I heard this one only once. Dwight Yoakam, I later discovered, had spent six years driving trucks.

And as he sang a flood of moments came out of recent memory: Keith talking in a half-whisper to his wife on the phone that late night in the truckstop diner somewhere in North Pennsylvania; the image of Bill taking his German shepherd Chrissie down to the river in Montana for a quiet walk to listen to the sounds; Earl stowing his golf clubs under his bunk for the prospect of a round of golf in Missoula, or Seattle, or wherever he found himself; and now here was Tim, driving like hell into the night with a bed at his grandmother's to do for home.

By ten that evening we'd reached the Pilot services on the New Jersey–Pennsylvania state line, where Neil caught us up. There was no restaurant here to sit down in, just a shop with a fast-food counter. Tim and I prowled wearily around the racks of sweets and chips and pens and batteries avoiding each other, intent in our separate affected scrutinies, wanting nothing. A cup of scalding Styrofoam coffee to burn your mouth, a sweet cookie sweating inside its Cellophane to consume standing up, and off again. You have to stop to give yourself a rest, walk on your wobbly legs, give yourself some refreshment – but when there is nowhere to go, nowhere to put yourself, you loll and drift and blink about until it's time to return to your prison and drive on. Your itinerancy has been confirmed in the most desultory, hapless, restless way. It doesn't matter how far away you are if you know where you're measuring from: it's those times when you're between everywhere.

At eleven-thirty Tim had had enough for the night: 375

miles wasn't bad for an afternoon start after a heavy night. The Mack didn't have a walk-in sleeper cab, just a single bunk behind the seat, so we stopped over at an isolated and gloomy twenty-buck motel off the Interstate at Bethel, Pennsylvania. A little elderly elf of a man shuffled into Reception in a baggy white vest and a battered baseball cap. When he read my address off the registration card he became gruffly loquacious. 'Emm . . . Mister Coster, I see you're from England . . . emmm . . . May I call you a *Limey*?' His long grey Seven Dwarves' beard twitched and fidgeted; he spoke in a pedantic, busying mutter. 'I suppose you like a . . . *pint of bitter*? Do you eat *bangers*? I gather they're real big over there for breakfast, along with beans . . .'

I didn't tell him I had a 70-foot Mack truck parked outside his front door, with the engine running all night for Tim's air-conditioning.

Chapter Sixteen

The next morning had an uneasy start when Tim's first-light inspection showed up a nail in the Mack's front offside tyre. It went in half an inch, and when he pulled it out the hole it had made in the rubber didn't close up. It was about evens, Tim reckoned, whether this tyre would make it all the way to California; in any case, from now on it meant 'no tearing it up.'

But things looked up again when we drove down the road to the Harrisburg truckstop, and met a guy who said the California scale at Banning was closed. This was the weigh-station halfway between the Arizona state line and LA that you had to pass if you entered the state on Interstate 10 as we'd be doing, where its assiduous officials could find all sorts of things *you* didn't know were wrong with your rig. Bars of sunlight broke through the clouds and shone mother-of-pearl down the sky. This trucker had a 1987 Ford – an unusual motor, but in modest evangelism he pressed upon me a glossy brochure for the new sleek Ford conventional he was about to buy – and he hauled shampoos and toothpastes in a reefer from Iowa up to St Paul, Minnesota, and he'd bumped into Tim a few years earlier when Tim had broken down. We met him this time in the line for the truckwash: Tim was getting his trailer a good wash-and-brush-up now so we'd be clear for the gimlet scrutiny of California: a dirty truck would get a ticket anyway, but it would also set the inspectors looking for other recondite instances of sloppiness and disrepair to call down apocalyptic fines. The Ford trucker had been through Banning only a couple of weeks ago, he said, and it was closed then. Busted by the Feds, was the word out, suspicious of some state highway officials tampering with trucks' brakes during their inspections, and then giving the drivers $150 tickets for faulty brakes. The sun had risen high and blazing.

'If you can't pay your fines,' Tim said, underway again in a gleaming Mack, 'they knock off twenty dollars for each day you spend in jail. You might be there a long time – I might be skinny like you when I came out! The boss says you should get a Bible and go and tell 'em you found Jesus. I said, George, I don't think that'd work.' He rummaged a hand back under the bunk. 'I got a coupla Bibles in here somewhere' – his voice bellowed into a laugh – 'but I ain't read 'em!'

We waved a final goodbye to Neil and his little girl as they turned off towards Iowa and Nebraska. 'I'm thinking of changing my route,' Tim mused out loud. 'I was gonna cut down through the woods in Virginia down 29 to join 85, but we were pulling the hills OK last night, so I'm thinking maybe I'll take 81 down through Tennessee; 29's flat but it's a slow road – there's some small towns along it and red lights and things. It'll take you half a day to get down through the Carolinas . . .'

Bill and Earl had talked all the time about their trucks: about modifying this, tightening that; they mutually admired other trucks, picked away at their own, swapped tips on finessing them, knew about every option available on every model. Tim just drove: as long as his truck didn't break down he was concerned only to lay down miles. He talked about the shit he was taking from some punk upstairs at the office about the fuel consumption figures he was getting because he left his engine running all night. 'I told this guy: my truck earns all the money for this business, don't give me no shit about fuel. I get paid by the mile. One day I'll go in their office and turn their air-conditioning off.' Earl and Bill peered out through the twin shallow panes of flat glass that constituted a Kenworth's windscreen: they were quite happy with an antique look of a lumbering Russian ZIL, because it was what they'd always had, and with it they could ride the route they always rode. The wider world beyond the compass of the empty land around them was where the rocket scientists lived, and Hillary and Billary were conspiring to invent ever-more taxes, and all of it all the time closin' in on you. A tiny windscreen was just fine. In this new Mack we looked out through a deep curved wraparound of glass, and Tim kept up a pugnacious monologue about how he'd had it with this job and all the options he'd got of going to drive somewhere else. 'He's a cheap prick,' he huffed and puffed of his boss. 'He pays me twenty-three cents a mile. He should pay us a quarter a mile. My truck does 200,000 miles a year. My truck makes all the money for his business!' He thought he might go and work for Schneider, the orange 'pumpkin trucks' fleet. They paid twenty-eight cents a mile, thirty-one cents a mile! – gave you really good health and pension benefits, your own truck – cabovers, but they were OK – and round his neck of the woods Schneider had a lot of work hauling the tissue paper that was made up in New England.

Or he'd had a chance a few years ago – he wasn't sure if it was still on offer – to join the Teamsters. These days the legendary truckers' union was far less powerful than when the notorious Jimmy Hoffa was its boss, and Robert Kennedy had been the Attorney-General trying to nail it conclusively for its racketeering and links with the Mob. I'd read tales of old about guys who crossed the Teamsters being rushed to hospital in excruciating pain after waking up from a spiked drink – and having large cucumbers extracted from their rectum. But after the Teamsters' 1987 truck strike had closed down the States for three days – non-union independent hauliers had been intimidated into staying off the roads with fire bombs and nail traps – the Reagan administration had deregulated the trucking industry, making it far easier for non-unionized fleets to obtain work, and breaking for good the Teamsters' remaining stranglehold. Nowadays the union's main power base – and the source of continuing allegations of gross corruption – was the freight-handling branches at the airports, but the big trunking fleets like Continental Freightways and Roadway were still Teamster companies. Such fleets ran relays across the country, each driver doing an eight-hour day, earning a guaranteed salary of sixteen dollars an hour, running from one terminal to the next, staying in the motel there overnight, and coming back the next day. It was a long way from over-the-road work, and there sounded little scope for encountering big pink dragons or nesting eagles or golf courses, but if you could get in with them you'd have a solid job. But if Tim joined he'd have to start as a casual driver on call. The Teamsters made you work up from the bottom: they didn't just let anybody in.

After a break at the Sadler truckstop in Virginia – a muscular redneck pull-in so far impervious to the sanitizing anodyne culture of the Flying J, we spent the afternoon rolling south past the hazy grey silhouette of the Blue

Ridge Mountain range, and I heard how life's road had brought Tim to the wheel of a big truck.

'I don't want my son to go into the trucking industry,' he said. 'I want him to use his brain, not his muscles. I started out down here in the army, four years in Virginia and Oklahoma. I was running a computer warehouse – I shoulda kept that job. I had it made. Eight to four, an hour for a coffee break, hour for lunch. But after a while you get tired of taking orders.

'I was in bars from sixteen, man – I had a beard like this, everyone thought I was twenty, twenty-two. Drinkin' in bars, chasin' women . . . but that life *ages* you, man. I'm tellin' ya, it ages you quickly. I'm thirty-seven, but I feel fifty. And my body – sometimes it feels eighty!

'So I came out of the army and went to work in a plastics factory punching the lettering on the childproof tops of medicine bottles. And I rose up to run the shipping and receiving sides as well. But then I got put on the night shift. Couldn't sleep, couldn't do the job properly, and one day I got my hand caught in the machine. Didn't hurt, but scared me real bad, man. I got right out.'

Then he'd gone to a company that made machines for folding cardboard boxes: 'Shoulda stayed in that job, too. That was a good job . . .' But meanwhile he'd gone and bought himself a 'junk' truck – a 1965 International cabover: with what his grandmother lent him towards it he was only left with a monthly payment of a hundred and fifty dollars. He taught himself to drive it, and 'ran it around' for a year, picking up the odd trailer here and there and delivering it from Massachusetts to New Hampshire. 'Then I got a contract with the Coca-Cola bottling plant, delivering them the plastic bottles from the factory. It was good money – I could make three hundred dollars a day from that, on top of the box machine job. Around that time I got married, had a coupla kids.

'Then I bought a brand new truck – that was a Peterbilt.' (I had had Tim marked down as not a Kenworth kind of guy.) 'That was a mistake. The payments were too high, I couldn't make it pay, my wife wanted a divorce, then my parents died in the same year . . . and I went and lost it . . .' He'd tried his sandwich bar in Nashua for a year, made reasonable money from it and sold it for a bit of a profit – 'and then George put me back together.'

In the Roanoke truck stop that afternoon – we were down in Virginia's ski-resort region – we shot the breeze over Styrofoam coffees with a couple of guys from New Jersey driving a four-wheeler for United Van Lines, shifting furniture from San Jose and San Diego to Memphis and Nashville, and then on up to Massachusetts. Tim switched off the winking scanner he had propped up on the dashboard – these devices gave you advance warning of a Smokey Bear by picking up his speed-trap radar, but they were illegal within the state of Virginia – and we took a detour around the backwoods to avoid the hassle of the weigh-station down the road. Tim wound down his window and hung his elbow out to make it look like he always cruised around here: if he got stopped, he said, pointing to all the truck dealers along the road, he'd say he was just going to call in at one of them for some parts.

'I took my old grandmother with me on a coupla trips,' he said. 'My sister went nuts – she said, "She's eighty-two! You're crazy!" But I threw her in the truck with me and we went all round Florida. I had ten drops all over – fluorescent lights for construction sites. New schools, that sort of thing. It was all I did for a whole year: haul fluorescent lights. Then J.B. Hunt came in and undercut the rates and that was that. But we had a pretty good time – 'cause she really likes talking on the CB.'

Back on the Interstate near Pulaski an old London Transport double-decker bus stood marooned outside a drive-in diner.

We crossed into Tennessee after seven, with the grey-blue hills north of Knoxville ahead of us, and soon a glimpse of the Great Smoky Mountains behind the rolling wooded hills to the east. Knoxville in the dusk a couple of hours later was an episode of hairy nip-and-tuck with a woman in a little red Toyota tootling along in the hammer lane at fifty. Even a big brute of a Mack truck looming in her mirror didn't make her pull over: she clutched the wheel and strained towards the windscreen. I could see a child in the front seat beside her; neither wore a seatbelt. As soon as we had overtaken her on the inside to get safely ahead, the little red saloon scrambled past us again at seventy. Another two hours, and Chattanooga a sea of lapping, spangled lights in the night; one more hour, past midnight already, and a HoJo motel at Collinsville, already 1,100 miles from North Billerica, Massachusetts, and a few breaths on your face of warm-washing silent-soughing Alabama night.

'Or I could go work for this other company,' said Tim. 'Bud Myers – they're just south of Minneapolis. Offer you twenty-five cents a mile straight off, a brand new truck . . . The Midwest companies always need drivers who want to go to New York, New Jersey, the east coast. That's why they offered me work right away.'

I was getting the hang of Tim's speculative monologues. It was what he did, where Earl and Bill would talk about seat design and extended hoods. It was what he did to get all his ducks in a row. It was how he talked some adrenalin into himself for the day ahead, how he gave himself another hit when the day and his energy had started to wane. It was a way of keeping himself sat in that seat in that cab all those hours, all those days: by minutely arguing the toss with himself about all the better alternatives to what he was actually doing. At the end of it, out on that road all by himself, George's only hope of getting that load delivered, when Tim had this full deck of aces in hand of better places he could be going, he'd become the one who was offering the boss employment. The blow that does not break me makes me strong.

Past Smoke City – the city of Birmingham, Alabama, where in mid-morning an unhealthy haze hung across the skyscrapers and a roadside sign announced the Thirteenth Annual American Deerhunters' Expo at the convention centre – Tim chatted over the CB to a guy in a white Peterbilt droop-snoop about news of a truck overturned ahead near the intersection of 59 and 65. 'Where you goin'?'

'I'm on m'way to Shaky,' the Southern drawl came back. 'M'first trip there on m'own.'

'When you gotta be there?'

'Thursday mornin'. I like to rush it . . .' Two days from here to California: he'd have to.

'We had a woman driver on the firm for a while,' Tim said when the Pete had disappeared ahead. 'She was a tough cookie, lemme tell ya – she used to be in the Marines. And everyone used to be amazed at how she'd do California in sixty hours every time – until she did it once too often by keeping the foot to the floor the whole way and blew the engine and the boss fired her.' In his old Mack Superliner Tim had once done Florida from Massa-

chusetts with his buddy Brad 'The Booster', a real hard-
drivin' man, in a day and a half. Took a load of books
down to Miami that had to catch a boat: left Saturday at
noon and got them there at midnight on Sunday, each
truck pushing the other all the way. You couldn't do it in
these new Macks, he said: they had speed governors. And
then down in Florida the firm had a regular account with a
factory in Tallahassee that made kitty litter, so they'd
loaded up with that on Monday morning and been back
home by the end of Tuesday.

The middle of the day brought us through the flat
forest of central Alabama, and then as we neared the
Mississippi border the trees dropped away to leave hum-
mocky grassland, and once across the state line they rolled
back right up to the road again. Mississippi's big forestry
industry sent lumber to woodyards and sawmills in Merid-
ian, which then supplied the furniture factories back up
in Virginia. Heavy rain was pelting down and smearing
the forest to a dark green shimmer; muddy water stood
high around the tree trunks; the sloughs were flooding.
Rain and flood around the Mississippi, all the way down.
Three hours to cross Mississippi on Interstate 20, and
stormy rain smashing and staggering across the wide lush
prairie.

'I broke down along here a while back. Broke a spring
on the trailer and the thing sat down on the frame and
blew two tyres. I limped it into that rest area over there
and had to spend the night there. Got out in the middle of
the night to take a leak over by the ditch, and I was
standing there, and I heard a noise a little way away. Then
I heard it again, over in the bushes. I looked down, and
there was a fucken alligator in front of me! Hell, I put that
thing away and headed back for the truck. Couldn't get to

sleep for hours, and then I dreamt about alligators all night.'

In Monroe, Louisiana, at a meal in the Western Sizzler steakhouse, Tim lived up to the preceding myths about his gargantuan appetite by stowing away a plate-sized steak with side vegetables and salad and bread roll. It was a tired, pensive man who'd heaved this big truck up and down Monroe's main drag looking for a place with a gateway wide enough to allow us to pull in and eat – sometimes in a big truck you felt like a cat peering inside the inaccessibly tiny mousehole at your food. But it was the booming bantam-cock who emerged into the hard evening sunshine, good for a few hundred more miles.

Putting the last hundred miles of Louisiana behind us that evening, and then starting to eat into Texas, the biggest haul of all, had the same sense that had come to me, creeping across North Dakota with Earl, of a slow sea crossing. This wide, unvariegated prairie, verdant with some dense crop, for hour after hour, where cities were the interruption: crossing Mississippi we'd passed only two; Louisiana reeled by punctuated by two more; there were 125 miles of Texas before you hit the outskirts of Dallas. All these miles already across so many states that had been flat traverses of arable green for days on end: Pennsylvania, Wisconsin, Minnesota, North Dakota, Washington, Virginia, Alabama, Mississippi ... The sensation I'd had for an hour or two with Tony in Europe when we were crossing the flat fields of western France, of a countryside factory, an industrial landscape built-up no higher than ground level, but as densely productive as a car plant: land worked to the last granule of soil and drop of water to produce food to fill refrigerated lorries so that other lorries could run to the supermarket halls so that supermarket

halls could fill home freezers and fridges – here in America
that sensation almost never went. The landscape was endlessly self-replicating. It seemed you could never drive out
of it: over the horizon would be another whole state's-
worth. The time-lapse camera of trucking made America
exude its immense richness and lushness: America was one
huge farm.

'Tim, where's your favourite place in the States? If you
could take your truck anywhere, where would you ride?'

'Oh, Route 90. Along the Gulf Coast of Mississippi
from Mobile. I rode it a few years ago all the way round to
Ocean Strips. That's the *balls*, man. That ocean is *real*
pretty. People ask me why I do this job. Man, I say, have
you ever seen the sunset over Colorado? Have you ever
seen the sunset over the California ocean?'

In front of us was a slow-moving truckload of livestock:
between the side slats of the trailer the cows' mournful
eyes mooned out at us. Tim pulled out to overtake. 'They
call them bull wagons. You don't wanna get behind one of
them. Bull decides to take a leak and you get it all over
your windscreen.'

A roadside hoarding flashed past:

1–713 – REVERSE:
NEUROSURGICAL VASECTOMY REVERSAL

Terrell, Texas, ten miles outside Dallas, we made just
before midnight, 1,816 miles now clocked up between us
and the Cargo depot, and a night-stop at another low-
down motel next to the Outlaws porn-movie shop. Interstate 20 had been busy with traffic during the night ride
through eastern Texas, and the CB was busy with truckers
keeping a paranoid look-out. Tim kept the radio on all the

time, a maddening, fractious wash of fizzes and booms and sudden eardrum-piercing volleys of jabber. Sometimes the blare sounded as though the guy was holding a megaphone to his lips, at others as though he were fathoms deep in an underground cavern – you could easily spend a thousand dollars on boosters and echo boxes to play around with your personal CB sound. More than once a trucker's mutterings were introduced by the sepulchral call-and-response signature tune from *The Good, the Bad and the Ugly.*

In all those miles I heard perhaps five minutes of interesting or memorable conversation. CBs were by now nothing new, and the novelty of rapping into them about K-wobblers and Kojaks-with-Kodaks and county-mounties would have worn off ages ago. But the *Convoy* myth of a rich, demotic art-form – a kind of redneck *ragga* – struck me as probably and regrettably always wishful thinking. It's a similar fallacy to presuming that radio hams must have access to the most extraordinary oral traditions. In fact, just like the radio ham, the CB user has interest only in the medium, not the message. The radio ham wants to talk to Afghanistan or Vanuatu only because it challenges his knob-twiddling proficiency in establishing grainy contact; the trucker with his CB only switches on because he wants to know about *Bears*!

Tonight the air waves were busy. A Bear had just snuck in behind us! (Outrage.) Another Smokey Bear up ahead was workin' the highway real hard. Thinks he's Mister America. Whenever someone gave you some news the protocol was always to answer in a good-ol'-boy Southern drawl – even Tim, whose normal accent was *hward-twalking* New York machine gun, would lapse into a sing-song 'Ahh 'preciate it.' A motorcyclist was cutting in on the channel to chew the fat with someone about the best rides west. (This was the other breed of CB user: the fastidious bore – the lonely limpet at the party who locked on to you with his endless advice on the best holiday route for driving to the seaside: out here you endured dogged exchanges of 'Yeah, I like 65, yeah, and the 28 and 493 ... 59, yeah, 59 on to 188, yeah, that's good too ...') The truckers were getting irritated – but only because it was blocking their Bear-watch. 'Would you mind usin' another channel?' came an ornery voice.

It was late at night, and all the trucks around us were barrelling along at sixty-five, seventy. It all seemed silly and juvenile and humourless. *Slow down, then!* I wanted to bawl down their stupid CBs. Wouldn't it be more fun to listen to the motorcyclist than play schoolboys' games of cops and robbers and cowboys and Indians and hide-and-seek with the police?

Then a dynamite blonde saved the night for everyone. A black BMW with the soft-top down came gliding down the hammer lane and passed us all at magnificently excessive, swelling speed. All you could see of its driver was a rippling blur of golden hair and a pair of Ray-Bans for night-hipness more than headlight-glare. An awed silence filled the air waves. Eventually, of course, the blue disco-lights came winking along the fast lane in pursuit. Tim and I got level with the two cars on the hard shoulder just as the blonde was easing out of her convertible, fingers running through her locks in languid inquiry: *You wanted to talk to me?*

The CB came alive again with gruff voices and worldly bemusement.

'Do you *rilly* think he's gonna give her a *ticket*?

'Mo' likely take down her number 'n' give her a date for dinner . . .'

Chapter Seventeen

Our trucking iconography comes from the movies. But no one has yet made a trucking film that comes near to capturing the texture of the driving life. Instead, we have merely transpositions of common genres. *Duel* is a persecution movie: instead of the Thing, or *Jurassic Park*'s dinosaurs, the nightmarish antagonist is a big blaring rig, whose anonymous driver you never see, whose motive for homicidal pursuit of the sweating motorist is never known. *Duel* plays on our fear of the big radiator suddenly looming in our rear-view mirror, on the inequity of proportion between the super-compact and the semi that could smash it without even a tremor – but it's an exercise in suspense, not a depiction of a world.

Smoky and the Bandit is a tiresome comedy caper in cops-and-robbers mould: a facile exploitation of the trucker-as-outlaw cliché as an excuse for a script of pleased-with-itself CB demotic. *Convoy*: CB-talk plus outlaw-syndrome with a justice-seeking moralism. *White Line Fever*: justice-seeking moralism melded with mawkish love story. In each case there's plenty of scope for hairy stunt driving and writing off police cars, and the kind of avenging individualistic heroics that John Wayne or Clint Eastwood would dust his hands and get down to in a western. But even *White Line Fever* isn't about white line fever: that tremulous delirium born of way too much driving when the mark down the middle of the road starts to waver and wobble and presage the arrival of the big pink dragons. In none of these movies is there any sense of distance: of the attritional mileage the over-the-road driver has to punish himself with. Hollywood's trucking films, predictably, are always thrilling, fast-paced, hammer down, determinate. In none is there any sense of what always seemed to me the central fact of the trucking life: its rootlessness, its indeterminacy: the countless times when you hole up a thousand miles from nowhere: the road that never ends anywhere, but only ever continues on, and then on.

In the European trucking classic, *Le Salaire de la Peur* (*The Wages of Fear*), the two drivers may have a load of volatile nitro-glycerine behind them that could blow them sky-high any second, but they are still only going *three hundred miles*. As Cargo Transportation's foreman would say, 'That's New York! Half a day!' *The Wages of Fear* is not a road movie, but an exploration – often melodramatically overblown – of men under stress, their bluff called on the swaggering bravado they have shown in volunteering for a dangerous job to get some money. The film – unlike the driving life – bids for extreme existential climax. Only in its first twenty minutes – a boldly long sequence in a flyblown Mexican town that prowls through bars and along dusty streets tracking shiftless men rolling yet another cigarette, picking quarrels, drifting into fights, waiting for work – do you recognize something of the world of border queues, Wide Load permits, truckstops, motels and Truckworld.

There is only one movie that comes close, and it is the least-known of them all. *Hell Drivers* – the title is its worst failing – is a black and white British movie of the fifties starring Stanley Baker, supported by a heterogeneous cast juxtaposing Jill Ireland and David McCallum with Gordon Jackson and Sid James. It is the best and almost certainly the only tipper-movie – about a crooked haulage firm, with a contract to transport gravel from the quarry to the building site, that encourages its drivers to compete in achieving the most daily loads because its managers are receiving a rake-off from each one. Stanley Baker, newly released from prison for an undisclosed offence, is victimized by the foreman driver who holds the record, and decides to take him on. The tippers run only ten miles from quarry to construction site – but they thunder back and forth all day. The film brims with reckless, careering, dizzying driving. It switches from hurtling trucks to grimy boarding houses and muscular truckers' pull-ins and back to more driving. The runs speed up and, as Stanley Baker closes on the surly record-holder, the tactics become more and more reckless. But none of this helter-skelter recklessness is to be admired: it is suicidal. There is no glamour to the movie, no heroism, no swagger – and no point. The end of it all is not worth the journey, and everyone in it knows it: it is a shabby, twilit, attritional world in which you don't reach where you're going, because you don't know where that might be.

One day, perhaps, someone will apply such a treatment to the long-haul guys, and come up with a trucking movie that captures not the chromium accoutrements but the existence: not the climactic but the plotless: a movie that doesn't get to the centre of things, but is always halted and turned back on the periphery, that looks over at the action from the road that bypasses it: a movie that lets all the wide open space in the world in. One day, perhaps, someone will make a *Paris, Texas* with Peterbilts.

*

For Texas can trip you up. You can get lost in Texas, even in a big truck. In the frantic old days – heading straight across the middle down through Denver – Tim had trans-navigated America coast-to-coast in four days. It took us four days to get clear of Texas. It was Monday night when we'd crossed over from the east, and Friday evening before we got out into New Mexico. Tim had been looking forward to Texas, he'd said, so he could really stretch his legs – but in Texas you could stretch your legs all day and by nightfall you were still in the middle of the state. Continental truckers in Europe had the border queues for Russia and Hungary; in America you had Texas. Texas was an antsy, lethargic, wearisome week, and most of the people we bumped into seemed to be finding it so, too. The radio station talked like the forces radio Tony and I had tuned in to on the German–Polish border, as though the other side of the state line were eastern Europe – it didn't matter whether its portentousness was tongue-in-cheek or not: everywhere else was an age away.

'One hundred per cent American. No foreign stuff allowed. This is 105 FM Young Country . . . Where are you calling from?'

'California.'

'California!'

'Yeah.'

'Well, what can we do for you?'

'I just wanned to call and say how much I hate missin' your station, 'cause it's so hard to find a station playin' country in California . . .'

We dropped the Acme Print Company brochures at Adventure Printing next to Dallas's rail freight yard; by lunchtime we'd got rid of the first lot of faulty computer monitors to the software company at Grapevine opposite the Dallas–Fort Worth airport, at a gleaming new mirror-glass headquarters that hid the trucks out of sight round the back via an access road so narrow and a loading bay so shallow you almost took out several employees' cars manoeuvring in.

'I used to have to wear glasses,' said a shocked woman on the radio while Tim was round the back supervising the unloading of the pallets – it was a commercial for laser correction of short sight. 'And it was *terrible* to have to wake up in the morning and *depend* on something . . .'

I was getting *very* sick of Alan Jackson and a lot-about-livin'-and-a-little-'bout-love.

At the Dallas Flying J, Tim rang North Billerica and discovered that one of Cargo's young kid drivers had been holed up at the 76 truckstop in Fort Worth for a *week* saying he couldn't find anything to bring back. The kid drove a tilt, and was looking around for a suitable load for it. The news prompted a fusillade of monologue. 'Man, you can't just wait, you gotta go look for it, take what they got. Down here, man, this time of year it's always melons, you can always haul a load of melons – if you got a tilt you break up some pallets, build up the sides of your trailer with the boards, then you can fill it up with melons, take them to Florida, fill up with a load of bricks for New York City – always haul bricks up to Massachusetts and Connect-icut, lemme tell ya, that's what I do, man, maybe I should go sort him out . . .'

But the boss had said keep headed for Laredo, so we hit Interstate 35 south out of Dallas and made for Austin and San Antone. 'Texas to Florida,' announced Tim – the Colorado River through the middle of Austin sparkled deep blue in the early evening sunshine: 'If I could get a job just doing that run I'd do it for the rest of my life. I did it once – couldn't get a load home, so I loaded out of San Antone for Orlando, it was a Harden's Restaurant that had gone out of business and this guy in Florida who owned a chain of them bought all the equipment. Down on the Gulf, reee-all pretty.' He fished around for a magazine cutting in the mess of papers on the cab floor and handed me an advertisement from a Southern trucking firm offering finance arrangements for guys to set up as owner–drivers with a new Freightliner. 'This girl I've been dating for a few years, she said she'd go halves with me and we'd run it together.' The contract work ran out of Texarkana, on the Texas–Arkansas line: it would be a way of running down to the Gulf. 'I'm thinkin' about it,' said Tim.

In the Flying J at San Antonio I browsed through the cassette racks while Tim refuelled the Mack, and amongst the standard fare of Clint Black and Alabama and Reba McEntire I found a tape of Steve Earle's *Guitar Town* knocked down to four bucks. It was one of my favourite tapes back in England, I'd found myself listening to it again waiting at the Russian border at Brest, and now here it was turning up in the place it was written for. I hadn't expected it to. None of the truckers I'd met in the States had ever even heard of Steve Earle. Guides to country music tended to leave him out, along with the other 'New Country' musicians like Lyle Lovett and k.d. lang. The truckers preferred the traditional stuff, with its reedy, hiccupping vocals. I preferred the other stuff: the 'redneck rock', as it was sometimes dubbed, hailing from Texas rather than Nashville. *Rolling Stone* once said that Steve Earle's music owed more to Keith Richards than Chet Atkins. That was fine by me – it was a way of saying that the blues had got into him. In those fragile moments on night roads, pure blues – Muddy Waters's ghostly holler out to the Delta fields, the bottleneck shivering on the strings – would be too true, too naked to bear. And in the moments when there was a new strip of black top under your wheels, when the miles had slipped down easy and you were glad to be one small piece of rolling motion on earth all by yourself, with a horizon you didn't mind how far away – well, then you wanted more than a quaint and tidy diddle-iddle with a smug sentiment, but no heavy-metal bluster either: you just wanted someone to sing it sanguine and spring-heeled, how it was. We hit the night road out of San Antone, Tim punched the tape doubtfully into the stereo, the guitar hit that thunking ticking-over twang, and Steve Earle sang

> Hey pretty baby are you ready for me
> It's your good rockin' daddy down from Tennessee
> I'm just out of Austin bound for San Antone
> With the radio blastin' and the bird dog on . . .

A dead straight road with invisible immense flatlands either side of you, a hundred and forty miles through the night. At first the lights of Laredo were a faint peachy hue on the horizon; as we came near they became a braid of gold baubles stretching across the bottom of the sky. Sometimes everything else falls away, and it becomes very simple: you are what you do.

Laredo is a sprawling frontier town under a tall blue sky, its main drag miles long, a procession of neon signs, low shacks and tousled palm trees, draped with low tangles of telegraph wires. Nothing stands more than a few storeys high; the downtown district is dusty and gimcrack. New trailer homes are going for five dollars a day. Historically,

Laredo was the poor cross-border smuggling town. But on the approach to the city we'd passed a giant distribution warehouse going up for the Wal-Mart discount hyper-market chain. ('Guys like that . . .' said Tim, 'start with nothing, build up something like that – they interest the shit outta me.') Laredo's wealth is not in its real estate, or tourist condos, or silver ore reserves. Arriving with a truckload of goods for across the border is the best way to see where the money is in Laredo. Mercury Forwarding, for whom our pumps were bound, had an address of Number several-thousand-and-something Mines Road – out of the way behind a maze of potholed streets – which then took us miles out of Laredo's northern corner, and then further, and all the way past huge depots of trucks and trailers: hundreds of yellow Hunts, hundreds of orange Schneiders; trailers batched up for putting on trains. And all the way new warehouses were going up in the free pockets of land, new sewers were being laid, new water mains, gas supplies. The Interstate in from San Antonio had been newly resurfaced and shone like fresh leather. Laredo was a swirling building site, spreading out and filling in fast to accommodate the burgeoning import–export trade between the US and Mexico. Buckets on Caterpillar diggers like the one Keith and I had wrestled with up in New Hampshire – they were shipped from Mexico all the way up to Illinois.

We left our four vertical swing pumps at Mercury in a warehouse littered with imperfectly wrapped stuffed deer and a female lion, and headed back into town to see if there were any loads for the West Coast showing on the board at the truckstop. We still had our second consign-ment of computer monitors for Long Beach, but the scarcity of good back loads from Shaky meant that this last leg would hardly pay its way unless Tim could find a partial to make up the weight.

The truckstop was an evil hovel in a yard packed with trucks. The sun struck down hard and white – this far south the midday temperature was in the nineties. The yard was a maelstrom of white dust every time a truck moved. At the back a blonde hooker was hanging about behind the trailers.

'You know when even the fleet trucks are hanging around the truckstop that things are real quiet,' Tim said. The dingy TV lounge was thick with lethargic guys and stale smoke. No loads. Some of these guys had been here days. The lot lizard outside, they said, was going for five bucks.

'Guy I know stopped in here,' piped up one trucker, 'girl comes up to him and says, "Do you wanna sucky?" He says no. She says, "Well, how 'bout a room, we got them for seventeen dollars!"'

Tim rang the office and came off with the news that Neil was holed up too. The Cookie Duster had dropped his daughter off with her grandparents, and now he was still stranded in Des Moines: flooded in – hadn't even got rid of his load yet. With the catastrophic flooding of the Mississippi all the highways out were closed; he couldn't move. Tim had been noticing how much rain had even reached Texas: a year ago the road from Dallas down to San Antone had run through desert. Now he'd marvelled at how all the water had 'turned the state green'.

There was no point hanging around here: there'd be more hope of a load in the east of Texas, so we set off back to San Antone. On the CB outside Laredo a trucker was asking around for a girl. 'Boy, you sure keen to have ya dick drop off,' said Tim.

*

Now your head had come up to speed – your mental momentum had hit top gear for the idea of making a coast-to-coast in a handful of days, and you didn't want to slow down. How could you hang about when you could be rolling on?

But we hung about the San Antonio Flying J till halfway through the next day. It felt like a week. It cured me of ever imagining I was fond of service stations. All you knew was that there was no load, and whether that load materialized in an hour or a fortnight, until it came up on the board or down the phone your entire world was in desperate limbo. For days your life had become a sacramental discipline of waking, and riding till midnight, and collapsing into sleep until you woke to ride again. Now you had to make decisions, for hour after hour, about how to organize your consciousness! I went for a baking walk up a side lane amongst fields of cow pasture ticking with crickets, and had to decline a lift from a pick-up full of farm workers – incredulously speechless – who would have dropped me back at the truckstop in ten minutes instead of twenty. I drank a can of Pepsi. Tim bought a lottery card. He rubbed the numbers on the lottery card. He threw away the lottery card. He told the cashier in the shop how he'd been waiting for the results in the newspaper from the national lottery. But when they'd come through, and he'd looked at them, although he had had a feeling he was going to be in with a chance, he hadn't won anything after all. Tim put his clothes in the wash. Twenty minutes later I'd come round to thinking that, on balance, I should put my clothes in the wash, too. We joined the sprawled gathering in the TV room to watch the feature film channel, and I found myself looking at Stanley Baker in the sixties British fictionalization of the Great Train

Robbery – full of bemused bobbies and bulbous Jaguars and accents that divided into clipped toff and gorblimey-spiv. I couldn't believe that my life was making time for me to watch *Robbery* in San Antonio.

'Hell, Peggy,' a quiet, perplexed man was saying in one of the phone booths, 'this must be the worstest trip I ever made.' His glasses clung across his face like a spreadeagled rock climber. 'I bust m'glasses, only got one side on to hold 'em on to m'face, and then I had to deadhead six hundred miles, and then –' The rest of his litany of disaster was drowned out by the explosion of guffaws. Imagine having to run empty – a wild goose chase with no load at the end of it – for *six hundred miles*! 'Yeah, I'll take it, Peggy,' the man was saying ruefully. 'I don't rilly wanna go down there, but I wanna git outta *this* place . . .'

Finally, after three years' waiting since we'd got up that morning, Tim pestered North Billerica with one more phone call and there was a load for us. South-east of San Antone in Victoria was the plastics factory Tim had been to before, which had a load of recycled plastic trash bags to go to Pomona in the Los Angeles conurbation. It was less than an inch away on my little Rand McNally pocket atlas, but that still meant a hundred and twenty-five miles, and nearly two and a half hours' drive. But it was a pretty road through rich rolling fields and orchards and the antique town square of Gonzales – the first town centre I'd seen through a truck windscreen since I'd started riding over here – and by the early evening we had 18,000 lb of black Tuffies in back, special heavy-duty 'Rhino' specification, and we were all set for Shaky. On the way back to San Antone I began to notice how every pick-up and Winnebago and Cadillac we came up behind – this highway was only two lanes – pulled over on to the hard shoulder

and bumped along there until it had let us pass. 'Don't
happen nowhere else in the States,' Tim said. 'Just Texas.
Down here the trucker's supposed to be the boss – always
got the right of way. People know we got to go.'

Someone called Joe Diffie; sang,

> Prop me up beside the jukebox if I die,
> . . .
> You can pay your last respects
> One quarter at a time

But we'd done two hundred miles, the day had gone,
and we'd hardly reached San Antone where we'd started
out. We stocked up at the services at the junction of Route
183 and Interstate 10 with tuna sandwiches in clingfilm,
Snickers bars and Styrofoam coffee, and it was time at last
to head west.

We did 450 miles that day, and by midnight we'd got as
far as the Ozona Services, still 350 miles inside Texas. Here
and there the headlights had lit up small delicate deer
grazing quietly on the grass verge; at the 591-mile marker
the Interstate had gone over Woman Hollering Creek; a
billboard shouted that HOLLIS GRIZZARD HAS HIS
EYE ON CRIME; at ten Tim had shot the shit with a
portable parking lot surging past us on its way to Arizona.
The distances these guys did – he was due to drop there in
the morning! 'Man, that's 650 miles where he's going,'
wondered Tim. 'That's an eleven-hour ride!'

> Hey pretty baby don't you know it ain't my fault
> Love to hear the steel belts hummin' on the asphalt
> Wake up in the middle of the night at a truckstop
> Stumble in the restaurant wonderin' why it don't stop . . .

We were up and buzzing when we got to the 76 truckstop at Ozona, so we sat at the diner with some coffee and burgers. At a quarter to one a guy felt his way over to us, his face and eyes pulled into the bulging tightness of someone deep underwater. 'I'd forgot how big Texas was,' he mumbled to the trucker in a baseball hat next to him – he could hardly heave himself up on to his stool. He twitched and stared ahead like a fragile fish under a stone. After a while a thought struck him. 'Has Texas grown recently?'

On our last day in Texas I counted our time down by the mile markers.

257 to the state line was a pick-up towing a trailer full of ostriches from Folsom, Louisiana at the Fort Stockton truckstop. Tim looked in at the garage to check there was a wrecker on its way out for the Freightliner pulled up under an over-bridge at 265 with both rear trailer tyres peeled. You wouldn't want to leave a guy stranded out there in the summer heat for too long.

242: a 'full-grown Bear' – a State Trooper, with some four-wheeler customers on the hard shoulder. 'I'll give him a little room,' Tim said, pulling the Mack out into the hammer lane. 'I don't want to blow his hat off. I did that once, and I watched him in my mirror shakin' his finger at me as he was chasing his hat down the road!'

206: a skinny rubber chicken was dangling from the door locks on the back of a Peterbilt reefer from Tucson.

Tim picked up his CB handset. 'Hey there, Tucson – looks like that chicken of yours could use a little water . . .'

'Well, man, that there chicken o' mine couldn't stand the pressure 'n' he went 'n' hung himself. When I get home I'm gonna give him a decent burial.'

Lightning flashed inside the thick grey belt of cloud

hanging over the Rio Grande mountains ahead. Soon the cloud was upon us and rain scrambled on the screen in frenzied rivulets.

'You sure put a curse on that there bird o' mine, buddy – sayin' he needed a drink. At least he'll git a good wash 'fore I bury him.'

164: the land opened out suddenly into a huge green plain, bounded by distant mountains in pastel browns, blues and greys.

El Paso, a few miles from the state line at last, sprawling to the horizon under scoured, whorled mountains, and a trucker sitting on the steps of the Petro truckstop, dazed and disconsolate beneath his stetson and wraparound shades. 'I'm broke down – I come outta LA on m'way to Flarrda. I'm gone be here three days 'fore I get help from Flarrda . . . I been doin' this for eight years – gettin' kinda tired of it, all the waitin'-around shit . . . I came outta LA, I was all charged up 'n' ready to run *fast*. I like to run fast . . . You like to git high? I like to git high. I do crack – none of the smokin' stuff. Crack gits me easy 'n' readied up . . .'

But we could go, so we did go, and as we crossed over into the rest of the world the impenetrable grey screen of the sky trembled with lightning and then split with giant flashes.

Chapter Eighteen

That evening the sun set in front of us in a colossal conflagration. After the storm steam hung above the ground. A bug shower spattered and blackened the windscreen with insect bodies. The sky bruised from apricot to lilac, and the clouds were boiling white surf. At last, in the dying rage of colour, we drove under a ceiling of smouldering embers, the sky ahead a mess of flayed meat, and a single lilac bird's wing of cloud – you could see the delicate quilting of feathers around the pinions – flagging our way west. Against the northern horizon an immeasurably long freight train slid slowly along like a conveyor-belt.

Tim had been looking at the atlas during our stop at the El Paso Petro. 'I know the way to get into California without going through any scales,' he said. 'It's all coming back to me ... I was just outside of Barstow a few years ago loading onions for Long Beach – you know, you load 'em across your trailer in a layer about halfway up. And there's this little guy beside me – from Idaho, nice truck – and he's stacking these onions in up to the roof! More and more! I said to him, "What kind of load are you gonna make?" He says, "About 110,000 pounds!"' – Tim said it with a great laughing shout. 'He was getting eleven hundred dollars for the delivery – it was only a 300-mile ride –

but it was costing him a hundred and fifty dollars to get all those onions taken off, 'cause it was a double load. He said, "I'll show you how I get round the scales" – he says, "There's the scale out on 58, it closes every night from midnight till four in the morning." I followed him down to this truckstop just past Barstow before the scale, and it's about midnight, and there's like two hundred truckers all sittin' there. It gets to one in the morning and suddenly all these trucks haul ass out on to the highway, one after the other. So I let them go out in line and join on the end and we go straight through! This guy said to me, "I *like* making money!"'

New Mexico disappeared in the dark, and then half of Arizona, for by midnight we were already in Tucson. When we pulled away in the morning the country radio station was trailing its biography serial about a popular young country and western singer. 'And later on this morning,' announced the presenter, 'we'll be featuring the next instalment of "The John Anderson Story". And this week, the story of a period in John's life when he was going through a really bad time . . .' I was wondering if this was the same voice that had given Keith and me the tip about the barbecue hot-dogs over Independence weekend. 'He got divorced, he was trying to sort himself out and get things back together. And his father took him aside and said, "John, there are more important things in this life. More important than money. More important than your career . . . The most important thing of all – is that nobody finds out you're my son."'

Tim was running out of hours: by one o'clock he'd have used up the seventy hours' driving he was allowed since the previous weekend, and we'd have to hole up at another truckstop and cool our heels for another eight before we could head on. Tim checked his tyres at a rest area outside Phoenix, and they were pretty hot, so easing off was a good idea in any case. There was a beautiful warm wind washing over the desert, delicious on the face, but running at night would be kinder to the Mack. We sat out till nine that night at the Flying J at Ehrenberg just before the California state line: by then it would be midnight Eastern time, on which Tim's Log Book was calibrated, and he'd be able to start a new seven-day schedule. A little wizened guy in a cloth cap got up while we were watching TV in the lounge and muttered to excuse himself that he'd better go check if his truck was still there, 'dem brakes bin playin' up aller way'. We wandered across to the Colorado where the windsurfers on the sun-spangled river were teetering and wobbling and leaning like butterflies resting. I left Tim back at the Mack and wandered out behind the Flying J to the sandy foothills behind until I had a view over the pale purple desert and the scattered emerald squares of irrigated fields in the river's flood plain.

I sat down cross-legged amongst the sand and scrub and read my copy of *USA Today* until the light began to go – the latest on the Biblical inundation of Iowa where the rain was still falling and the Mississippi waters were no lower, and the President himself was arriving to meet the people without homes and workplaces and assess the relief needed. At least *USA Today* was a truly national newspaper – wherever you were, it gave you the news from all over, and even a little from abroad.

But where was I? Arizona: it was a low foothill with a desert view, and a corporate-design truckstop at my back – but where was it in America? By the end of tonight we'd be at Ontario on the fringe of LA, and North Billerica, Massachusetts to Los Angeles, California, by the route we'd taken, was 4,500 miles in less than ten days. I'd been to Arizona twice before – it was probably the state I knew best of all, from the Bright Angel trail down the Grand Canyon in the north to the square miles of redundant B-52s and Phantoms shining in the sun at Tucson's Davis–Monthan Air Force Base in the south. I'd shopped in Arizona's city malls, ridden its buses, driven its back roads, seen its new riches in the prosperous resort of Scottsdale, shooting its precious water resources into the air as though the ornamental fountains trilled champagne; I'd seen its history in the ghostly gold-town relic of Jerome; its raucous down-home side in the rackety music bars of Prescott, and its twee New Age-ery in the boutiques of Sedona. I had a handle on Arizona.

But right now I couldn't place it. This was just a day of blazing heat, fiercer than Pennsylvania, drier than Alabama. Just another Flying J. The wide flat Interstate ahead of us and wide flat Interstate narrowing to a point behind. I measured out my life with yet another Snickers bar. Arizona was not where we were meant to be, was waiting for the chance to be somewhere else. But so, it was starting to feel, was everywhere. Arizona was more miles, a line on a map: after all this way I was developing some of Earl's incuriosity. Wherever you were there was always another place after it, so it was best to keep on going.

Time to roll: climb up into the little twilit capsule and swing out on to the Interstate for the last time. The dark always sharpened the senses – moving off at night was always a crisp, wide-awake, expectant moment, always felt good no matter how tired you were.

'I did a lot of sitting around here a few years ago,' said Tim. 'I took an oversize load of stuff to Seattle for some electric dam project, and I couldn't get no load home. So I found a load of Christmas trees, and brought them down to Yuma, over there on the Mexican border. Cop pulled me over, said I was speeding – he said, "How can I give you a ticket when you've got Christmas trees with you?" Then I still couldn't find a load back home. Eventually I found a load of polished bricks and took them back, but I was gone a full *month* – a whole fucken month. I didn't make no money that trip, lemme tell ya.'

Tim had decided against taking the route of the overloaded-onion-hauler from Idaho: detouring north up to Barstow meant ducking and diving along Highway 95: a full-grown Bear finding you up there in the middle of the night would certainly think you were trying to hide something. At Ehrenberg every trucker's story about the Banning scale was different – for all we knew it could have re-opened, so it was a chance after all. We bought our seven-dollar trailer permit to allow our Maine-registered trailer into Shaky – no point pulling down a heap of trouble by overlooking a teeny bit of bureaucracy at the last, however officious and hairsplitting, and we were all set to brave the Banning scale.

On the radio Delbert and Tania were singing 'Tell Me About It' as we saw the SCALE CLOSED sign and cruised past.

Trucks rolled into the vast T/A truckstop at Ontario all through Sunday – like us, getting into town before the end of the weekend to be ready to drop first thing Monday morning. There must have been room for five hundred rigs there, and by the end of the day the place was packed. I saw plenty of really smart machines – mostly classic Petes across from the South: loads of chrome, immaculate paint-jobs, mirror-polished; a bright yellow beast receiving a coat of wax; a magnificent orange and silver Pete I wanted to drive away and call my own right there. All across the lot guys were out working on their charges as though they were thoroughbred racehorses: pulling rocks out of the tyres, leathering the paintwork, bent over behind the open hood offering drinks of oil and water. NO-STRESS EXPRESS went the slogan on the back of the trailer opposite; amongst these groovy giant tourers, the Mack's bull nose branded us straight away as a message from the rock-solid north-east.

At ten that morning a dapper grey-haired man poked a copy of *Wheels Alive* through our cab window, bade us a polite good morning and said he'd come round to invite us to church today and, if we'd like to, they'd be pleased to see us. Half an hour later a dozen men sat with bowed heads underneath the canopy on the truckstop terrace while the preacher talked into his microphone – but I couldn't join them to see if any excessive loads were being gratefully shed, because our trailer stood on its legs, uncoupled for the day, and we were driving out on our way to the beach.

We parked the Mack on the seafront at Huntingdon Beach and spent the day walking along the immense stretch of sand, out to the end of the pier, in and out of the gift shops along the promenade for a couple of T-shirts to take back to the east coast for Tim's kids, amongst the smart Ray-Banned young couples taking a stroll, the bronzed hunks throwing a ball around, the toddlers pottering around their sand castles. Then, as the day waned, up and down the beach all the barbecues were lit up – great hampers and cool boxes of provisions, sacks of charcoal, folding chairs and tables, a fully-staffed army field kitchen intently self-absorbed. Perhaps my memory should afford ironic reflections that all the detritus of a summer Sunday like this – the discarded silver foil unwrapped from the chicken drumsticks, the popsicle sticks, the Coke cans, the Cellophane – would all soon be collected and bagged up in Rhino Tuffies like those we'd just come all the way from Texas with; or that we'd come this whole distance from the north-east corner of a vast country to its far opposite corner in the south-west for the sake of a few hundred-weight of busted VDUs. But it doesn't. It recalls simply a whole day of stretched legs and fresh air and the edge of the ocean foaming around your toes – and, best of all, oblivious lives teeming at their own secret pace all around you, instead of the anchoritic solipsism of trucking travel. No longer on the way to somewhere else; no longer a thousand miles from nowhere: just, *here*.

At the truckstop the talk was of *loads* – lots of them! The DAT screens had pages of them! Normally, said the two Massachusetts truckers Tim had been chatting to, there might be one page of loads out of here if you were lucky. Today there was three times as much. Certainly this was the time of year – high summer – for the produce season, with all California's onions, grapes, tomatoes and peppers coming to harvest, and its specialist produce haulers, who out of season would muscle in on the freight haulage, full up shipping them all out.

But this year the difference was the Mississippi floods. At St. Louis, Missouri, the main railroad across the country linking west coast with east was inundated. Tim and I had been surprised at how many freight trains we'd seen rolling along the southern line through New Mexico and Arizona: here was the reason. As much rail freight for the east coast as possible was going across through the South – but the rest, and all the loads delayed by the flood until they were now urgent, were going by road! Temporarily, improbably, wondrously — for perhaps a few weeks in a lifetime — Los Angeles was pay dirt, a truckers' Klondike! Tim found one guy who was just setting off for New York with a load of furniture and a fee of $6,200. Our partial of computers from Massachusetts had paid less than $1,200: now the talk was of *seven thousand dollars* to take a load back to Boston.

Tim already had a back load for Connecticut waiting for him in Torrance, but when we backed into Standard Paints' loading bay on Monday morning, the Tuffies dropped in the City of Industry, the computers offloaded at the Tatung warehouse, it was to watch a mere handful of skips of paint tubs being forklifted into the back. There was still three-quarters of the trailer that Tim could fill! The Tim Brown who got back into the cab seemed to have grown in stature and bearing, to have assumed some of the straining pugnacity of the little bulldog leading the way at the end of the Mack's hood. I jumped out beside LAX airport and waved him goodbye: for him it was time, as he occasionally used to exclaim, 'to continue my mission!' He was going straight back to the truckstop to clean up on some more loads. They weren't going to get to the east coast any other way.

Discography

To ensure suitability for in-cab stereo systems, catalogue numbers for all recommended road music refer to the cassette format.

Steve Earle, *Guitar Town*: MCA MCFC 3335

Dwight Yoakam, *This Time* (including 'A Thousand Miles from Nowhere'): Reprise 9362–45241–4

Delbert McClinton, *Delbert McClinton* (including 'Tell Me About It'): Curb CUR MC 008

Delbert McClinton, *I'm With You*: Curb D4–77252

Anson Funderburgh and the Rockets, featuring Sam Myers, *Rack 'Em Up* (including 'Hold That Train, Conductor'): Black Top C–BT–1049

Anson Funderburgh and the Rockets, *Sins*: Black Top C–BT–1038

Little Feat, *As Time Goes By – The Very Best of . . .*: WEA 9548–32247–4

B.B. King, *There's Always One More Time*: MCA MCC 10295

The Blues Band, *Fat City*: RCA PK 75100

Discography

Dion, *The Best of Dion*: CBS BT 18917

Stevie Ray Vaughan and Double Trouble, *Live Alive*: Epic 466839 4

George Thorogood and the Destroyers, *The Baddest Of . . .*: EMI America 0777 797718 4 4

George Thorogood and the Destroyers, *Maverick*: EMI America E J 24 0282 4

Tammy Wynette, *The Classic Collection*: Epic 40 22136

Allegri, *Miserere* and Palestrina, *Missa Papae Marcelli*, sung by the Tallis Scholars, conducted by Peter Phillips: Gimell 1585T–39

READ MORE IN PENGUIN

In every corner of the world, on every subject under the sun, Penguin represents quality and variety – the very best in publishing today.

For complete information about books available from Penguin – including Puffins, Penguin Classics and Arkana – and how to order them, write to us at the appropriate address below. Please note that for copyright reasons the selection of books varies from country to country.

In the United Kingdom: Please write to *Dept. EP, Penguin Books Ltd, Bath Road, Harmondsworth, West Drayton, Middlesex UB7 ODA*

In the United States: Please write to *Consumer Sales, Penguin USA, P.O. Box 999, Dept. 17109, Bergenfield, New Jersey 07621-0120*. VISA and MasterCard holders call 1-800-253-6476 to order Penguin titles

In Canada: Please write to *Penguin Books Canada Ltd, 10 Alcorn Avenue, Suite 300, Toronto, Ontario M4V 3B2*

In Australia: Please write to *Penguin Books Australia Ltd, P.O. Box 257, Ringwood, Victoria 3134*

In New Zealand: Please write to *Penguin Books (NZ) Ltd, Private Bag 102902, North Shore Mail Centre, Auckland 10*

In India: Please write to *Penguin Books India Pvt Ltd, 706 Eros Apartments, 56 Nehru Place, New Delhi 110 019*

In the Netherlands: Please write to *Penguin Books Netherlands bv, Postbus 3507, NL-1001 AH Amsterdam*

In Germany: Please write to *Penguin Books Deutschland GmbH, Metzlerstrasse 26, 60594 Frankfurt am Main*

In Spain: Please write to *Penguin Books S. A., Bravo Murillo 19, 1° B, 28015 Madrid*

In Italy: Please write to *Penguin Italia s.r.l., Via Felice Casati 20, I-20124 Milano*

In France: Please write to *Penguin France S. A., 17 rue Lejeune, F-31000 Toulouse*

In Japan: Please write to *Penguin Books Japan, Ishikiribashi Building, 2-5-4, Suido, Bunkyo-ku, Tokyo 112*

In Greece: Please write to *Penguin Hellas Ltd, Dimocritou 3, GR-106 71 Athens*

In South Africa: Please write to *Longman Penguin Southern Africa (Pty) Ltd, Private Bag X08, Bertsham 2013*

READ MORE IN PENGUIN

A CHOICE OF NON-FICTION

The Time Out Film Guide   Edited by Tom Milne

The definitive, up-to-the minute directory of over 9,500 films – world cinema from classics and silent epics to reissues and the latest releases – assessed by two decades of *Time Out* reviewers. 'In my opinion the best and most comprehensive' – Barry Norman

The Remarkable Expedition   Olivia Manning

The events of an extraordinary attempt in 1887 to rescue Emin Pasha, Governor of Equatoria, are recounted here by the author of *The Balkan Trilogy* and *The Levant Trilogy* and vividly reveal unprecedented heights of magnificent folly in the perennial human search for glorious conquest.

Skulduggery   Mark Shand

Mark Shand, his friend and business partner Harry Fane and world-famous but war-weary photographer Don McCullin wanted adventure. So, accompanied by a fat Batak guide, armed only with a first-aid kit and with T-shirts, beads and tobacco for trading, they plunged deep into the heart of Indonesian cannibal country . . .

Lenin's Tomb   David Remnick

'This account by David Remnick, Moscow correspondent for the *Washington Post* from 1988 to 1992, of the last days of the Soviet Empire is one of the most vivid to date' – *Observer*

Roots Schmoots   Howard Jacobson

'This is no exercise in sentimental journeys. Jacobson writes with a rare wit and the book sparkles with his gritty humour . . . he displays a deliciously caustic edge in his analysis of what is wrong, and right, with modern Jewry' – *Mail on Sunday*